Payables Management

A Practitioner's Guide

Third Edition

Steven M. Bragg

AccountingTools®

Copyright © 2020 by AccountingTools, Inc. All rights reserved.

Published by AccountingTools, Inc., Centennial, Colorado.

No part of this publication may be reproduced, stored in a retrieval system, or transmitted in any form or by any means, except as permitted under Section 107 or 108 of the 1976 United States Copyright Act, without the prior written permission of the Publisher. Requests to the Publisher for permission should be addressed to Steven M. Bragg, 6727 E. Fremont Place, Centennial, CO 80112.

Limit of Liability/Disclaimer of Warranty: While the publisher and author have used their best efforts in preparing this book, they make no representations or warranties with respect to the accuracy or completeness of the contents of this book and specifically disclaim any implied warranties of merchantability or fitness for a particular purpose. No warranty may be created or extended by written sales materials. The advice and strategies contained herein may not be suitable for your situation. You should consult with a professional where appropriate. Neither the publisher nor author shall be liable for any loss of profit or any other commercial damages, including but not limited to special, incidental, consequential, or other damages.

For more information about AccountingTools® products, visit our Web site at www.accountingtools.com.

ISBN-13: 978-1-64221-050-7

Printed in the United States of America

Table of Contents

Chapter 1 - Overview of Payables 1
   Transaction Cycles 1
   Organizational Structure of the Accounting Department 2
   Payables Functions 4
   Payables Job Descriptions 7

Chapter 2 - Invoice Processing 9
   The Need for Precise Invoice Processing 9
   The Supplier Invoice Processing Procedure (Manual System) 10
   The Supplier Invoice Processing Procedure (Integrated System) 15
   Accounts Payable Credits Processing Procedure 17
   The Evaluated Receipts Processing Procedure 19
   The Check Payment Issuance Procedure 20
   Payment Alternatives 24
   The Void Checks Procedure 24
   Enhancements to Invoice Processing 26
      Direct Invoice Delivery 26
      Centralize E-mailed Invoice Processing 27
      Return Incomplete Invoices 27
      Invoice Numbering Convention 27
      Request Aggregated Invoice 27
      Minimize Approvals 28
      Analyze Matching Discrepancies 28
      Monitor Invoice Disputes 29
      Recurring Payment Automation 29
      Manual Check Reduction 29
      Analyze Manual Checks 30
      Restrict Manual Delivery of Checks 30
      Restrict Cash Advances 30
      Schedule Frequent Check Runs 30
      Use a Signature Stamp or Plate 31
      Reduce the Need for Second Signatures 31
      Encourage use of ACH 31
      Clean the Payables Aging Report 32
      Search for Open Credits 32
      Reduce the Number of Suppliers 32
      Final Thoughts 32

Chapter 3 - Types of Payments 34

    Cash Payments (Petty Cash) *34*
    Check Payments *38*
    Foreign Check Clearing *40*
        Float 41
        Advantages of Checks 42
        Disadvantages of Checks 42
    Bank Drafts *42*
    Automated Clearing House Payments *43*
        Advantages of ACH 44
        Impact on Float 45
        Global ACH 45
    Wire Transfers *45*
    The Letter of Credit *47*
        The Standby Letter of Credit 48

Chapter 4 - Expense Reimbursement **50**

    The Need for Expense Reimbursement *50*
    The Expense Report Submission Procedure (Manual System) *50*
    The On-Line Expense Report Submission Procedure *54*
    The Expense Report Review Procedure *55*
    The Travel and Entertainment Policy *57*
    Additional Expense Reimbursement Topics *59*
        Form of Documentation 59
        Cash Advances 60
        Expense Report Auditing 60
        Expense Report Outsourcing 61
    Spend Management *61*
    Employee Reviews *61*

Chapter 5 - Procurement Cards **63**

    When and How to Use Procurement Cards *63*
    The Card Reconciliation Procedure *65*
    The Lost Card Procedure *70*
    Additional Procurement Card Topics *73*
        Card Issuer Relations 73
        Card Rebates 73
        Cash Flow Management 73
        Card User Relations 74
        Departure of Card Users 74

Chapter 6 - Use Taxes 76
   Sales and Use Tax Overview 76
   Use Tax Systems 77
        Additional Use Tax Issues 78
   Use Tax Audits 79
   Sales Tax Exemption Certificate 79
   Multiple Points of Use Certificate 80

Chapter 7 - Finance Issues 81
   Early Payment Discounts 81
   Payment Timing 83
   Supply Chain Financing 84

Chapter 8 - Accounting for Payables 86
   Routine Accounts Payable Entries 86
   Gross and Net Price Methods 88
   Period-end Accounts Payable Entries 88
   Applicable Accounts to Charge 89

Chapter 9 - Closing Payables 93
   Accounts Payable Accruals 93
   Expense Reports 94
   Issues with the Credit Card Close 95
   Accounts Payable Suspense Items 96
   Discrepancy Invoices 97
   Uncashed Checks 98
   Reconciling Accounts Payable 98
   Additional Year-end Tasks 99
   Closing the Ledger 100

Chapter 10 - Department Management 101
   Payables Manager Responsibilities 101
   Schedule of Activities 101
   Error Tracking System 102
   Process Reviews 103
   Queue Management 104

 Department Layout 105
 Skills Review and Training 106
 Measuring the Results of Training 107
 Consolidate Accounting 108
 Quality of the Work Environment 109
 Flexible Work Hours 109
 Job Sharing 110
 Permanent Part-Time Work 110
 Supplier Relations 110

Chapter 11 - Payables Controls 113
 Accounts Payable Processing Controls 113
 Alternative Accounts Payable Control Systems 118
 Control System for Manual Accounts Payable 118
 Control System for Computerized Accounts Payable 119
 Additional Payables Controls – Trend Analysis 119
 Additional Payables Controls – Fraud Related 120
 Additional Payables Controls – Periodic Actions 122
 Expense Report Processing Controls 123
 Alternative Expense Report Control Systems 124
  Control System for Manual Expense Reporting 124
  Control System for Computerized Expense Reporting 124
 Additional Expense Report Controls – Fraud Related 125
 Additional Expense Report Controls – Periodic Actions 126
 In-Process Procurement Card Controls 127
 Alternative Procurement Card Control Systems 128
  Procurement Card Control System without a Transaction Log 128
  Procurement Card Control System with a Transaction Log 129
 Additional Payables Controls – Fraud Related 129
 Additional Payables Controls – Periodic Actions 130
 Petty Cash Controls 131
 Additional Payables Controls – Fraud Related 133
 Payables Policies 133
  Payables Policies 134
  Expense Report Policies 135
  Procurement Card Policies 136

    Petty Cash Policies 136

Chapter 12 - Payables Fraud 138
Personal Purchases 138
Refunds of Personal Purchases 138
Fake Suppliers 139
Supplier Overbillings 139
Unauthorized Shipments 139
Supplier-Staff Collusion 140
Authorization Limit Avoidance 140
Petty Cash Theft 140
Redirected Payments 140
Check Fraud 141
Check Theft 141
ACH Debits 141
Keystroke Logging 142
The Need for Controls Reviews 142

Chapter 13 - Payables Technology 144
The Payment Factory 144
Automated Expense Report Submissions 145
Automated Payables Matching 145
The Reverse Lockbox 146
Supplier Portals 147
Automated W-9 Forms 147

Chapter 14 - Payables Record Keeping 149
The Vendor Master File 149
Vendor Master File Usage 150
Supplier Naming Conventions 151
Vendor Master File Errors 152
Duplicate Record Detection and Prevention 153
TIN Matching 154
The Payables Filing System 154
Off-site Storage 155

  Document Imaging *156*
  Document Destruction *157*

Chapter 15 - Government Reporting **158**
  The Form 1099-MISC *158*
  The Form 1099-NEC *162*
  Treatment of Incorrect Filings *165*
  The Form W-9 .... *166*
  The Backup Withholding Rule *167*
  Form 1099 Administrative Issues *168*
  Form W-9 Administrative Issues *168*

Chapter 16 - Unclaimed Property **171**
  The Unclaimed Property Liability *171*
  Uncashed Checks *172*
  Treatment of Credits *172*
  Due Diligence Letters *173*
  The Dormancy Period *173*
  The Unclaimed Property Audit *174*
  Document Retention Policy *175*
  Filing Unclaimed Property Reports *176*
  Claiming Unclaimed Property *177*

Chapter 17 - Cost Recovery **178**
  Internal Cost Recovery Targets *178*
    Advertising Expenditures 178
    Allowances 178
    Contracts 179
    Duplicate Payments 179
    Freight Billings 179
    Health Plan Enrollment 180
    Legal Billings 180
    Spend Compliance 180
    Supplier Credits 181
    Telecommunications Billings 181
    Unclaimed Property 181
    Unreturned Deposits 181
  Internal Cost Recovery Staff *182*
  Recovery Auditors *182*

Cost-Benefit of Cost Recovery Activities *184*
Cost Recovery Timing *186*
Fertile Ground for Cost Recovery Efforts *186*

Chapter 18 - Payables Measurements **188**
Days Payables Outstanding *188*
Supplier Billed Price Variance *189*
Transaction Error Rate *190*
Full-Time Equivalent Measurements *191*
    FTEs per $1 Million of Revenue 192
    Staff Cost per FTE 192
    Line Items per FTE 193
Paperless Measurements *193*
    Percent of Paperless Invoices 193
    Percent of Paperless Payments 193
Additional Payables Measurements *194*

Glossary **196**

Index **199**

Preface

The typical organization must deal with a continuing flood of supplier invoices and check requests from employees. There are usually demands to also issue payments as expeditiously as possible, despite an offsetting need to investigate each request to ensure that it is valid. *Payables Management* describes a number of alternatives for creating an efficient payables system that processes invoices at low cost, while still maintaining close control over the payments made. The book also covers an array of related topics, including procurement cards, use taxes, closing the books, payables controls, unclaimed property, and more.

The book is divided into two sections. In Chapters 1 through 9, the focus is on day-to-day payables activities, including invoice processing, alternative payment methods, and the accounting for a number of different payables transactions. In Chapters 10 through 18, the focus shifts to the management of and systems related to payables. These topics include department management, control systems, payables technology, record keeping, and those performance measurements most relevant to payables.

You can find the answers to many questions about payables in the following chapters, including:

- Which job descriptions should I use for the payables staff?
- Which alternatives are available for processing invoices?
- How can I make the review of expense reports more efficient?
- What process flow is needed to generate a use tax liability?
- How can I calculate the interest rate associated with an early payment discount?
- How can I make the physical layout of the payables department more efficient?
- Are there any naming conventions to follow when setting up new suppliers?
- How can I minimize the amount of property that must be reported as unclaimed?
- What are some of the targets of a cost recovery effort?

Payables Management is designed primarily for professionals, who can use it as a reference tool for developing payables systems and researching the correct accounting to deal with various transactions. Given its complete coverage of these topics, *Payables Management* may earn a permanent place on your book shelf.

Centennial, Colorado
August 2020

About the Author

Steven Bragg, CPA, has been the chief financial officer or controller of four companies, as well as a consulting manager at Ernst & Young. He received a master's degree in finance from Bentley College, an MBA from Babson College, and a Bachelor's degree in Economics from the University of Maine. He has been a two-time president of the Colorado Mountain Club, and is an avid alpine skier, mountain biker, and certified master diver. Mr. Bragg resides in Centennial, Colorado. He has written more than 200 books and courses, including *New Controller Guidebook*, *GAAP Guidebook*, and *Payroll Management*.

Steven maintains the accountingtools.com web site, which contains continuing professional education courses, the Accounting Best Practices podcast, and thousands of articles on accounting subjects.

Buy Additional AccountingTools Courses

AccountingTools offers more than 1,000 hours of CPE courses, with concentrations in accounting, auditing, finance, taxation, and ethics. Related courses that you might like include:

- Expense Report Best Practices
- Form 1099 Compliance
- How to Audit Liabilities
- How to Audit Procurement
- Purchasing Guidebook

Go to accountingtools.com/cpe to view these additional courses.

AccountingTools®

Chapter 1
Overview of Payables

Introduction

The following chapters delve into the exact functions of the payables department. But before we dive into the details, it is useful to understand where the payables function is placed within a company, how it is positioned within the accounting department, the range of activities for which it is responsible, and the types of individuals who should work within the department. In addressing these topics in the following sections, we also note which of the following chapters contain additional information.

Transaction Cycles

Before discussing the management of payables, it is useful to understand where this function fits into the structure of a business. One way to look at this structure is in terms of the transaction cycles that comprise the operations of a business.

A transaction cycle is an interlocking set of business transactions. Most business transactions can be aggregated into a relatively small number of transaction cycles related to the sale of goods, payments to suppliers, payments to employees, and payments to lenders. We explore the nature of these transaction cycles in the following bullet points:

- *Sales cycle*. A company receives an order from a customer, examines the order for creditworthiness, ships goods or provides services to the customer, issues an invoice, and collects payment. This set of sequential, interrelated activities is known as the sales cycle, or revenue cycle.
- *Purchasing cycle*. A company issues a purchase order to a supplier for goods, receives the goods, records an account payable, and pays the supplier. There are several ancillary activities, such as the use of petty cash or procurement cards for smaller purchases. This set of sequential, interrelated activities is known as the purchasing cycle, or expenditure cycle.
- *Payroll cycle*. A company records the time of its employees, verifies hours and overtime worked, calculates gross pay, deducts taxes and other withholdings, and issues paychecks to employees. Other related activities include the payment of withheld income taxes to the government, as well as the issuance of annual W-2 forms to employees. This cluster of activities is known as the payroll cycle.
- *Financing cycle*. A company issues debt instruments to lenders, followed by a series of interest payments and repayments of the debt. Also, a company issues stock to investors in exchange for periodic dividend payments and other payouts if the entity is dissolved. These clusters of transactions are more

diverse than the preceding transaction cycles, but may involve substantially more money.

The payables function is a key part of the purchasing cycle, but can also be involved in the payroll cycle and the financing cycle. The payables function may be used to cut rush checks intended for employees, as well as to issue payroll advances. Any debt or interest payments arising under the financing cycle are also issued through the payables function. Thus, payables is one of the most pervasive activities in an organization.

Organizational Structure of the Accounting Department

When a business is quite small, there is little need for a formal organizational structure for the accounting department, since it is comprised of just one or two bookkeepers and perhaps an outside accounting specialist who advises the staff. This group informally handles the payables function amongst themselves. However, as the company becomes larger and the trickle of business transactions turns into a flood, it will be necessary to devise a formal structure for the department. Initially, this will require the hiring of a corporate controller, who manages a small staff of general-purpose accountants. Over time, additional positions will be added, until the organizational structure comes close to the configuration noted in the following exhibit.

Single Entity Accounting Organization

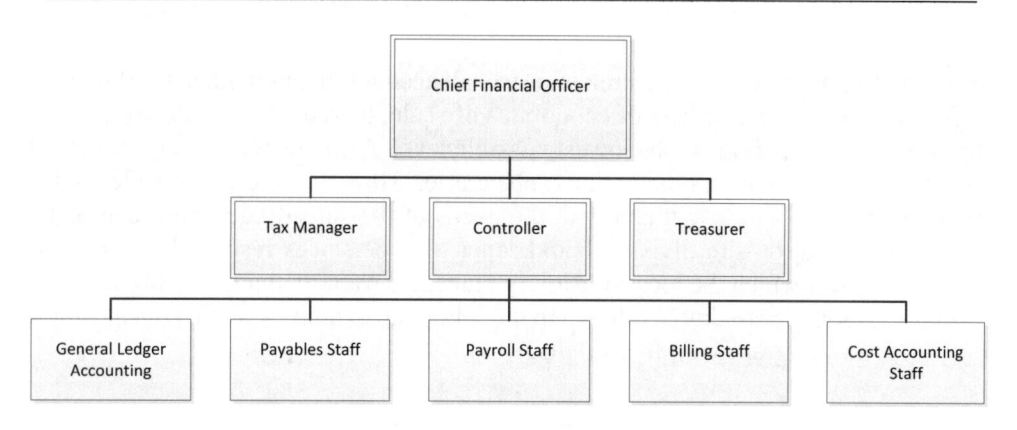

```
                    Chief Financial Officer
                              |
         ┌────────────────────┼────────────────────┐
     Tax Manager          Controller           Treasurer
                              |
    ┌──────────┬──────────────┼──────────────┬──────────┐
  General    Payables      Payroll         Billing    Cost
  Ledger      Staff         Staff           Staff   Accounting
 Accounting                                           Staff
```

In the preceding organization chart, the payables function appears as one of many accounting functions. However, it may have the largest headcount of these groups, depending on the volume of payables activities that are generated, and so comprises a disproportionate amount of the total activity in the department.

If a company splits its operations into several subsidiaries (or acquires subsidiaries), then it must decide whether to adopt a decentralized or centralized accounting structure. Under a decentralized structure, the handling of all normal business transactions is handled at the level of the subsidiary, with a small number of corporate-level positions that address such issues as parent-level taxation, budgeting, and transfer pricing. The advantage of this configuration is that the accounting staff is highly knowledgeable about local subsidiary activities. However, this approach also means that a number of positions are duplicated across the company, and that there is no way to take advantage of economies of scale. A typical decentralized accounting organization is shown in the following exhibit. Note the large number of payables groups scattered across the organization.

Decentralized Accounting Organization

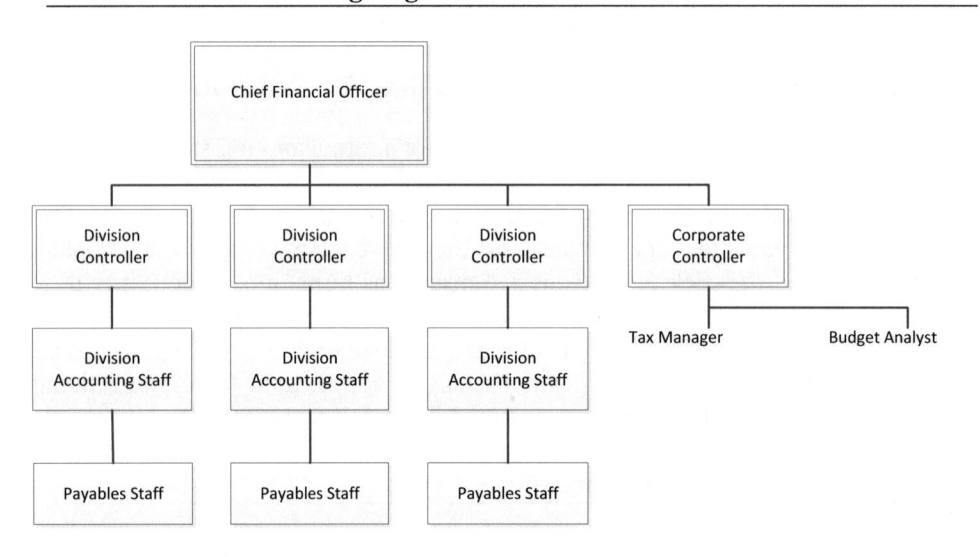

```
                          Chief Financial Officer
            ┌──────────────┬──────────────┬──────────────┐
       Division        Division       Division        Corporate
       Controller     Controller     Controller       Controller
            │              │              │          ┌─────┴─────┐
            │              │              │       Tax Manager  Budget Analyst
       Division        Division       Division
    Accounting Staff Accounting Staff Accounting Staff
            │              │              │
       Payables Staff  Payables Staff  Payables Staff
```

An alternative approach is to centralize nearly all accounting operations. By doing so, a company can take advantage of economies of scale, thereby driving down the cost of processing transactions to the lowest possible level. Also, there is no duplication of accounting positions across the various subsidiaries. However, there is a tendency for the accounting staff to lose touch with the needs of the subsidiaries, so it can make sense to retain an on-site division bookkeeper; this person is responsible for those transactions over which the local subsidiary managers want to maintain a higher level of control. A sample structure is shown in the following exhibit. Note that the payables function is now aggregated into a single group.

Centralized Accounting Organization

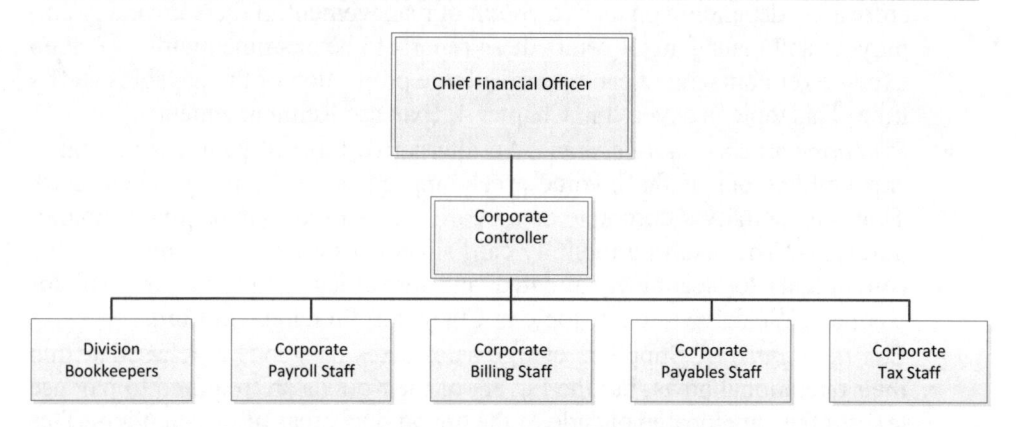

```
                    ┌──────────────────────┐
                    │ Chief Financial Officer │
                    └──────────┬───────────┘
                               │
                       ┌───────┴────────┐
                       │   Corporate    │
                       │   Controller   │
                       └───────┬────────┘
          ┌────────┬───────────┼───────────┬────────┐
    ┌─────┴────┐ ┌─┴──────┐ ┌──┴─────┐ ┌───┴────┐ ┌─┴──────┐
    │ Division │ │Corporate│ │Corporate│ │Corporate│ │Corporate│
    │Bookkeepers│ │ Payroll │ │ Billing │ │Payables │ │  Tax   │
    │          │ │  Staff  │ │  Staff  │ │  Staff  │ │ Staff  │
    └──────────┘ └─────────┘ └─────────┘ └─────────┘ └────────┘
```

There is no ideal organizational structure that will work for all accounting departments. Instead, the structure should match the conditions that an organization encounters. For example, an acquisition may only be possible if the local management team is given control over its accounting function – if so, a decentralized structure is the only possible option. Alternatively, a chain of retail stores may find that a local bookkeeper is always needed to process cash receipts, with all other functions being handled from a central location. As a third example, a consulting firm with locations around the world may find that it must centralize the billing function in order to ensure that contract funding levels are properly monitored, while allowing local branches to process their own payroll. As a final example, if a company operates under the strategy of being the low-cost leader, it may be compelled to reduce its accounting costs to the bare minimum by centralizing all functions in a single, massive accounting operations center.

Payables Functions

The classic perception of payables is that it simply pays the bills. Actually, the payables department is comprised of many activities that extend well beyond the payment of bills. These activities include:

- *Invoice processing*. The department is charged with collecting invoices from suppliers and check requests from employees, verifying that these items are authorized for payment, and issuing payments in a prompt manner. A key element of invoice processing has traditionally been the three-way match, where supplier invoices are checked against an authorizing purchase order to verify the price, and against a receiving document to ensure that the requested quantity was received. There are alternatives to the three-way match that can reduce the manual labor of the payables staff. Invoice processing and payments are addressed in Chapter 2, Invoice Processing.
- *Expense reimbursements*. A significant additional chore is the processing of employee expense reports, which can require detailed review efforts, or

occasional audits, or the use of automated expense reimbursement analysis software – depending on the viewpoint of management. If there are many employees and management wants these reports to be examined with care, then expense reimbursement can require a large proportion of the payables staff's time. This topic is covered in Chapter 4, Expense Reimbursement.

- *Procurement card management.* An alternative form of payment that takes expenditures out of the invoice processing queue is the procurement card. This is essentially a corporate credit card that is used to make many smaller purchases. The resulting monthly card statements are then examined by the card holders for accuracy, validated, and forwarded to the payables staff for payment. We delve into this topic in Chapter 5, Procurement Cards.
- *Use tax reporting.* Suppliers charge sales taxes on goods purchased within their operational areas, but the buyers of their goods are required to pay use taxes if they are located outside of the operational areas of the suppliers. This can require an involved process of determining which purchases were subject to use tax, applying the correct tax rate, and forwarding tax payments to the applicable government entity. This requirement is covered in Chapter 6, Use Taxes.
- *Discount taking and payment timing.* The payables manager is responsible for determining which early payment discount offers from suppliers are sufficiently worthwhile to take, and for scheduling invoice payments to ensure that the business is entitled to the discounts. It is also necessary to properly schedule the invoice approval and payment process so that the payments are made by the dates at which the company is obligated to make payments. These financing topics are covered in Chapter 7, Finance Issues.
- *Account for payables.* Intermixed with all of the preceding activities is the need to properly record payables in the accounting system. This involves determining which standard accounts to use for recording the expense and asset payments that flow through the payables system, as well as the layout of the entries used to record invoices, early payment discounts, and credit memos. Accounting entries are addressed in Chapter 8, Accounting for Payables.
- *Closing the books.* The payables staff is responsible for several key activities at the end of each reporting period. They must create accrual journal entries for expenses for which no supplier invoice has yet been received, process all remaining expense reports, clear pending items and discrepant invoices, and reconcile the ending balance in the accounts payable general ledger account. These activities are so significant that they can delay the closing process for the entire company. Closing the books is described in Chapter 9, Closing Payables.

The preceding activities list covers the main activities of the payables staff. In addition, there are a number of administrative tasks that the payables manager must ensure are completed, ranging from controls monitoring to unclaimed property reporting. These tasks include:

- *Department management*. The payables manager is responsible for maintaining a schedule of activities for the department and ensuring that all tasks listed on the schedule are completed in a timely manner. The manager should also use process reviews and an error tracking database to gather information about how the various payables activities can be improved upon. There are a number of specific techniques that can assist this transaction-heavy department, including queue analysis, work flow analysis, and skills reviews. These topics and more are covered in Chapter 10, Department Management.
- *Controls*. Given the payment volume that flows through the payables department, this is an excellent place to install a comprehensive set of controls. There are a massive number of possible controls to choose from that cover invoice processing, expense reports, procurement cards, and petty cash. These controls will vary, depending on the existence of manual or computerized payables systems. We cover a large number of controls and related payables policies in Chapter 11, Payables Controls. In addition, we describe the types of payables fraud in Chapter 12, so that the reader can gain some perspective on the need for controls.
- *Payables technology*. Given the industrial level of processing needed to handle the large number of invoices and payments in a typical company, there is a strong need for a high level of process automation. A multi-division company may find it cost-efficient to set up a payment factory that handles the payables for all of the divisions from one central location. For those businesses not able to make such a large investment, other alternatives include computerized expense report submissions, automated payables matching, and supplier portals. These technologies and more are described in Chapter 13, Payables Technology.
- *Record keeping*. The payables department is responsible for a large amount of paperwork, including supplier invoices, expense reports, procurement card statements, receiving documents, and purchase orders. An appropriate filing system must be created for all of these documents, as well as a master vendor file that is closely monitored for errors and duplicate records. These issues and more are noted in Chapter 14, Payables Record Keeping.
- *Government reporting*. In the United States, companies are required to issue the annual Form 1099 to the government and to suppliers, which documents the payments made to certain suppliers. This can be a major task, for the payables staff must first collect identifying information from all suppliers on the Form W-9, which is then used to create the Form 1099. If this identifying information is incorrect, the government requires the company to repeatedly contact suppliers to obtain the necessary information. This difficult requirement is covered in Chapter 15, Government Reporting.

- *Unclaimed property.* Every business in the United States is liable to the state governments to report unclaimed property, which can arise from a number of transactions. The payables department is deeply involved in unclaimed property reporting, since uncashed checks sent to suppliers are considered to be unclaimed property. The types of unclaimed property, state audits, document retention requirements, and several related issues are addressed in Chapter 16, Unclaimed Property.
- *Cost recovery.* The payables department may have a dedicated group of employees who are responsible for examining payment records to see if the expenditures made by the company can be reduced. Areas into which they may delve include contractual compliance, duplicate payments, freight billings, supplier credits, and unreturned deposits. This group may be supplemented or replaced by an outside group of recovery auditors. This excellent approach to cost management is described in Chapter 17, Cost Recovery.
- *Measurements* There are several measurements that can be of use to the payables manager in running the department, including days payables outstanding, the transaction error rate, and the percent of paperless payments made. These and other measurements are presented in Chapter 18, Payables Measurements.

Based on the broad range of activities for which the payables department is responsible, it should be clear that this is an area that must handle large incoming flows of payables documents, process them with minimal errors, and issue payments in a timely manner. In the next section, we discuss the types of individuals who can accomplish these tasks.

Payables Job Descriptions

Now that we have defined the payables function within the transaction cycles of a business, its place within the accounting department's organizational structure, and its specific functions, we can now turn to the job descriptions within the department.

The most important job description is for the payables clerk, since this description covers most of the staff in the department. The accountabilities of the payables clerk are as follows:

- Match supplier invoices to authorizing purchase orders and proofs of receipt
- Take all economical supplier discounts
- Obtain payment approvals for non-cost of goods sold invoices
- Issue notices to suppliers regarding rejected invoice line items
- Process expense reports
- Process procurement card payments
- Issue stop payments and void checks
- Issue reminders to suppliers regarding uncashed checks
- Pay supplier invoices when due
- Incorporate all applicable supplier credits into payments made

- Properly record payables transactions in the accounting software
- Monitor supplier Form W-9 submissions
- Update the supplier master file
- Reconcile accounts payable to the general ledger

The other key position in the department is the cost recovery person, who may be referred to as an internal auditor or cost auditor. The accountabilities of this person are as follows:

- Compare supplier contracts to the rates stated on supplier invoices
- Investigate the company's use of allowances permitted by suppliers
- Examine the payables database to detect duplicate payments to suppliers
- Review freight, legal, health care, and telecommunications invoices for excessive billings
- Examine payables records to determine which suppliers are being used in contravention of the corporate spend management program
- Verify that all supplier credits are being appropriately used
- Verify that all deposits made are being returned as per expectations
- Support any cost recovery staff contractually working for the company

These two job descriptions are quite different. Someone in a cost recovery position must be inclined toward the detailed examination of records, while a payables clerk must be highly procedures-oriented, understanding exactly how all types of incoming transactions are to be sorted through and dispositioned.

Summary

Having laid out a general outline of the responsibilities and positioning of the payables department and its staff within a business, we turn in the following chapters to a more detailed examination of the activities outlined in the Payables Functions section.

Chapter 2
Invoice Processing

Introduction

The payables process involves the examination and scheduling of supplier invoices and other payment requests, which can be accomplished through manual, computerized, and evaluated receipts systems. It is also necessary to have procedures in place to issue checks, process supplier credits, and void checks. These are mostly high-volume applications, and therefore require detailed processes that are rigidly followed to ensure that payments are properly authorized and paid.

In this chapter, we provide examples of the various invoice processing procedures. We provide separate procedures for:

- Supplier invoice processing (manual system)
- Supplier invoice processing (integrated system)
- Accounts payable credits processing
- Evaluated receipts processing
- Check payment issuance
- Void checks

Process improvement tips are provided throughout the text and in a separate section near the end of the chapter, as well as flowcharts showing a streamlined view of each procedure.

> **Related Podcast Episodes:** Episodes 81, 82, and 138 of the Accounting Best Practices Podcast discuss accounts payable best practices, accounts payable matching, and a lean system for accounts payable, respectively. They are available at: **accountingtools.com/podcasts** or **iTunes**

The Need for Precise Invoice Processing

The typical organization is flooded with thousands of supplier invoices each year. If each invoice were to be handled as a separate and unique document, there would be a highly variable treatment of each one, with invoices being recorded inconsistently and paid individually. The result would be inaccurate record keeping, as well as some payments being made early, late, or multiple times. We avoid these problems by engaging in a highly regimented process flow that handles each invoice in exactly the same way. The result is a set of procedures that the payables staff is trained to use when dealing with invoices. In the following sections, we describe the differing approaches taken to invoice processing when using different types of computer systems.

To clarify the many steps required for these processes, we also include flowcharts that contain the key processing steps.

> **Note:** It is critical for the entire payables staff to follow the same invoice processing procedure, every time. Otherwise, some people will develop their own unique approaches that result in a few invoices being processed incorrectly. Possible outcomes are invoices being charged to the wrong accounts and – worst of all – duplicate payments to suppliers.

The Supplier Invoice Processing Procedure (Manual System)

Though most companies operate with a computer-based accounting system, it is considerably less likely that they coordinate the information between the accounting, purchasing, and receiving databases. When there is no inter-linking of this information, use the following procedure to process supplier invoices:

1. **Store purchase order.** When the purchasing department creates a purchase order to authorize the purchase of goods or services, they send a copy of the purchase order to the payables staff. Upon receipt, the payables staff stores the copy in an unmatched purchase orders file, sorted by supplier name. A sample purchase order form follows.
2. **Store receiving report.** When a supplier delivers goods to the receiving dock, the receiving staff completes a receiving report that references the supplier name, purchase order number, and number of units received, and sends a copy (sometimes including a copy of the bill of lading) to the payables staff. Upon receipt, the payables staff stores the copy in an unmatched receiving reports file, sorted by supplier name.
3. **Review supplier invoice.** When a supplier invoice is received, examine it to ensure that it contains the following information:

    - Supplier pay-to address
    - Payment terms
    - Purchase order reference number (optional)
    - List of services provided (for service contracts)
    - List of hours worked (for service contracts)

    If the required information is not listed, obtain it from the supplier and add it to the invoice.

Sample Purchase Order

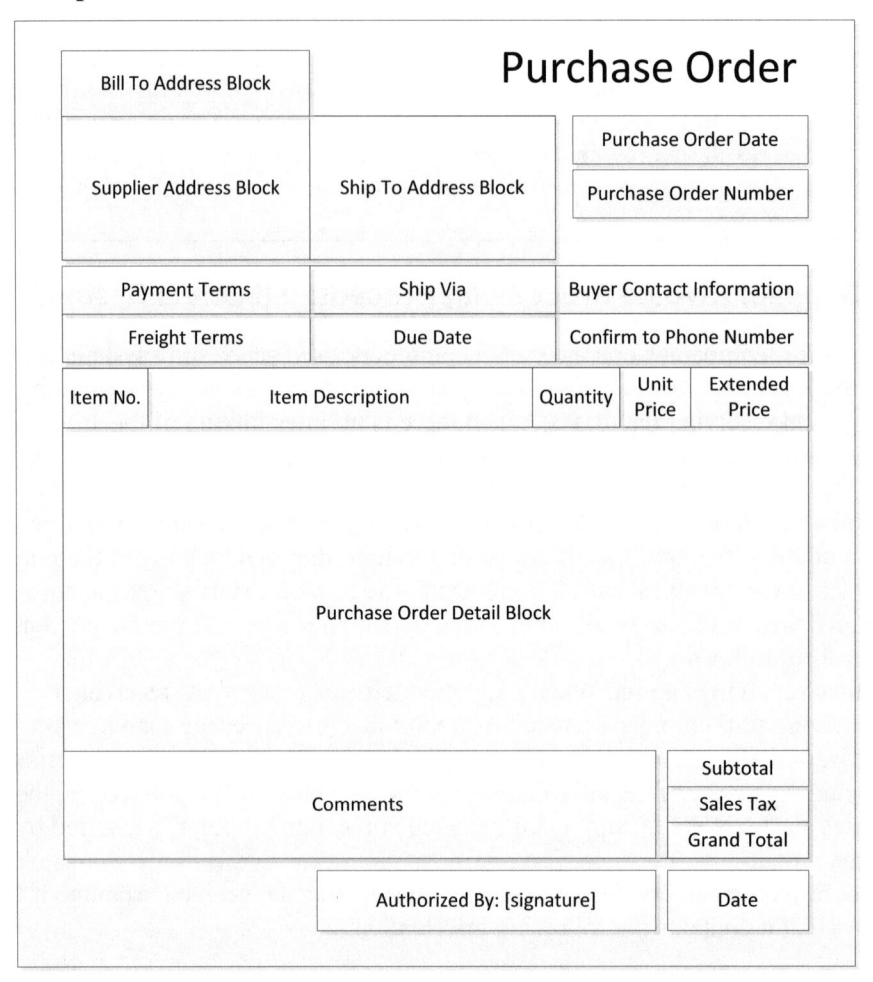

		Purchase Order	
Bill To Address Block			
Supplier Address Block	Ship To Address Block	Purchase Order Date	
		Purchase Order Number	
Payment Terms	Ship Via	Buyer Contact Information	
Freight Terms	Due Date	Confirm to Phone Number	
Item No.	Item Description	Quantity	Unit Price	Extended Price
	Purchase Order Detail Block			
Comments		Subtotal	
		Sales Tax	
		Grand Total	
	Authorized By: [signature]	Date	

A payment can also be initiated by a check request form, which must be signed by the person whose budget will be impacted by the resulting expense. The form should contain payment information, the reason for the expenditure, and the appropriate approvals for the expenditure level required. A sample form follows.

Sample Check Request Form

Check Request Form	
Payee Name	Payee Vendor Number
Payee Mailing Address	Tax ID Number
	Amount to Pay
Check Mailing Instructions	Account to Charge
Reason for Check Request	
Check Request Approvals Block	

This form states the name and mailing address of the entity to be paid, as well as the vendor identification number under which the entity's information is stored in the accounting system (if any). The form also includes the tax identification number for the entity, since it may be necessary to issue a Form 1099 tax report to them at the end of the calendar year. The account to be charged for the expense can be stated on the form, though many employees may not use it, since their knowledge of account codes may be limited. Finally, there should be a check request approvals block, on which are noted the varying levels of authorization needed, based on the amount requested.

4. **Conduct a three-way match.** Match the invoice with the receiving report issued by the receiving department and the purchase order issued by the purchasing department. If there is no receiving report or purchase order, contact the issuing department to see if there is a missing document. If the price stated on the supplier invoice does not match the price stated on the purchase order, contact the purchasing department for further instructions. If the quantity stated on the supplier invoice does not match the amount stated on the receiving report, contact the receiving department for further instructions.

> **Tip:** If some suppliers persistently submit incorrect billing information, the payables staff may need to discuss the issue with them. This takes time, but is more efficient over the long-term if payment problems can be eliminated. Thus, there may need to be an additional step following the matching process, to contact suppliers about problems found.

> **Tip:** Three-way matching can be a very good control, but it is also very inefficient. A more cost-effective alternative is to only require it for supplier invoices that exceed a certain dollar amount. It is also not needed for such ongoing payments as taxes, utilities, insurance, legal and accounting fees, and royalties.

5. **Obtain approval** (optional). If there is no purchase order for a supplier invoice, or if the invoice is an expense report from an employee, or if the invoice is for services (for which there is no receiving report), send the invoice to the person whose budget will be impacted by it and ask for an approval signature. It is customary to first make a copy of the invoice before sending the document to the approver, to ensure that the invoice will not be lost. It may also be useful to maintain a log of all invoices that have been sent out for approval, and cross them off the list as they are returned. The payables staff can use the log to follow up on any unapproved invoices.

> **Tip:** Approvers may not know why they were sent an invoice, or may not know where to write their approval on the document. To mitigate these issues, create an approval stamp that contains an approval line, and use this stamp on all invoices before sending them out for approval.

6. **Create vendor master file record** (optional). If the company has not done business with a supplier before, create a vendor master file record for it in the accounting system. This record contains such information as the supplier's payment address, tax identification number, contact information, and payment terms.

7. **Obtain Form W-9** (optional). Check the Form W-9 file to see if there is a completed form for the supplier. Alternatively, check the vendor master file to see if a tax identification number has been listed for the supplier. If not, contact the supplier and request that a form be sent. Upon receipt, file the form in the Form W-9 file.

> **Tip:** The Form W-9 is the source document for the tax identification number used in the Form 1099 that is sent to qualifying suppliers at year-end. The company is in the best position to obtain this document when it can withhold payments from suppliers, so be sure to tell suppliers that no payment will be forthcoming until a completed form is received.

Invoice Processing

8. **Enter invoice.** Enter the invoice into the accounting system for payment. Set the invoice date in the system at the invoice date noted on the invoice, rather than the current date (otherwise it will be paid late). Also, set the system to take advantage of any early payment discounts allowed by the supplier.

> **Tip:** When invoices contain no unique invoice number, there is a significant risk of paying them twice, since the accounting software cannot uniquely identify them. To avoid this issue, enforce a policy for creating invoice numbers. Such a policy typically converts the invoice date into an invoice number.

9. **Issue adjustment letter** (optional). If the amount to be paid differs from the amount stated on the supplier invoice, consider sending an adjustment letter to the supplier, stating the amount of and reason for the difference. This can keep the supplier from charging late payment fees and pestering the payables staff with questions about the unpaid difference. A sample adjustment letter follows.

Sample Adjustment Letter

Adjustment Notification

| Supplier Address Block | Company Logo | Company Address Block |

To whom it may concern:

[Company name] has short-paid your invoice number _____ by the amount of $_____, for the following reasons:

- ☐ Damaged goods
- ☐ Incorrect items delivered
- ☐ Incorrect quantity delivered
- ☐ Items delivered after requested due date
- ☐ Price on invoice does not match purchase order
- ☐ Quality test failed

Additional Comments Block

If you would like to discuss these issues with us, please contact the accounts payable department at [phone number].

Invoice Processing

> **Tip:** It may be useful to include more detailed information about an adjustment in a supplier's file, in case the supplier's collections staff asks for more detail at a later date.

The following exhibit shows a streamlined view of the supplier invoice processing procedure in a manual environment. It only includes those optional steps most likely to occur on an ongoing basis.

Supplier Invoice Process Flow

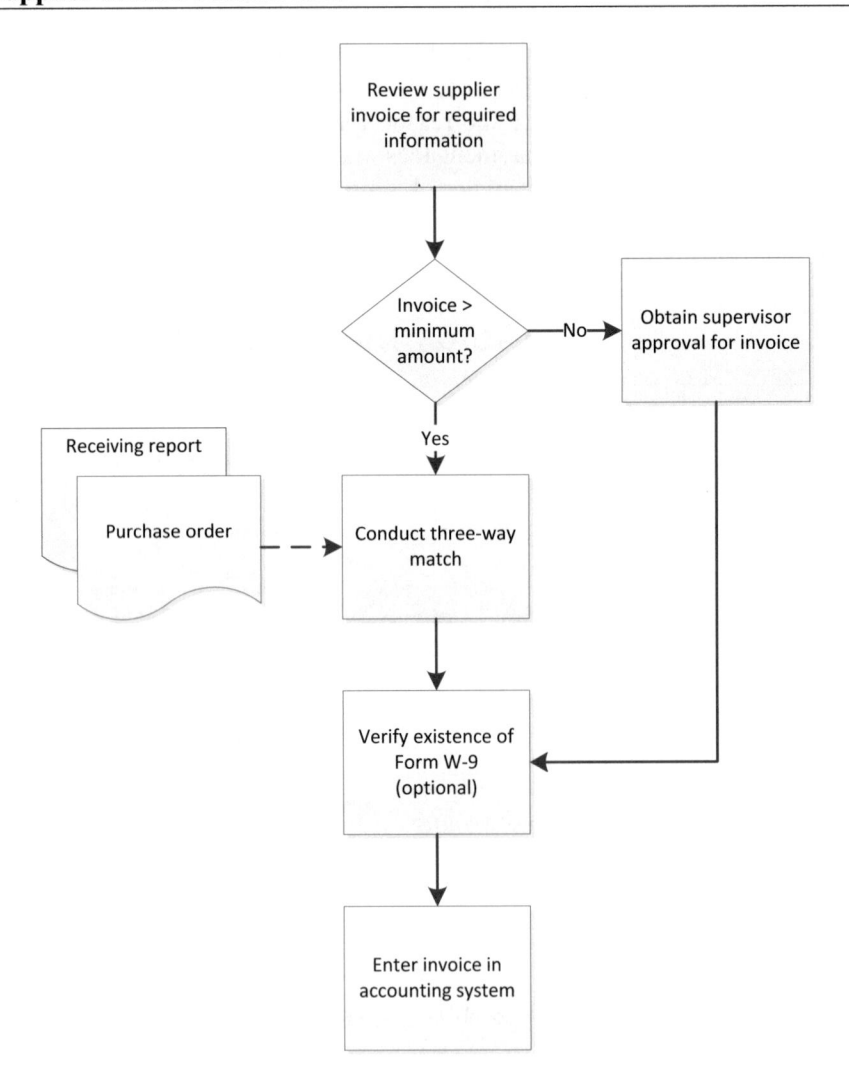

```
                    ┌─────────────────────┐
                    │  Review supplier    │
                    │ invoice for required│
                    │    information      │
                    └──────────┬──────────┘
                               │
                               ▼
                         ╱ Invoice >  ╲
                        ╱   minimum    ╲───No──┐
                        ╲   amount?    ╱       │
                         ╲_____╱        ▼
                               │        ┌──────────────┐
                              Yes       │   Obtain     │
                               │        │  supervisor  │
   ┌──────────────┐            │        │ approval for │
   │  Receiving   │            │        │   invoice    │
   │    report    │            │        └──────┬───────┘
   ├──────────────┤            ▼               │
   │   Purchase   │─ ─ ─▶ ┌──────────────┐     │
   │    order     │       │Conduct three-│     │
   └──────────────┘       │  way match   │     │
                          └──────┬───────┘     │
                                 │             │
                                 ▼             │
                          ┌──────────────┐     │
                          │ Verify       │     │
                          │ existence of │◀────┘
                          │ Form W-9     │
                          │ (optional)   │
                          └──────┬───────┘
                                 │
                                 ▼
                          ┌──────────────┐
                          │Enter invoice │
                          │in accounting │
                          │   system     │
                          └──────────────┘
```

The Supplier Invoice Processing Procedure (Integrated System)

If a company has a computer system that comprehensively integrates the information stored in all of its departments, there is an opportunity to streamline the payables process by shifting a portion of the three-way matching process (described in the last procedure) to the receiving department. The following procedure shows how this more advanced approach to invoice processing can be used.

1. **Conduct match at receiving dock.** When the purchasing staff creates a purchase order to authorize a purchase, they create a purchase order record in the computer system. This record is made available to the receiving department in the computer terminals at the receiving dock. They take the purchase order number from the shipping information provided by the supplier and enter it into the computer, which presents them with the purchase order record. The receiving staff then enters the quantity received into the purchase order record.
2. **Review supplier invoice.** This is the same step described earlier in the manual invoice processing procedure.
3. **Conduct two-way match.** Upon receipt of an invoice from the supplier, match the invoice with the purchase order in the computer system, against which receipts have already been logged. If there is a difference between the quantity received and the quantity stated on the invoice, the company should pay the quantity recorded by the receiving staff. If the price stated on the supplier invoice does not match the price stated on the purchase order, contact the purchasing department for further instructions.
4. **Obtain approval** (optional). This is the same step described earlier in the manual invoice processing procedure.
5. **Obtain Form W-9** (optional). This is the same step described earlier in the manual invoice processing procedure.
6. **Enter invoice.** This is the same step described earlier for the manual invoice processing procedure. A variation is for the payables staff to enter each line item in the invoice into the computer system, which then automatically conducts the three-way match described for the preceding procedure. However, it can be time-consuming to enter longer invoices in this manner.

> **Tip:** It is also possible to scan supplier invoices into the computer system. The scanning software is preconfigured to know where key information is located on each supplier's invoice, which the software then extracts and stores. This method is time-consuming to set up, and is likely to reject the invoices of suppliers whose invoice characteristics have not been entered into the system.

7. **Issue adjustment letter** (optional). This is the same step described earlier in the manual invoice processing procedure.

Note the absence of a step to create a vendor master file record, since the purchasing staff should have already created this record when they issued the initiating purchase order.

The following exhibit shows a streamlined view of the supplier invoice processing procedure in an integrated system.

Invoice Processing

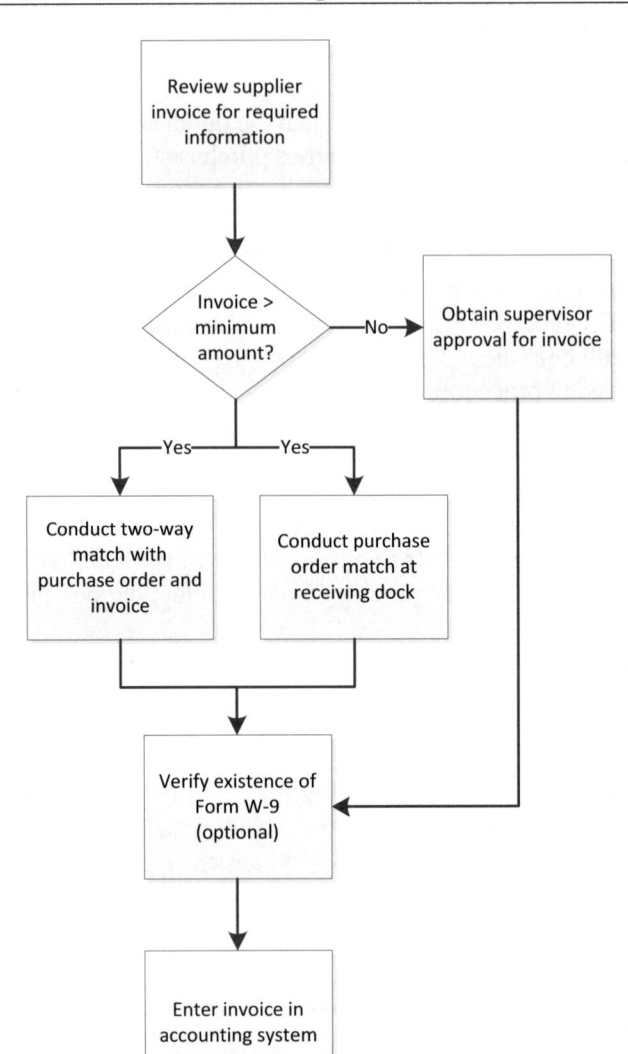

Supplier Invoice Process Flow (Integrated System)

```
            ┌─────────────────────┐
            │ Review supplier     │
            │ invoice for required│
            │ information         │
            └──────────┬──────────┘
                       │
                       ▼
                 ╱ Invoice >  ╲         ┌─────────────────────┐
                ╱  minimum     ╲──No──▶│ Obtain supervisor   │
                ╲  amount?     ╱        │ approval for invoice│
                 ╲            ╱         └──────────┬──────────┘
                  Yes    Yes                       │
            ┌──────┘      └──────┐                 │
            ▼                    ▼                 │
    ┌──────────────┐     ┌──────────────┐          │
    │Conduct two-way│     │Conduct purchase│        │
    │match with    │     │order match at │          │
    │purchase order│     │receiving dock │          │
    │and invoice   │     │               │          │
    └──────┬───────┘     └──────┬────────┘          │
           │                    │                   │
           └────────┬───────────┘                   │
                    ▼                               │
           ┌──────────────────┐                     │
           │ Verify existence │◀────────────────────┘
           │ of Form W-9      │
           │ (optional)       │
           └────────┬─────────┘
                    ▼
           ┌──────────────────┐
           │ Enter invoice in │
           │ accounting system│
           └──────────────────┘
```

Accounts Payable Credits Processing Procedure

It will sometimes be necessary to apply to a supplier for a credit against an invoice, and to appropriately record this credit in the accounting system. The procedure for accounts payable credits processing is outlined below:

1. **Notify accounts payable.** When an employee wants to request the reduction of a supplier invoice by obtaining a credit, he or she notifies the payables staff, which records the following information regarding the proposed credit:
    - Supplier contact information

- Related supplier invoice number
- Related company purchase order number
- Reason for the proposed credit
- Status of any returned goods

2. **Issue credit request** (optional). Complete a form letter, requesting a credit and stating the reason for the request. Retain a copy for monitoring purposes, and send the original to the supplier.

> **Tip:** Wherever possible, have either the purchasing department or the payables staff handle all product returns and credits. If individual employees handle this task, they are likely to not follow through on supplier submission requirements, resulting in no credits being issued.

3. **Obtain return merchandise authorization (RMA) and ship** (optional). Contact the supplier's order entry or customer service staff and request an RMA. If granted, have the shipping department return the relevant goods to the supplier, identified by the RMA number.
4. **Enter supplier credit.** Upon receipt of a credit from a supplier, enter it into the accounts payable system.

> **Tip:** It is possible that there are multiple vendor master file records for a single supplier, so first verify which record is being used to store invoices, and then enter the credit against that same record. Otherwise, the credit may be applied to the wrong record and so will not be applied against a payment.

The following exhibit shows a streamlined view of the accounts payable credits processing procedure.

Accounts Payable Credits Process Flow

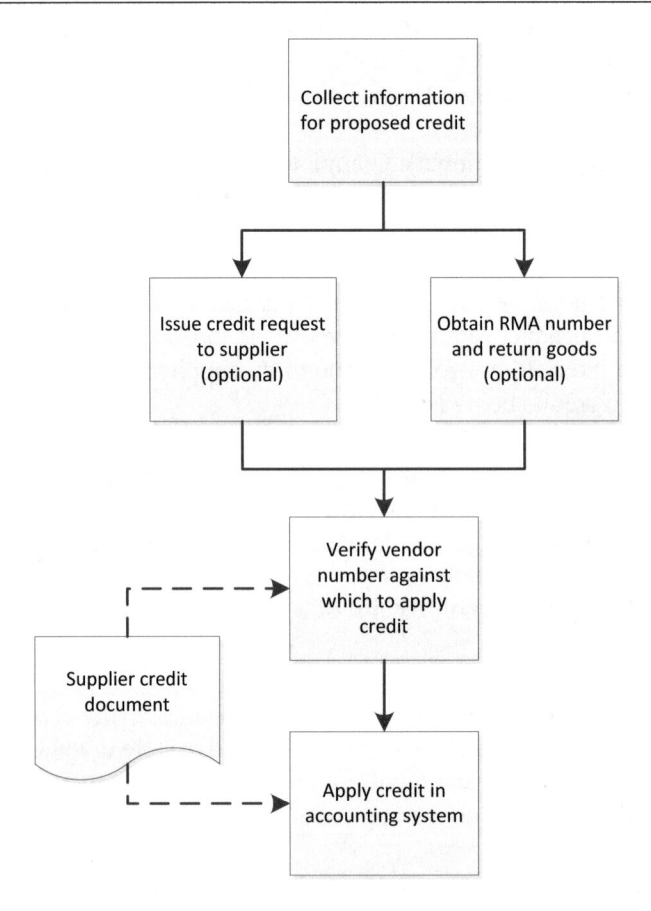

```
                    ┌─────────────────┐
                    │ Collect information │
                    │ for proposed credit │
                    └─────────┬───────┘
                    ┌─────────┴─────────┐
                    ▼                   ▼
         ┌──────────────────┐  ┌──────────────────┐
         │ Issue credit request │  │ Obtain RMA number │
         │    to supplier    │  │  and return goods │
         │    (optional)    │  │    (optional)    │
         └─────────┬────────┘  └─────────┬────────┘
                   └──────────┬──────────┘
                              ▼
                    ┌──────────────────┐
                    │  Verify vendor   │
                    │ number against   │
                    │ which to apply   │
                    │      credit      │
                    └─────────┬────────┘
    ┌──────────────┐          │
    │Supplier credit│─ ─ ─ ─ ─│
    │   document   │          ▼
    └──────────────┘  ┌──────────────────┐
                      │ Apply credit in  │
                      │ accounting system │
                      └──────────────────┘
```

The Evaluated Receipts Processing Procedure

The evaluated receipts system involves sourcing all cost of goods sold items through a small number of suppliers, who are then authorized to deliver their raw materials on a just-in-time basis directly to the company's production lines. Once manufacturing has been completed, the company uses its bills of material to determine what must have been delivered to the company, and pays based on this information and the price listed in its authorizing purchase order. The supplier does not have to send an invoice, and may even be discouraged from doing so. Though this approach is extremely efficient, it also requires a very well-organized manufacturing and purchasing system. The procedure for evaluated receipts processing is outlined below:

1. **Issue master purchase order.** The purchasing department issues a master purchase order to a supplier, authorizing a general quantity of goods to be acquired over the purchasing period, at a specific price.
2. **Issue purchase order release.** The purchasing department issues a release against the purchase order, detailing exactly how many units are to be delivered, and the

date and time of delivery. This may be an automated release from the materials management system.

3. **Calculate production totals.** Once production has been completed, compile the grand total of all units produced. An automated counting system, such as a fixed bar code scanner on a conveyor belt, may be sufficient for conducting this count.

> **Tip:** There should also be a system in place for tracking materials that were scrapped during the production process, since the company must add this information to the production totals to arrive at the supplier payment information described in the next step.

4. **Calculate delivered amount.** The payables system multiplies the number of units produced by the unit quantities stated in the bill of materials for each unit to arrive at the amount of materials delivered by the supplier. The system then multiplies the amount of materials delivered by the unit cost specified in the master purchase order to arrive at the payment due to the supplier, and automatically authorizes payment to the supplier.

> **Tip:** There is no need for a supplier invoice in the evaluated receipts system. In fact, an invoice increases the amount of paperwork that the payables staff must sort through, and so should be discouraged.

The following exhibit shows a streamlined view of the evaluated receipts processing procedure.

The Check Payment Issuance Procedure

The predominant mode of payment to suppliers is to print a check, though the use of direct deposit and wire transfers is also common. The check payment issuance procedure is outlined below, while the procedural variations for direct deposits and wire transfers are noted in the next section.

1. **Print payment due dates report.** Any accounting software package includes a standard report that itemizes the invoices that are now due for payment. The payables staff should print this report prior to the next scheduled date on which it makes payments. This report only works if the payables staff has previously entered the standard payment terms for each supplier in the vendor master file in the accounting software. The system should automatically present invoices that are available for early payment discounts.

> **Tip:** If a manual accounts payable system is being used, store supplier invoices in folders that are organized by due date.

Evaluated Receipts Process Flow

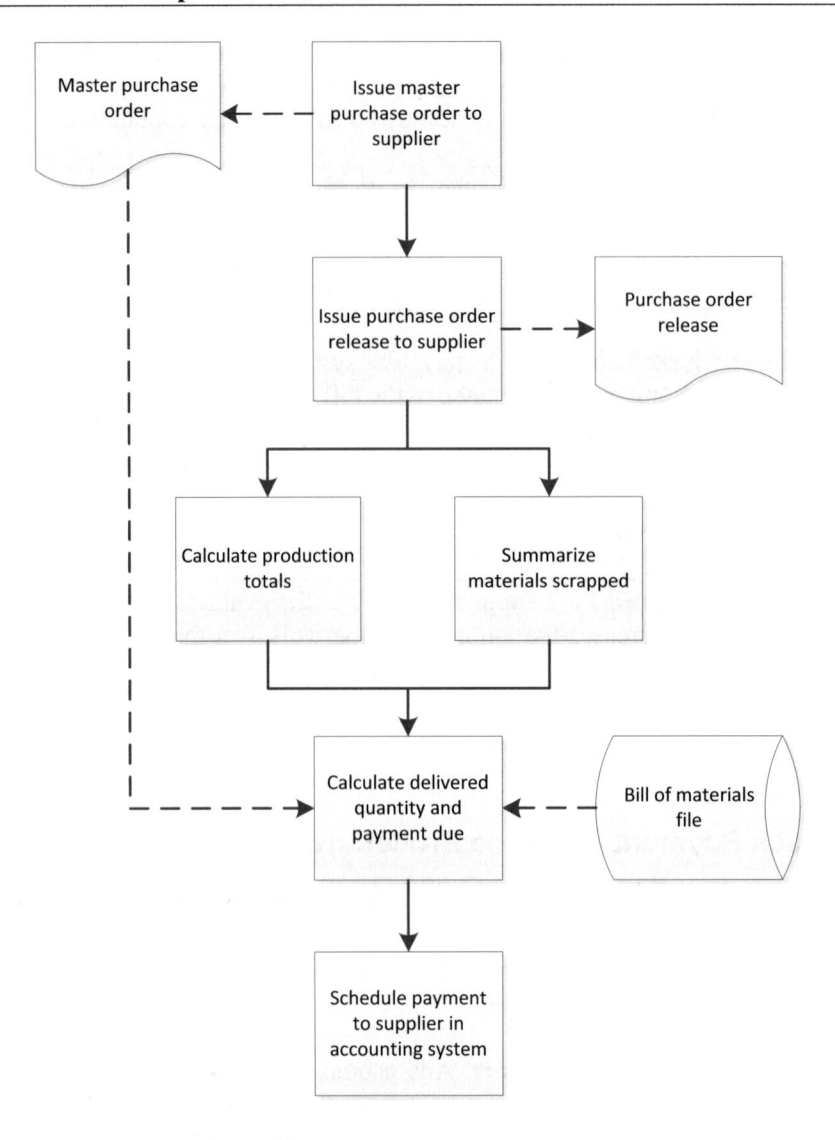

Flowchart:
- Issue master purchase order to supplier → Master purchase order
- Issue master purchase order to supplier → Issue purchase order release to supplier
- Issue purchase order release to supplier → Purchase order release
- Issue purchase order release to supplier → Calculate production totals; Summarize materials scrapped
- Calculate production totals & Summarize materials scrapped → Calculate delivered quantity and payment due
- Master purchase order ┄→ Calculate delivered quantity and payment due
- Bill of materials file ┄→ Calculate delivered quantity and payment due
- Calculate delivered quantity and payment due → Schedule payment to supplier in accounting system

2. **Approve payments.** The payables manager or controller review the report to see if any prospective payments should be delayed. If so, they cross out these items.
3. **Select payments.** Access the payments module in the accounting software and select all approved invoices listed on the payment due dates report. Print a preliminary check register and match it against the approved payment due dates report to ensure that only approved invoices are being paid.
4. **Obtain check stock.** Go to the locked cabinet where check stock is stored, and extract a sufficient number of checks for the check run. Re-lock the cabinet.
5. **Print checks.** Enter the beginning check number for the unused checks into the accounting software. Print the checks. Verify that the checks were properly

aligned and that all checks were printed. If not, re-print the batch of checks. Otherwise, accept the check run in the software and print a final check register.

> **Tip:** It is customary to retain a copy of the final check register, but there is no particular reason to do so, since the accounting system stores this information and can usually print a replacement report on demand.

6. **Return unused checks.** Return all unused checks to the locked cabinet. Note in a check usage log the check number range that was used. This step is needed to uncover cases where checks may have been fraudulently removed from the stock of unused checks.
7. **Sign checks.** Attach all supporting documentation to each check. Then schedule a check signing meeting with an authorized check signer. Be available during the meeting to answer any questions posed by the check signer. The check signer examines the supporting materials for any check where there is a concern about the payment. If a check is for an unusually large amount, consider requiring an additional signature on the check, thereby providing another level of authorization.
8. **Issue checks.** Attach any required remittance advices to checks, and mail them to recipients. Then attach the company's copy of remittance advices to supporting documents, and file them by supplier name.
9. **Issue positive pay file** (optional). If the company uses a positive pay system, compile information about the newly-printed checks into a file and send it to the bank. The bank then matches submitted checks against this file and rejects those not listed in the file.

The following exhibit shows a streamlined view of the check payment issuance procedure, not including the optional use of positive pay.

Invoice Processing

Check Payment Issuance Process Flow

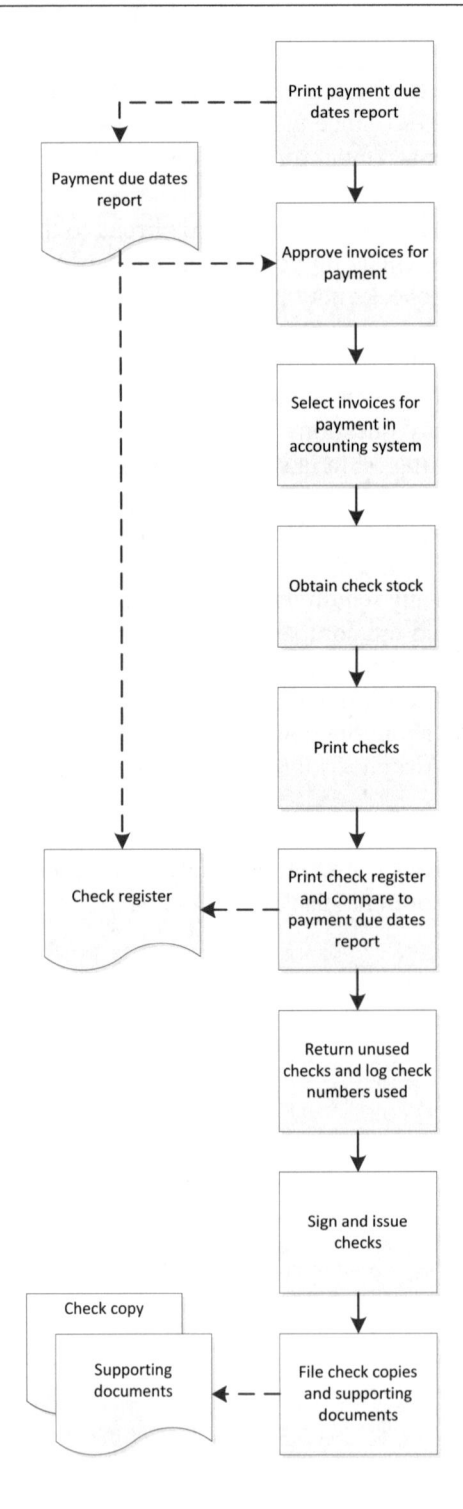

```
Print payment due dates report
        ↓
Payment due dates report
        ↓
Approve invoices for payment
        ↓
Select invoices for payment in accounting system
        ↓
Obtain check stock
        ↓
Print checks
        ↓
Print check register and compare to payment due dates report  →  Check register
        ↓
Return unused checks and log check numbers used
        ↓
Sign and issue checks
        ↓
File check copies and supporting documents  →  Check copy / Supporting documents
```

23

Payment Alternatives

The preceding procedure was designed for the issuance of payments by check. However, payments can also be made by direct deposit or wire transfer. These two alternatives are:

- *Direct deposit.* This involves payments using the Automated Clearing House (ACH) system, which is a digital payment that is usually completed in one or two business days. The direct deposit procedure is the same as the one used for check payments, through the point where payments are approved. After that point, the payables staff either prepares a direct deposit file for transmission to the company's bank, or accesses the bank's secure direct deposit site and manually sets up each payment. The bank then sends a confirmation to the company, stating the amounts and payees associated with each direct deposit transaction. The payables staff notes in the accounting system that the related invoices were paid by direct deposit.
- *Wire transfer.* This involves an electronic payment from the company's bank to the supplier's bank. It is typically completed within one day, though some international wire transfers can require a longer clearing period. The procedure is identical to the one used for direct deposit, except that the approval of an authorized person is usually required. Wire transfers are not recommended, since the associated fees are much higher than for other payment methods.

> **Tip:** Electronic payments are frequently made outside of the normal flow of accounts payable transactions, which means that someone has to manually record these payments in the accounts payable system. If they forget to do so, there is a risk that duplicate payments will be made. To mitigate this risk, set up a default payment type for each supplier in the vendor master file, and consider any variation from that payment type to be a policy violation that requires extra approvals.

More information about these payment alternatives is provided in the following Types of Payments chapter.

The Void Checks Procedure

There will be times when a check is created but is either replaced internally or lost in transit to the recipient. These checks should be voided in the payables system in order to avoid having a checks-in-transit figure on the bank reconciliation that is higher than the actual amount in transit. The void checks procedure is outlined below:

1. **Deface check.** If the check is still on-hand internally, deface the check with a "Void" perforation or stamp.

Invoice Processing

> **Tip:** For informational purposes, it may be useful to write the reason for the void on the back of the check.

2. **Issue a stop payment** (optional). If the check was lost in transit to the recipient, there is still a chance that it may eventually be received and cashed. In these situations, it is best to contact the bank and issue a stop payment flag on the check, which means that the bank will not accept the check if someone ever tries to cash it. The bank will charge a fee for this service.

> **Tip:** Depending on the circumstances, it may be possible to charge the check recipient for the bank's stop payment fee.

3. **Designate as void.** Access the payables module in the accounting system and flag the check as being void. This will remove the check from the "checks in transit" portion of the bank reconciliation, as well as re-designate the supplier invoice being paid by the check as unpaid.
4. **File voided check.** File the voided check in a separate voided checks folder. It is possible that the voided checks will be reviewed by the auditors as part of their year-end audit, so keep these checks segregated for their use.

The following exhibit shows a streamlined view of the void checks procedure.

Void Checks Process Flow

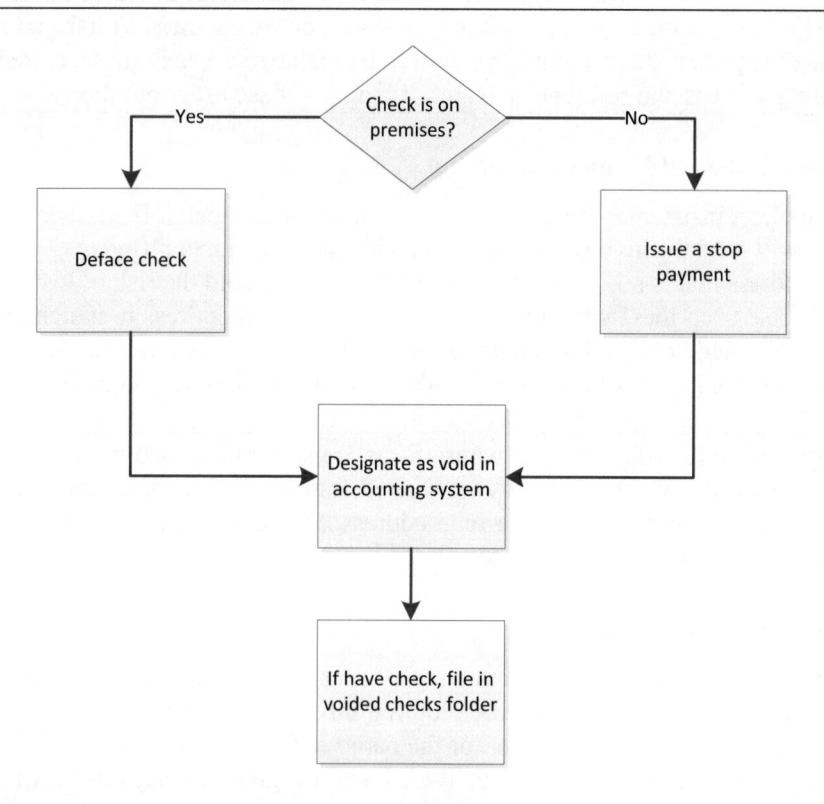

```
                    Check is on
        ──Yes──     premises?    ──No──
                        │
        ▼                               ▼
   Deface check                    Issue a stop
                                     payment
        │                               │
        └──────►  Designate as void in  ◄──────┘
                   accounting system
                        │
                        ▼
                  If have check, file in
                  voided checks folder
```

Enhancements to Invoice Processing

The primary focus of this chapter has been on the basic process flow for dealing with supplier invoices. We have inserted a number of improvement suggestions into the text of these processes. In addition, this section contains additional suggestions for other types of improvements. More enhancements are noted in the Payables Technology chapter.

Direct Invoice Delivery

There is a large potential bottleneck when suppliers send invoices directly to their contacts at the company, since those contacts may not forward the invoices to the payables staff in an overly brisk manner. Instead, the payables staff should contact the billing departments of all suppliers that persist in sending invoices to their contacts, and request that the billing contact be changed to the payables department. This may require multiple conversations with the more recalcitrant suppliers.

> **Tip:** An alternative to badgering suppliers after-the-fact is to do so in advance, by sending them a welcome packet when they first start doing business with the company. The welcome packet states the information to be included on each invoice, including the mailing address and references to authorizing purchase order numbers.

Centralize E-mailed Invoice Processing

Some suppliers insist on e-mailing their invoices to the company. If so, there is a risk that they will send the invoices to an e-mail address located in a different department, or to an address that is no longer used or monitored. To avoid the risk of lost invoices that will arise from these situations, create a single e-mail address to which invoices are to be sent, and notify all suppliers of this address. Also, assign specific responsibility for the monitoring of this e-mail address, so that no invoices languish there.

> **Tip:** Sign up for an e-fax service, where faxes are sent to a phone number at which the transmissions are automatically converted into electronic documents and forwarded to the corporate invoicing e-mail address. Doing so centralizes the receipt of all possible types of electronic invoices.

Return Incomplete Invoices

If a supplier invoice does not contain a sufficient amount of information, return it to the supplier with a request to add the required information. For example, there may be a missing purchase order number, or the name of the person who placed the order is missing, or the nature of the item delivered is too vague. The payables staff should not have to waste time tracking down this information, so put the burden of proof back on the supplier.

Invoice Numbering Convention

Adopt a standard procedure for creating invoice numbers for any invoices that do not already have an invoice number. By doing so, anyone entering an invoice should derive exactly the same invoice number from the information on the invoice, thereby mitigating the risk that such an invoice will be entered into the computer system more than once (the computer should reject any invoice number that already resides in the system). Examples of an invoice numbering convention are:

- Use the invoice date as the invoice number
- Use the packing slip number as the invoice number
- Never enter the leading zeros in an invoice number
- Never enter any dashes or other punctuation in an invoice number

Request Aggregated Invoice

An interesting variation on paying from invoices is to negotiate with suppliers to send a single invoice each month, containing all goods and services provided to the company for the past month. Doing so can considerably reduce the amount of invoicing volume that the payables staff must deal with.

The issuance of a single invoice departs from the standard invoicing procedure for most suppliers, where the shipment of goods automatically triggers the creation of an invoice. Also, there may be cash flow concerns when a supplier provides goods or services near the beginning of a month, but is not allowed to send an invoice until the end of the month. These concerns can be reduced by offering faster payment terms, or perhaps by offering to sole source with the supplier.

Minimize Approvals

Approvals should be avoided as much as possible in the payables process. There is a significant bottleneck involved in waiting for a manager to approve an invoice, so use as many other alternatives as possible. For example:

- *Use purchase order as approval*. If the purchasing department has already issued a purchase order, then the purchase order itself should be sufficient evidence that an invoice can be paid.
- *Eliminate approvals for small amounts*. Establish a threshold invoice amount, below which there is no need for an approval. If using this option, conduct an occasional examination of small invoices to see if anyone is engaging in fraudulent purchasing behavior.
- *Use negative approvals*. Send an invoice copy to an approver, with instructions to only respond if there is a problem with the invoice. The payables staff will assume that all other invoices have been approved by default.
- *Obtain approvals in person*. If it is absolutely necessary to obtain an approval, have a payables person hand-deliver the invoice, answer any questions posed by the approver, and bring back the signed invoice. Doing so is time-consuming, but ensures that invoices will be returned in a timely manner. This approach is most effective when a manager has a history of rarely approving invoices in a timely manner.
- *Escalate approvals*. If an approval is needed but cannot be obtained within a reasonable period of time, immediately route the invoice to a backup approver.
- *Approve based on billing history*. If a supplier has a history of issuing flawless invoices to the company, assume that this trend will continue, and automatically approve its invoices for payment. If a pattern of billing flaws appears at a later date, remove this approval exemption from the supplier's invoices.

Analyze Matching Discrepancies

The three-way matching process will inevitably uncover a number of discrepancies between the supplier's invoice, the authorizing purchase order, and the related receiving documentation. The payables manager will likely approve minor variances with no further analysis, since doing so minimizes the time requirements of the payables staff and represents only a minor change in cost. However, additional analysis may be called for when there are significant and recurring discrepancies. For these larger discrepancies, maintain a database of the dates and amounts of the variances, as well as the names of the suppliers with which they are associated. It is likely that a summarization of the database will reveal that a small number of suppliers routinely cause most of the discrepancies. Possible solutions include discussions of the issues with the billing staff of the indicated suppliers and even terminating any further business transactions with them.

Monitor Invoice Disputes

There may be disputes between the company and a supplier regarding the contents of an invoice. Possible topics of concern are the presence or absence of a sales tax charge, the price billed per unit, and the number of units received. Spending time arguing about these discrepancies requires a notable amount of staff time, quite possibly representing a larger cost than the amount under dispute. The payables manager should maintain a log of all open invoice disputes and review it daily, to monitor the status of each one. It may be useful to develop a protocol for the different resolution options, and allow the payables manager a broad level of authority to settle most disputes without further input from senior management. This approach will eliminate all but the most serious disputes within a few days.

Automate Recurring Payments

A small number of invoices are probably paid in exactly the same amount and on the same date each month, such as rent and equipment lease payments. If so, set up recurring payments for these items in the payables software, with a designated termination date. It may not be necessary to attach any explanatory materials to these payments, as long as they are designated as recurring payments. Doing so slightly reduces the processing time required by the payables staff.

Restrict Manual Checks

There are a number of rush-payment situations where employees demand that a payment be made at once. These payments fall outside of the normal batch-oriented check payment process, which increases the time required per payment, as well as the risk that the payment will not be entered into the payables system (which causes bank reconciliation problems). There are a variety of ways to reduce the number of manual payments made, including:

- Charge the requesting department a large inter-company fee for each manual payment made.
- Follow up on each manual payment to see if similar payments can be addressed by the regular payment system in the future.

- Print manual checks through the computer system by creating batch sizes of one check (thereby ensuring that the information is at least properly recorded in the payables system).
- Increase the frequency of scheduled check runs, so that more manual payments can be incorporated into a standard payment batch.

Analyze Manual Checks

There may be good reasons why manual checks are created. Perhaps there is a flaw in the system that allows invoices to be lost, requiring a rush payment to an irate supplier. Or perhaps there is a manual process in place for identifying early payment discounts, and a last-minute manual check is requested in order to take advantage of a discount. Consider keeping a log of the reasons why manual checks are being created, and aggregate the information in the log from time to time, to see if there are recurring issues that can be corrected. For example, sending out invoices for approval before entering them in the payables system can result in missing invoices that are not paid, so change the system to log in the invoices first, and then send them out for approval.

Restrict Manual Delivery of Checks

Payables processing is essentially a high-volume process. When an employee wants to have a check delivered to him by hand, this requires the payables staff to search through the latest check run, extract the check, and walk it over to the requesting person. This extra labor can represent a significant extra workload for the payables staff, especially when the requesting person is located at a distance from the payables department. Consequently, manual deliveries should be discouraged, perhaps by requiring the prior approval of the company controller.

Restrict Cash Advances

Cash advances require an inordinate amount of staff time, first to cut a manual check for the requesting person, and then to track whether the person has repaid the advance. This issue is best sidestepped by imposing a policy that strongly restricts the situations in which cash advances are allowed.

Schedule Frequent Check Runs

When a business only prints checks once every few weeks, supplier payments are likely to be made late, which increases the amount of staff time spent responding to supplier inquiries, as well as in dealing with replacement invoices that were sent under the assumption that the original invoice was lost. In addition, the more irate suppliers will demand that they be issued a manual check payment at once. To eliminate all of these extra demands on the payables staff, schedule at least one check run per week, if not more. Doing so ensures that payments are made as close as possible to the due dates of invoices.

Use a Signature Stamp or Plate

Check signing is intended to be a final review of payments, but most check signers are in too much of a rush to conduct an in-depth review of each check. Further, the company is likely already contractually committed to making each payment by the time the check signer reviews a check, which makes this control even weaker. A reasonable alternative is to use a signature stamp or plate to sign checks, as long as some sort of review was conducted earlier in the purchasing process (such as the issuance of a purchase order or the approval of an invoice by a supervisor). If management is uncomfortable with this leaner approach, a mid-way solution is to require a check signer only for larger checks.

Reduce the Need for Second Signatures

Company management may require that larger check payments be signed by a second check signer, under the theory that two check signers are more likely to spot problems than a single signer. From the efficiency perspective of the payables department, second signatures are to be avoided, since the additional check signer must be tracked down before a check can be issued. To reduce this extra amount of work, discuss with senior management the number of instances in which second signatures were required, and the nature of the invoices covered by these signatures. The discussion could result in a higher threshold before second signatures are required.

Encourage use of ACH

There are a number of possible ways in which to encourage suppliers to accept payments by ACH, since this is a lower-cost payment alternative. Possible options include:

- Include ACH payments as a negotiating point when discussing terms with suppliers
- Include ACH signup information in the welcome packet sent to new suppliers
- Market this payment alternative to the controllers and treasurers of suppliers
- Offer to pay slightly faster when suppliers accept ACH payments
- Require that all accelerated "rush" checks be paid by ACH
- Schedule ACH payments more frequently than check runs
- Volunteer to also send a separate e-mail to suppliers that contains the remittance information related to each ACH payment

Tip: *Always* e-mail remittance information to suppliers who are about to receive an ACH payment. Otherwise, they will call the payables department to ask which invoices were paid, which wastes the time of the staff.

A potentially significant issue when converting suppliers to ACH payments is that the company no longer benefits from the lengthy float period associated with check payments, which can trigger a sharp decline in the cash balance. Be sure to discuss this issue with the treasurer before rolling out ACH payments; a possible solution is to make ACH payments a few days late, to compensate for the lost float.

Clean the Payables Aging Report

The main reporting tool in the payables area is the accounts payable aging report. This report categorizes payables to suppliers based on time buckets. The report is typically set up within 30-day time buckets, so that each successive column in the report lists supplier invoices that are:

- 0 to 30 days old
- 31 to 60 days old
- 61 to 90 days old
- Older than 90 days

The intent of the report is to provide a visual aid in determining which invoices are overdue for payment. For the report to be effective, it should be periodically cleaned up, so that stray debits and credits are removed from the report. Otherwise, it tends to become cluttered over time, and therefore more difficult to read.

Search for Open Credits

Ongoing transactions with suppliers may occasionally result in a few credits being granted by the supplier, perhaps as sales discounts or for returned goods. Request that suppliers send the company a quarterly statement of account, and review it for these open credits. The credits can then be used to offset other payments.

Reduce the Number of Suppliers

In general, the difficulty of running the payables function is increased when there are many suppliers. Each supplier requires a separate vendor master file in the payables system, and presents additional monitoring issues involving where invoices are sent, early payment discounts, and any other clerical minutiae required of the payables staff. Consequently, if the purchasing department can limit its purchases to a select group of prime suppliers, this can reduce the workload of the payables department.

Final Thoughts

Upgrading an existing payables process with any of the best practices noted here requires extensive analysis. The payables manager should ponder how a prospective change will impact the efficiency of the overall process, how to train the staff in the altered process, how existing controls will be impacted, whether new controls should be added, whether other departments will be impacted, and whether the alteration increases the risk of fraud. Further, because payables is a high-volume activity, it can make sense to roll out changes slowly, allowing time for each successive change to be fully integrated into the existing process before considering additional changes.

Once a change has been made, ask the internal audit staff to conduct a post-implementation review to determine how well the change has been accepted. It is quite possible that some payables personnel have slid back into their old processing habits and are ignoring the change, which will call for additional remediation activities.

Summary

The typical payables department processes thousands of payments each year. Given the high transaction volume, it is wise to have detailed procedures in place for all possible variations on the processing of invoices and related payments. If procedures are absent, not sufficiently detailed, or weakly enforced, there is a strong likelihood that incorrect payments will be made, which will require a substantial effort to investigate and correct.

It is useful to obtain the services of the internal audit department for periodic testing of the accounts payable system. Doing so may spot potential control weaknesses and lead to the enhancement of some procedures. By engaging in testing on a regular basis, it should be possible to operate an industrial-grade payables function with minimal errors.

In this chapter, we described several alternative methods for paying suppliers. In the next chapter, we delve more deeply into the nature of each of these payments, as well as the use of petty cash, bank drafts, and letters of credit to make payments.

Chapter 3
Types of Payments

Introduction

There are a number of alternatives available for the manner in which suppliers and employees can be paid through the payables system. The method chosen can accelerate or delay the consumption of cash. There are also notable differences in the cost of each payment method. This chapter reviews each of the payment types, including the best usage of each one, and their comparative advantages and disadvantages.

Cash Payments (Petty Cash)

While cash is still the predominant form of payment by customers in some retail environments, it is an increasingly rare mode of payment to a supplier. Cash as a form of payment is mostly relegated to unplanned expenditures for incidental items (which are commonly handled through petty cash reimbursements), and for tips. Cash still has some applicability when paying temporary workers who do not have bank accounts, as is the case in the agricultural sector.

Petty cash is a small amount of cash that is kept on the company premises to pay for minor cash needs, such as office supplies, cards, flowers, and so forth. It is stored in a petty cash drawer or box near where it is most needed. There may be several petty cash locations in a larger business, probably one per building or even one per department.

To set up a petty cash fund, the cashier creates a check in the amount of the funding assigned to a particular petty cash fund (usually a few hundred dollars). Alternatively, the cashier could simply count out the cash for the petty cash fund, if there are enough bills and coins on the premises. The petty cash transfer form is used to document the transfer of cash from the bookkeeper to the petty cash custodian. Both the bookkeeper and custodian retain a copy of the form as evidence of who has taken responsibility for the cash. A sample form follows.

Types of Payments

Sample Petty Cash Transfer Form

```
┌─────────────────────────────────────────────────────────────────┐
│                  Petty Cash Transfer Form                       │
│                                                                 │
│   ┌──────────────────────────┐      ┌──────────────────────┐    │
│   │ Petty Cash Fund Number   │      │        Date          │    │
│   └──────────────────────────┘      └──────────────────────┘    │
│                                                                 │
│   ┌──────────────────────────────────────┐  ┌──────────────┐    │
│   │            The Sum Of                │  │  Total Paid  │    │
│   └──────────────────────────────────────┘  └──────────────┘    │
│                                                                 │
│                      ┌──────────────────────────────────────┐   │
│  For funds received: │ Petty Cash Custodian: [signature]    │   │
│                      └──────────────────────────────────────┘   │
│                      ┌──────────────────────────────────────┐   │
│  For funds disbursed:│ Cashier: [signature]                 │   │
│                      └──────────────────────────────────────┘   │
└─────────────────────────────────────────────────────────────────┘
```

Note that the form requires the amount transferred to be written in words, not just in numbers. This makes it more difficult for someone to fraudulently alter the numerical amount listed to a larger number, and pocket the difference paid.

The petty cash custodian then disburses petty cash from the fund in exchange for receipts related to whatever the expense may be. When someone is paid from a petty cash fund, they must complete a petty cash voucher. The voucher provides evidence that the person was actually paid, since someone must sign for the payment received. It also provides detail regarding the type of expense being reimbursed, since it provides space for both an expense description and the account number to which the expense is to be charged. The following sample voucher contains two additional features to combat fraud. First, it includes a voucher number, so that auditors can investigate missing vouchers. Second, the form requires that the petty cash custodian not only enter the total amount paid, but also to state the amount in words; by doing so, it is much more difficult for someone to fraudulently increase the amount stated on the voucher and remove a corresponding amount from petty cash.

Sample Petty Cash Voucher

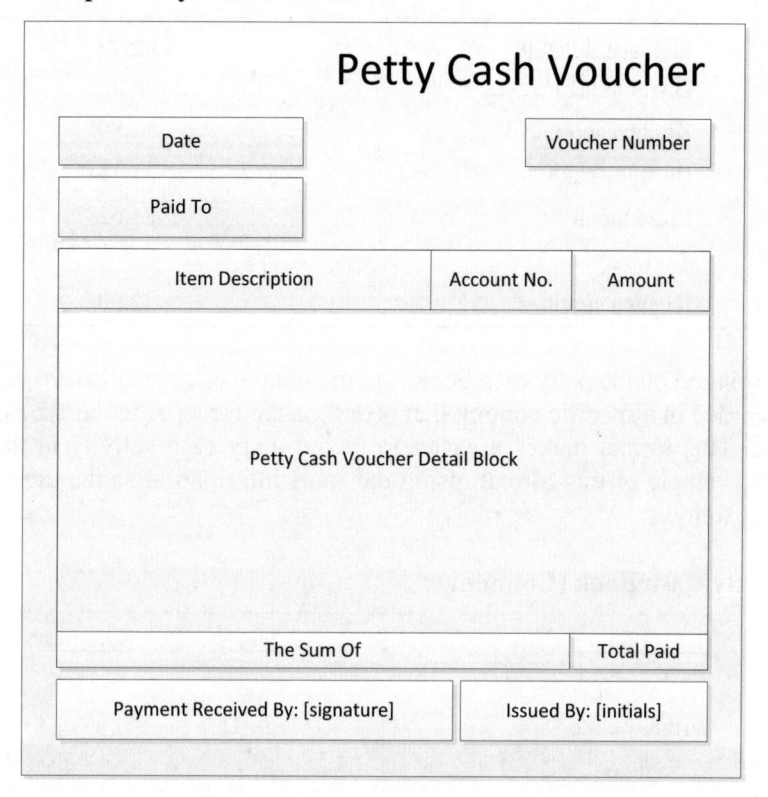

Petty Cash Voucher

Date		Voucher Number
Paid To		

Item Description	Account No.	Amount
Petty Cash Voucher Detail Block		
The Sum Of		Total Paid
Payment Received By: [signature]		Issued By: [initials]

The petty cash custodian summarizes all transactions in a petty cash book. The book is, in most cases, an actual ledger book, rather than a computer record. There are two primary types of entries in the book, which are a debit to record cash received by the petty cash custodian (usually in a single block of cash at infrequent intervals), and a large number of credits to reflect cash withdrawals from the petty cash fund. These credits can be for such transactions as payments for meals, flowers, office supplies, stamps, and so forth.

An alternative format is to record all debits and credits in a single column, with a running cash balance in the column furthest to the right, as shown in the following example. This format is an excellent way to monitor the current amount of petty cash remaining on hand.

Sample Petty Cash Book (Running Balance)

Date	Purchase/Receipt	Amount	Balance
4/01/xx	Opening balance	$250.00	$250.00
4/05/xx	Kitchen supplies	-52.80	197.20
4/08/xx	Birthday cake	-24.15	173.05
4/11/xx	Pizza lunch	-81.62	91.43
4/14/xx	Taxi fare	-25.00	66.43
4/23/xx	Kitchen supplies	-42.00	24.43

Another variation on the petty cash book is to maintain it as a spreadsheet, where each item is recorded in a specific column that is designated for a particular type of receipt or expense. This format makes it easier to record petty cash activity in the general ledger. An example of this format, using the same information as the preceding example, is as follows:

Sample Petty Cash Book (Columnar)

Date	Description		Meals	Supplies	Travel
4/05/xx	Kitchen supplies			$52.80	
4/08/xx	Birthday cake		$24.15		
4/11/xx	Pizza lunch		81.62		
4/14/xx	Taxi fare				$25.00
4/23/xx	Kitchen supplies			42.00	
		Totals	$105.77	$94.80	$25.00

The petty cash book is a useful control over petty cash expenditures, since it forces the petty cash custodian to formally record all cash inflows and outflows. The total of the receipts and remaining cash should equal the initial amount of petty cash funding at all times, though recordation errors and theft may result in a variance.

When the cash balance in a petty cash fund drops to a sufficiently minimal level, the petty cash custodian applies for more cash from the cashier. This takes the form of a summarization of all the receipts that the custodian has accumulated. The cashier creates a new check in the amount of the receipts, and swaps the check for the receipts. The check is then cashed and converted to bills and coins. The petty cash custodian refills the petty cash drawer, which should now contain the original amount of cash that was designated for the fund.

The tight level of control just noted for petty cash shows a key concern with any type of cash payment – there is a significant risk of theft. In sum, cash has become an incidental form of payment that requires an inordinate amount of control oversight.

Check Payments

The predominant form of payment is still the check payment. When a company issues a check payment, the payee deposits the check with its own bank. The payee's bank collects information from each check by scanning the bottom line of information on the check. This information is encoded using magnetic ink character recognition (MICR), which makes it easier to extract information from the check with a check scanner. The MICR line contains the routing information needed to route the check back to the payer's bank for reimbursement. The following information is encoded on the MICR line:

- *ABA number*. Contains the identification number of the bank on which the check was drawn. Also known as a transit routing number, or TRN. "ABA" is an acronym for American Bankers Association.
- *Account number*. Contains the number of the account assigned to the payer by the bank.
- *Check number*. States the number of the check, which is also shown in the upper right corner of the check.
- *Payment amount (optional)*. States the payment amount listed on the check. This code can be created by the payer when the check is printed, or by the payee when preparing the check for deposit. Most commonly, it is added by the bank at which the check is deposited.

A sample of the MICR information encoded on a check is shown in the following exhibit.

Sample Check Format

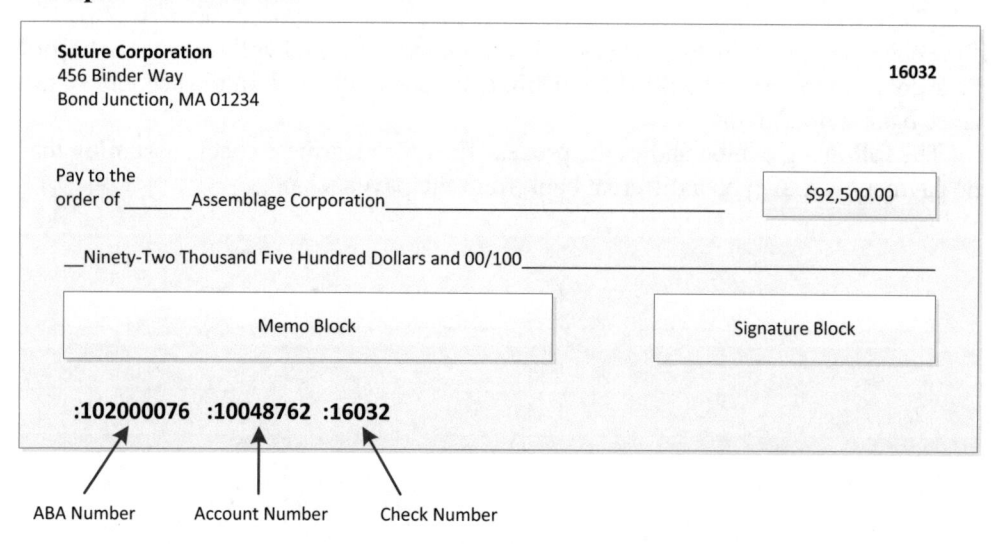

```
Suture Corporation
456 Binder Way                                                          16032
Bond Junction, MA 01234


Pay to the
order of _____ Assemblage Corporation_____     $92,500.00

__Ninety-Two Thousand Five Hundred Dollars and 00/100_____

       Memo Block                              Signature Block

   :102000076  :10048762  :16032
       |           |          |
   ABA Number  Account Number  Check Number
```

Technically, a check is paid "to the order of" a payee, which means that the drawee bank can pay anyone who presents the check to it, as long as the original payee endorsed the check. Thus, a check can become a negotiable instrument that could be sold to and cashed by a third party.

The payment amount stated on a check does not immediately appear in the payee's bank account, since the payee's bank has not yet received the funds from the payer's bank. Instead, the payee's bank makes a notation of the amount in the payee's account, and sets a date by which the funds will be available for use by the payee (known as the *value date*). A bank sets value dates based on its own availability schedule, which states the number of business days required before the cash stated on various types of checks will be made available to payees. Availability dates should approximately follow these timelines:

- *Zero-day delay*. *On-us* checks, which are checks deposited in the same bank on which they were drawn. U.S. Treasury checks should also be assigned a zero-day delay.
- *One-day delay*. Checks drawn on local banks or on banks located in major cities.
- *Two-day delay*. Checks drawn on more distant locations.

The payee's bank then has a choice of four possible methods for clearing the check, which are:

- *Clearinghouse*. Send the check to a check clearinghouse that aggregates and nets check payments forwarded from multiple banks.
- *Direct send*. Forward the check directly to the payer's bank.
- *Federal Reserve*. Send the check to the Fed's clearing service.
- *On-us processing*. Process the payment internally, if the check was drawn on an account with the same bank.

If the check is moving between banks, then ultimately the Fed will remove cash from the account of the payer bank with a debit, and deposit the cash in the account of the payee bank with a credit.

The following exhibit shows the process flow for clearing a check, assuming that the payment is drawn on a different bank from the payee's bank.

Types of Payments

Check Clearing Process Flow

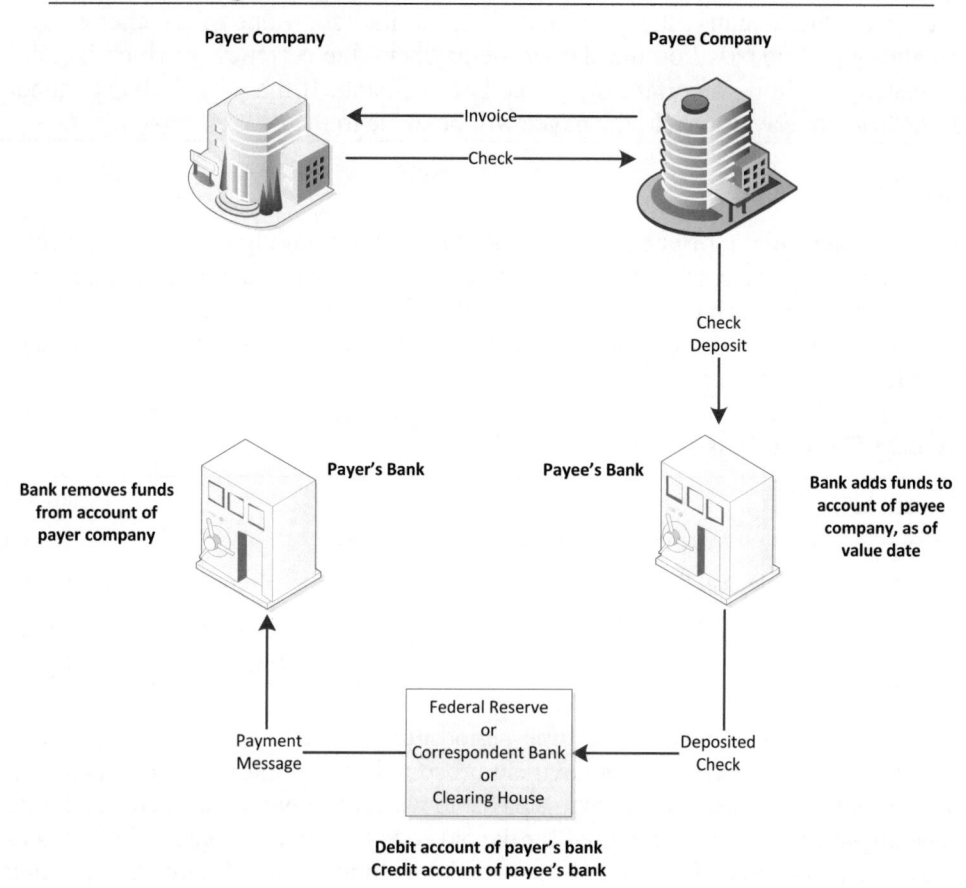

```
       Payer Company                      Payee Company
              ←──────── Invoice ────────
              ─────────  Check  ────────→
                                                │
                                          Check Deposit
                                                ↓
      Payer's Bank                        Payee's Bank
Bank removes funds                                    Bank adds funds to
from account of                                       account of payee
payer company                                         company, as of
                                                      value date
       ↑                                        │
       │         Federal Reserve                │
     Payment         or                      Deposited
     Message  ← Correspondent Bank ←          Check
                      or
                 Clearing House

         Debit account of payer's bank
         Credit account of payee's bank
```

Foreign Check Clearing

There are inevitable delays in the settlement of currencies, for every currency must be settled in its country of origin. Thus, if a check is paid out of the account of a bank that is not part of the U.S. payment system, the check is sent back to the payer's bank for collection. The payer's bank pays an in-country correspondent bank, which in turn remits the funds by electronic transfer to the payee's bank. This settlement process is very time-consuming and expensive, and may mean that the check recipient will not have access to the cash amount stated on the check for weeks.

There are countries in which there is heavy usage of a particular foreign currency – usually the U.S. dollar. In these cases, there are systems in place to clear locally drawn checks within those countries, using a local commercial settlement bank. For example, U.S. dollar clearing is available in Tokyo, Hong Kong, and the Philippines. These local settlement systems create a credit risk for the participants in a check clearing transaction, because the local settlement bank could fail while checks are being cleared, leaving liabilities outstanding between the payer and payee.

Types of Payments

> **Tip:** A few banks offer immediate availability of the cash noted on a check that originates in another country, though at a discount to the face value of the check. Cash availability will be based on the size of the payment, the currency in which it is denominated, and how important the payee is to its bank. If the payee's bank cannot collect from the payer's bank, the payee will be liable to its bank for repayment.

Float

There is a fair amount of uncertainty associated with the timing of check payments. Just because a paying company has cut a check does not mean that the recipient knows the exact date on which the related amount of cash will eventually appear in its bank account. Consider the timing uncertainties related to check payments that are noted in the following exhibit.

Typical Float Periods

Type of Float	Duration
Time to transport the check to the payee by mail (mail float)	2-5 Days
Time for payee to deposit the check (processing float)	1-2 Days
Time required for bank to make cash available to payee (availability float)	1-3 Days
Total Time	4-10 Days

In general, *float* is defined as the time period during which funds are in transition between the various stages in the payment process. For example, *mail float* is the interval from when a check is mailed to a payee to when the payee receives it. Similarly, *processing float* is the time required for the payee to record a payment in its accounting system and deposit the check at its financial institution. Finally, *availability float* is the time required for the funds stated on a check to be made available to the payee by its bank. In aggregate, these types of float are known as *net float*.

As the preceding table shows, even an immediate issuance of a check payment to a payee may not result in the cash appearing in the payee's bank account for as long as ten business days. The payer has no control over any of the three types of float, and so can only estimate how long it will have use of the cash amount stated on a check, before it is paid over to the payee.

> **Tip:** To increase the mail float, always deliver mail to a smaller ancillary post office. Pickups from these offices tend to be later in the day.

The float duration associated with checks has gradually compressed over time, especially since checks started to be digitized for electronic transmission to and between banks. Nonetheless, even the fastest-possible processing of a check payment is unlikely to result in a float of less than four business days.

Advantages of Checks

There are a number of reasons why check payments have succeeded so well, and for so long. First, they are a technologically simple form of payment from the perspective of the payer, since payments can be made entirely manually, and a copy can be retained to prove that payment was made. There is a significant amount of back end processing, but the payer and payee do not see the check clearing process. Second, the payer can take advantage of the substantial amount of float associated with checks, so that it is possible to continue to invest cash for several days after it has (theoretically) been paid to payees. Third, a remittance advice is commonly attached to a check, which contains information about the contents of each payment; the payee uses this information to assign the payment to outstanding accounts receivable.

Disadvantages of Checks

Against these advantages are arrayed a number of problems. First, the manual nature of a check makes it easy to fraudulently alter or replicate, which can lead to substantial fraud losses. Second, the recipient of a check has to wait several days to have use of the cash represented by the check. Further, if there is not enough cash in the payer's bank account to cover a check payment, the payee receives no cash at all. Third, checks are not always accepted as a form of payment across international boundaries. Fourth, the variability in float times associated with checks makes it difficult to accurately predict them in a cash forecast. Finally, the total system cost of processing a check is surprisingly high. Consider the following expenses:

- Cost of check stock
- Cost to print and mail checks
- Bank fee to process checks
- Cost to reconcile bank account
- Cost to enroll in a positive pay fraud-prevention program
- Cost to notify the bank of checks issued under a positive pay system
- Cost to cancel and replace checks that have been lost

Bank Drafts

There are circumstances where the payee wants a guarantee of payment by a bank. This situation arises when there are large payments due, such as for the purchase of real estate, and the seller does not want to take a chance that the check used to pay for the transaction will be returned due to not sufficient funds in the payer's bank account. In these situations, the payer asks its bank for a bank draft (also known as a cashier's check). The bank removes the cash from the payer's bank account and then prepares a bank draft, which is a liability of the bank. The bank earns a profit on the transaction not only by charging a fee to prepare the bank draft, but also by having use of the money until such time as the funds are made available to the payee.

A payer may also use a bank draft to make a payment in a foreign currency. In this case, the bank removes the cash from the payer's bank account, and then forwards payment to a foreign correspondent bank, which prepares the bank draft in the requested foreign currency.

The use of bank drafts has declined in favor of wire transfers directly into the bank account of the payee, since the transfer of funds is accomplished more quickly with a wire transfer.

Automated Clearing House Payments

The Automated Clearing House System is much better known as ACH. The system is designed for high-volume, low-value payments, and charges fees low enough to encourage the transfer of low-value payments. The system is designed to accept payment batches, so that large numbers of scheduled payments can be made at once. Given its convenience and reliability, the ACH system has replaced check payments to a considerable extent.

The system allows for the transfer of a limited amount of additional information along with payment instructions, though this information may be stripped away if a transaction is being transferred into a different national ACH system that does not allow for additional payment information.

ACH is primarily used to process payments from businesses to individuals. For example, ACH is used for payroll direct deposit payments, as well as for pension and annuity payments. There is also increasing usage of ACH for accounts payable payments from one business to another.

The basic process flow for the ACH system is as follows:

1. The payer submits a file to its bank, containing a batch of payment information.
2. The bank immediately pays any amounts directed to payee accounts within the bank, using an internal book transfer.
3. The bank assembles all remaining payments into a batch and sends it to the regional ACH operator to which it has been assigned.
4. The ACH operator nets the payment information submitted by the banks in its region and notifies them of the settlement amounts for which they are responsible.
5. The ACH operator summarizes the remaining transactions involving payments to banks located outside of its processing region, and sends the summaries to the other regional ACH operators for further settlement, which are completed on a gross basis.
6. When payments arrive in the accounts of payee banks, those banks forward the payments to payees, while the payers' banks debit the payers' accounts for the related and offsetting payment amounts.

The following exhibit shows the process flow when several payroll payments to employees are made using the ACH system (and employing a *very* simplified view of ACH processing).

Types of Payments

ACH Process Flow

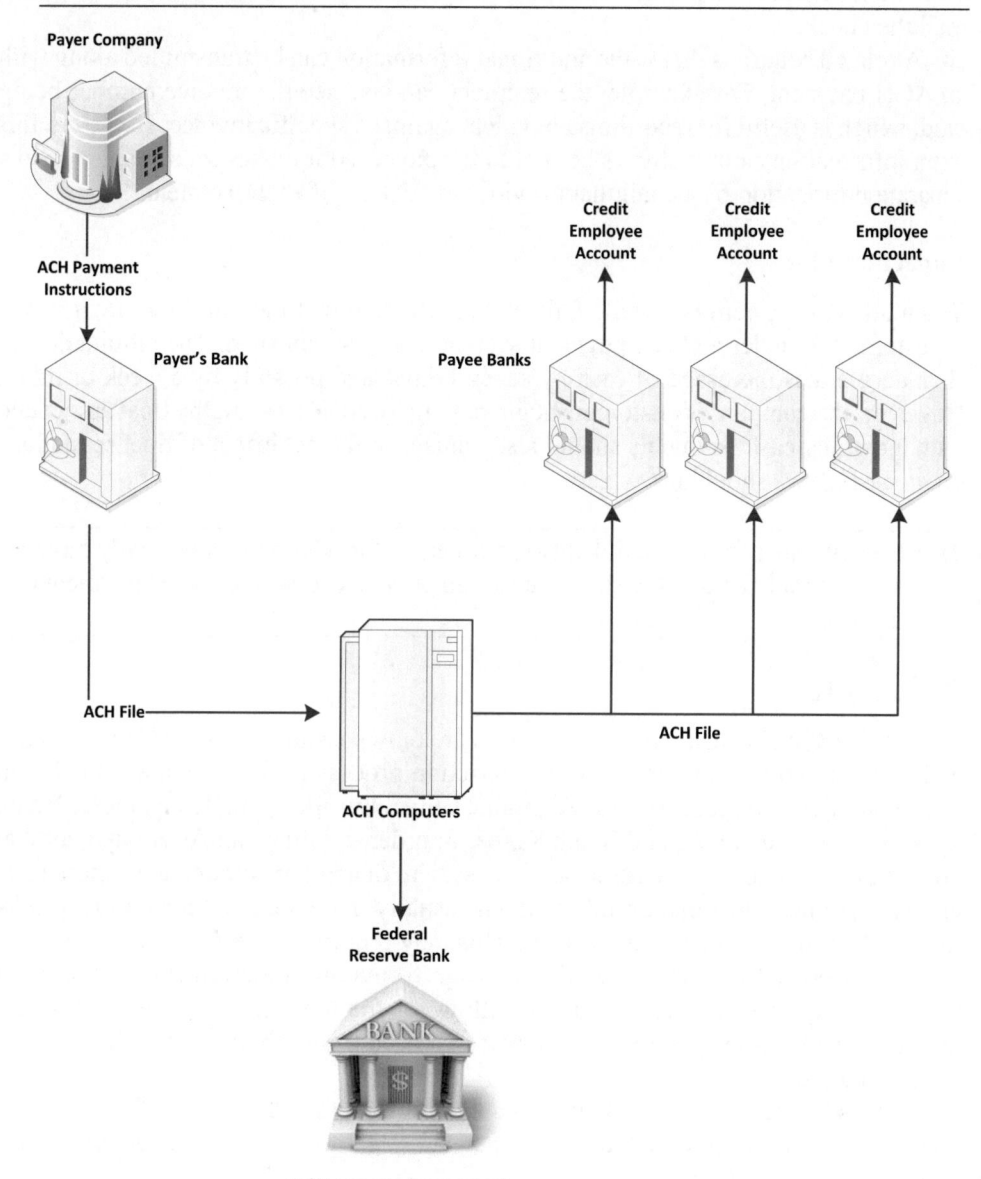

[Diagram: Payer Company sends ACH Payment Instructions to Payer's Bank, which sends an ACH File to ACH Computers. ACH Computers send ACH File to Payee Banks (crediting Employee Accounts) and to Federal Reserve Bank, which debits the payer's bank account and credits accounts of all designated payee banks.]

Advantages of ACH

A major advantage of ACH payments is the certainty of settlement timing. Once a transaction has been initiated, both parties know exactly when the related amount of cash will be removed from the payer's account and added to the payee's account.

Another major advantage of ACH is its low cost, which is just a few cents per transaction. Compare this cost to the total cost of issuing a check, which includes the cost of check stock, a mailing envelope, postage, and the labor required to prepare and mail the check.

A related benefit is that some additional information can be transmitted along with an ACH payment. For example, the recipient can also see the invoice number being paid, which is useful for recording a payment against a specific invoice. However, this extra information cannot always be sent to the payee, so it makes sense to also send a separate notification by e-mail that provides the details of each payment.

Impact on Float

When an ACH system is installed, the payer will find that the multi-day float it was accustomed to under a check payment system has now vanished. The elimination of float accelerates the usage of cash by several days, and possibly by a week or more. However, if a company's customers begin paying by ACH as well, the float associated with incoming cash payments should also vanish, so the net effect of float reductions on *all* cash flows should net to zero.

> **Tip:** If payments can be scheduled two days early for what would normally have required a wire transfer, a $20 wiring charge can be replaced with an ACH payment that costs a few cents.

Global ACH

Electronic payments using the ACH system are only possible within the United States and Canada, though similar types of transaction processing systems are available in other countries or regions, such as Australia, China, Europe, Hong Kong, India, Japan, New Zealand, Singapore, and South Korea. In order to initiate an ACH payment that crosses borders into the electronic payment system of another country, a business must enter its payment information into a portal (usually maintained by a bank) that links to the other country's payment system. This may require the entry of different types of data, in order to comply with the message formatting requirements of the other system. Many of these systems do not allow for the inclusion of remittance information along with a payment, so the payer will need to supply this information to the payee separately.

In those parts of the world that do not have systems similar to the ACH system, it may be necessary to pay by the more expensive wire transfer method, which we address in the next section.

Wire Transfers

A wire transfer is the fastest way to send funds to a payee. A wire transfer is usually confined to the larger payments, since the transaction cost is rather high, at about $20. In addition to the high cost, a wire transaction can require the most manual labor of any type of payment. Each bank to which a wire is sent may have its own unique ways of assigning funds to an account, so it is useful to contact the receiving bank for wiring instructions prior to initiating a transfer. At a minimum, the following information will be needed:

- The name and account number of the payee
- The name and address of the bank to which the funds are to be sent
- The routing number and account number to which the funds are to be sent
- The amount to be paid

The payables staff may be able to initiate a wire transfer by accessing an on-line form in a secure part of the bank's website, which gives the company the best level of control over funds being sent. Alternatively, the information can be sent to the company's representative at the bank, who issues the wire.

Though wired funds can be in the account of the payee within a very short period, there are several timing concerns to be aware of. First, every bank has a cutoff time, after which any wiring instructions received will not be processed until the next business day. The accounting staff must ensure that rush payments are initiated prior to the cutoff time. Second, there can be a substantial delay in the transfer of cash to a payee across international borders, possibly of several days. The international delay can be particularly prolonged when the bank initiating the wire transfer does not have a correspondent relationship with the intended recipient bank, and so has to route the payment through a third bank that has the required relationship. Third, a bank that receives a wire transfer may manually review it to ensure that the funds are applied to the correct account, which can take time. All of these factors can contribute to a delay in the receipt of wired funds.

> **Tip:** To ensure that payees receive funds quickly, see if they have an account at the same bank as the payer, and initiate a wire within that bank from the payer's account to the payee's account. This is an internal book transfer for the bank, which makes funds immediately available to the payee.

When the payer sends funds internationally and pays with its home currency, the receiving bank may charge the payee a startlingly high foreign currency translation fee. The payee cannot avoid this fee, since the funds must come through the receiving bank. To sidestep the fee, the payer can offer to remit payment in the currency of the payee in exchange for a reduced payment. By doing so, the payer can choose among multiple foreign exchange providers to obtain the best exchange rate, which will probably result in a better exchange rate than would be offered by the payee's bank.

Another issue the payee will encounter is a *lifting fee*, which is a transaction fee charged by the receiving bank. The lifting fee may match the wire transfer fee charged to the payer by the issuing bank. Given the size of the fees charged to both parties in a wire transfer transaction, it may make sense for the buyer and seller to agree to a different form of payment that is less expensive.

> **Tip:** To avoid payment delays and reduce wiring fees, consider funding an account within any country where the company routinely issues payments, and eliminate wire transfers in favor of in-country payment systems that are paid from that account.

The Letter of Credit

A letter of credit is used extensively in international trade, where it provides an assured form of payment for the exporter. The key element in the letter of credit is that a guarantee of payment is made by a bank, rather than the importer, which represents a major reduction in the credit risk of the exporter. The basic process flow for a letter of credit payment is:

1. The importer and exporter agree upon the terms and conditions under which the exporter will ship goods to the importer.
2. The importer applies to its bank, known as the *issuing bank*, for a letter of credit. This involves filling out a bank-provided letter of credit form.
3. The issuing bank issues a letter of credit to the exporter's bank, stating that it (the issuing bank) is obligated to pay the exporter's bank if the exporter fulfills the conditions stated in the letter of credit (usually the provision of an invoice and proof of delivery, though more comprehensive documentation may include certifications of insurance and product quality). To cover its liability, the issuing bank restricts an amount of cash in the importer's bank account equal to the amount of the line of credit, or it may restrict a portion of the line of credit that the importer has with the bank.
4. Once the shipment terms have been completed, the exporter presents the mandated documents to its bank (the *confirming bank*), which examines the documents and then issues payment. If the exporter's bank does not want to be involved in the payment, it transfers the documents to the issuing bank, which pays the exporter.
5. Upon notification of payment by the exporter's bank, the issuing bank removes the restricted cash from the importer's bank account or charges the importer's line of credit, and then forwards payment to the exporter's bank.

EXAMPLE

Suture Corporation is planning to sell one of its cancer scanning beds to Sydney Scientific, which is located in Australia. The sale transaction is priced at $350,000. Suture is delivering the unit to Sydney, with an expected arrival date of September 30. Suture's bank is Wells Fargo, and Sydney Scientific's bank is Commonwealth Bank. The process steps for the related letter of credit transaction are:

1. Sydney asks Commonwealth Bank to issue a letter of credit. Commonwealth does so after reviewing the deal documentation. Commonwealth also restricts $350,000 of the available funding on Sydney's line of credit with the bank.
2. Wells Fargo confirms the letter of credit and sends the documentation, plus a confirmation advice, to Suture.
3. Suture transports the scanning bed to Sydney.

4. Suture completes all required documentation and presents it to Wells Fargo. The bank reviews and approves the documentation and pays Suture the $350,000, less transaction fees.
5. Wells Fargo forwards the documentation to Commonwealth Bank, which pays Wells Fargo. Commonwealth also charges its line of credit with Sydney for $350,000, plus transaction fees.

The letter of credit has been a mainstay of international trade for many years, since it ensures the flow of funds from importers to exporters. However, there is also a great deal of paperwork, which increases the time required by the buyer, seller, and intermediary banks to process payment. Also, there is a risk that a flaw in submitted documentation will trigger a denial of payment by a bank, which is a serious problem for an exporter. Due to these deficiencies, it is increasingly common for international business partners to find other, less onerous ways to pay each other, such as through wire transfers or local electronic payment systems.

The Standby Letter of Credit

A variation on the basic letter of credit concept is the *standby letter of credit*. This is a guarantee by a bank that it will pay a supplier on behalf of a customer if the customer is unable to provide payment. A supplier is most likely to request a standby letter of credit in international trade situations, and especially when dealing with a new customer. If requested, the customer applies to its bank for the letter of credit, which reviews the credit quality of the customer. If the bank is willing to take the risk, it charges a fee to the customer, which is usually a percentage of the face amount of the letter of credit, and issues the letter of credit to the bank of the supplier. The term of a standby letter of credit is usually for one year, which is a sufficient period of time for the underlying transaction to be completed and paid. A standby letter of credit can be quite expensive, ranging from 1% to 10% of the face amount of the letter of credit, and so is to be avoided by the customer in a business transaction to the greatest extent possible.

Summary

A company will likely use a mix of payments. Over time, the types of payments have changed, resulting in the near-elimination of cash payments. However, we cannot so easily predict the demise of check payments. Given their extreme ease of use, check payments will probably continue to be used in great quantities through the foreseeable future, though ACH payments will certainly make inroads into the quantity of checks issued. Other forms of payment, such as wire transfers, bank drafts, and letters of credit, are designed for special situations, and so will likely continue to be used in roughly the same proportions in the future.

In the following table, we have noted the characteristics of the various types of payment, and the situations in which they should be used.

Types of Payments

Characteristics of Payment Methods

Payment Method	Characteristics and Applicability
Cash	Best for unplanned expenditures, tips, and payments to unbanked temporary workers. Requires strong controls due to risk of theft. Not recommended as a form of payment.
Checks	Easy to use in a manual system, and payers can temporarily retain the use of cash through float. Its total usage cost is high, and there is a risk of fraud.
Bank drafts	Limited to use when a supplier wants a guaranteed payment. Requires expensive manual processing and a bank fee. Not recommended for high volume usage.
ACH	Very efficient and low-cost form of electronic payment. Can require setup time, so not good for one-time payments. Highly recommended for repetitive payments to long-term business partners.
Wire transfers	Used for fast payments of large amounts. Can be delayed for cross-border payments, may require manual setup, and fees are high. Replace with ACH payments whenever possible.
Letter of credit	Established form of payment for international transactions. Requires considerable paperwork, and so may be avoided in favor of more efficient payment systems when business relations are well-established.

Chapter 4
Expense Reimbursement

Introduction

Expense reports are submitted by employees in order to be reimbursed for expenses they incurred on behalf of the company. Expense reports are quite different from normal expenditures that originate in the purchasing department, since there is no authorizing purchase order or receiving report to document an expense. Given these differences, an entirely different set of procedures are needed to process expense reports. In this chapter, we provide examples of several expense report processes, which are:

- Expense report submission (manual system)
- Expense report submission (automated system)
- Expense report review

We also make note of several techniques for improving the efficiency of the expense reimbursement process.

> **Related Podcast Episode:** Episode 113 of the Accounting Best Practices Podcast discusses employee spend management systems. It is available at: **accountingtools.com/podcasts** or **iTunes**

The Need for Expense Reimbursement

When a company has a mobile workforce, it is entirely likely that most employees will be expending funds on company business on a fairly regular basis. If so, the total expense incurred may comprise a notable portion of the total amount of company expenses. Given the amount of money involved, it is necessary to have a well-defined system under which employees summarize their expenditures and submit them to the company for reimbursement. Otherwise, expense reimbursements may be allowed for personal expenses or for excessive purchases, such as the use of first class seats on flights.

As an example of a structured expense reimbursement system, the following section describes the process flow that an employee and the payables department would follow to create an expense report and issue a payment to the employee.

The Expense Report Submission Procedure (Manual System)

When employees want to be reimbursed for expenditures, they fill out an expense report. This can be on a preprinted form, on an electronic spreadsheet, or in an on-line form. The expense report form comes in many varieties, of which there are two main types. The first is shown in the following sample format, where a common set of expense categories are listed across the top row, leaving space for many entries down the left side of the form. The alternative is to switch these placements, so that columns for each of the seven days of the week are listed across the top, with the most common expense categories listed down the left side. The format shown here has the advantage of being usable for longer periods than one week.

Sample Expense Report Form

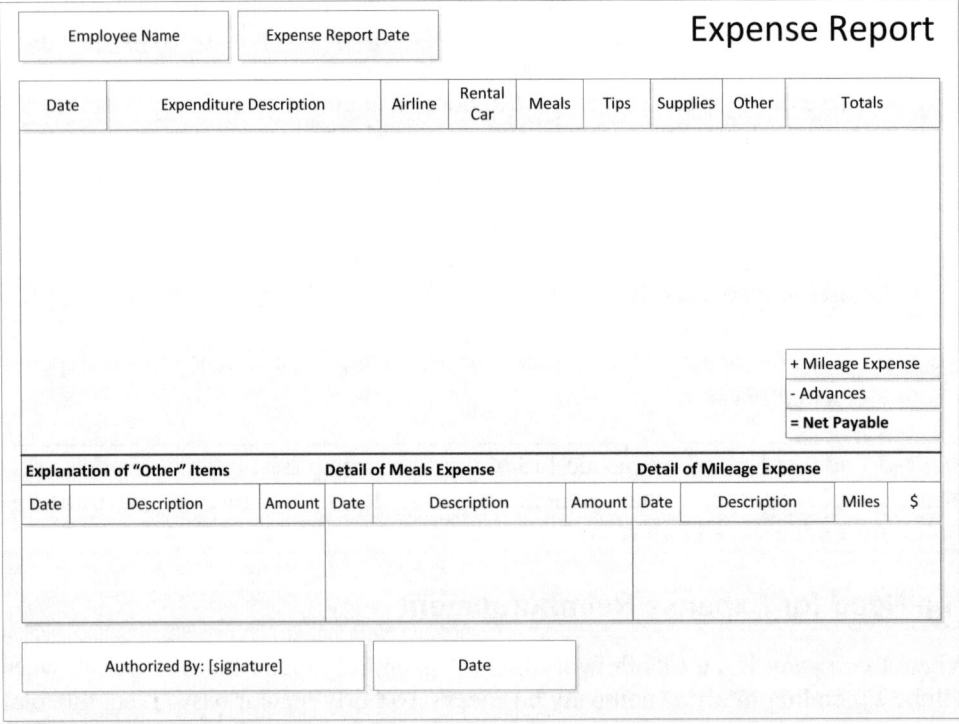

Employee Name	Expense Report Date							Expense Report	
Date	Expenditure Description	Airline	Rental Car	Meals	Tips	Supplies	Other	Totals	

+ Mileage Expense
- Advances
= Net Payable

Explanation of "Other" Items			Detail of Meals Expense			Detail of Mileage Expense			
Date	Description	Amount	Date	Description	Amount	Date	Description	Miles	$

Authorized By: [signature]	Date

Both expense report formats contain additional blocks at the bottom of the report, in which employees can enter additional detailed information about certain expense categories.

This procedure assumes the use of either a preprinted form or an electronic spreadsheet. The procedure includes steps for a number of expenditures commonly found on expense reports, including mileage reimbursements, per diem meals, and deductions for advances. The procedure for completing an expense report is outlined below:

1. **Enter expense items.** Enter all items to be reimbursed on the expense report, placing each one in the expense category to which it most closely relates. Attach *original* receipts for all expenses that exceed the minimum corporate receipt policy. Otherwise, if employees were to attach copies of receipts, they could then submit the originals in other expense reports and be reimbursed twice.

> **Tip:** Employees may not be aware of the company's travel policy, so consider summarizing its key points on the face or back of the expense report. This may keep some questionable expenses from being claimed.

> **Tip:** If employees paid in a foreign currency, the easiest way to reimburse them is at the exchange rate stated on the person's credit card statement for those expenditures, plus any foreign currency exchange fee (also listed on the credit card statement).

2. **Enter mileage.** State on the expense report the beginning and ending locations of travel on each date, as well as the miles driven between those locations. Multiply the miles driven by the mileage reimbursement rate to arrive at the total mileage amount for which to be reimbursed.
3. **Enter per diem meals** (optional). If the company pays its employees a fixed amount per meal (known as a per diem rate) rather than reimbursing actual meal expenses, itemize the travel dates to which per diem meals apply, and enter the per diem amounts as per the company travel policy.
4. **Enter entertainment expenses** (optional). It is customary for a business to allow its employees to spend much greater amounts for meals than normal if they are entertaining business customers. It is difficult to impose any restrictions on these expenses, but employees should at least be required to state who attended and the business purpose of the meal or meeting.
5. **Enter advances.** If a company pays an employee an advance to cover expenses during a trip, list the entire amount of the advance on the expense report as a deduction from the total expenses claimed.
6. **Explain non-corporate travel payments** (optional). The company may have a policy of having all airline and hotel payments be made by a central reservations group. If so, paying for airline or hotel arrangements with a personal credit card breaches company policy, and should be explained in an attachment to the expense report.
7. **Obtain approval.** All expense reports must be approved by the person whose budget will be impacted by the expense. This is usually the department manager. For higher-level positions, reports may be approved by the chief operating officer or a similar position.
8. **Retain copy.** Make a copy of the expense report and retain the copy.
9. **Forward to accounts payable.** Forward the expense report, with attached receipts, to the payables staff for payment processing.
10. **Review expense report.** The payables staff examines the expense report for several issues, as described later in the Expense Report Review Procedure section.
11. **Generate invoice number.** The payables staff assigns an invoice number to the expense report and records the expense report as an invoice in the accounts payable system for the amount payable, net of advances. Assigning an invoice number is not a minor issue, because there needs to be a way to differentiate employee expense reports in the accounting system. Since employees tend to submit multiple expense reports at the same time, it is not possible to base the invoice number

on the submission date or the approval date. Instead, consider using an invoice number that is derived from the date of the first or last expense stated in the expense report (which is more likely to be unique).

The following exhibit shows a streamlined view of the expense report submission procedure, with some optional tasks included.

Expense Report Submission Process Flow

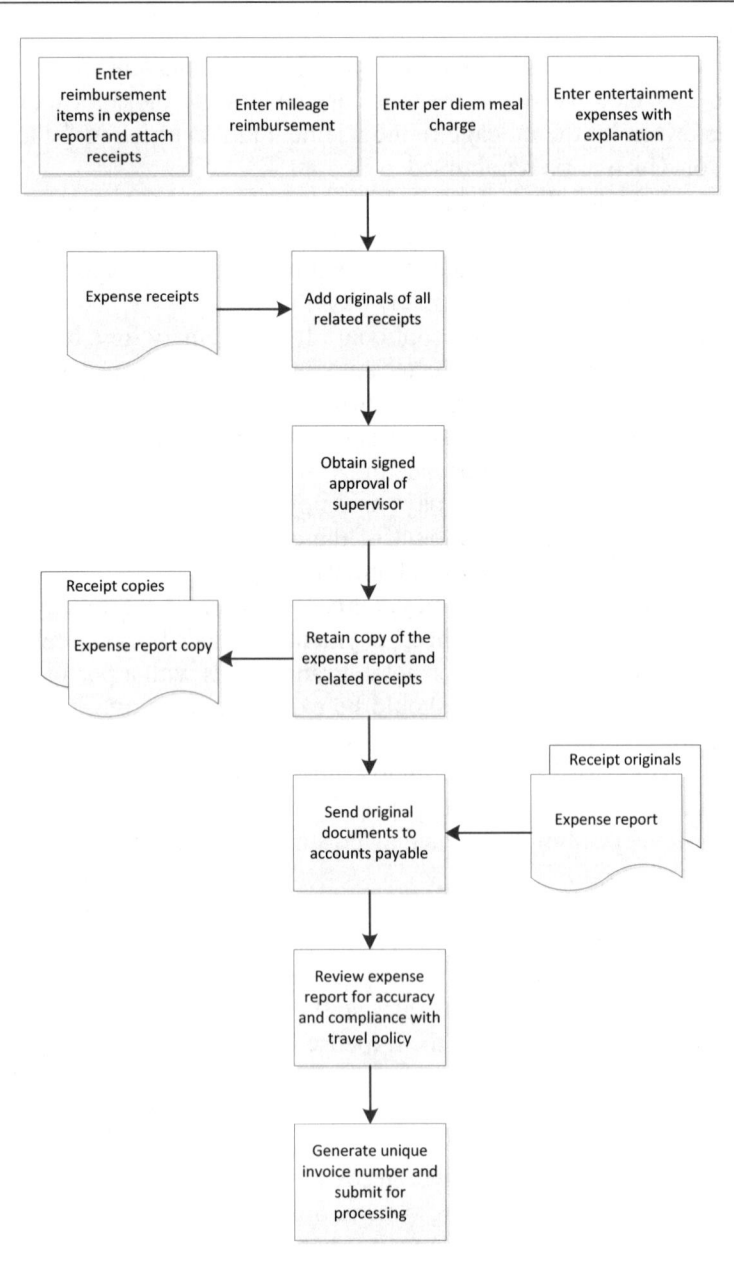

```
┌─────────────┐  ┌─────────────┐  ┌─────────────┐  ┌─────────────┐
│   Enter     │  │             │  │             │  │   Enter     │
│reimbursement│  │   Enter     │  │Enter per    │  │entertainment│
│items in     │  │  mileage    │  │diem meal    │  │expenses with│
│expense      │  │reimbursement│  │  charge     │  │explanation  │
│report and   │  │             │  │             │  │             │
│attach       │  │             │  │             │  │             │
│receipts     │  │             │  │             │  │             │
└─────────────┘  └─────────────┘  └─────────────┘  └─────────────┘
                         │
                         ▼
   ┌──────────────┐   ┌──────────────────┐
   │   Expense    │──▶│ Add originals of │
   │   receipts   │   │  all related     │
   │              │   │    receipts      │
   └──────────────┘   └──────────────────┘
                              │
                              ▼
                     ┌──────────────────┐
                     │  Obtain signed   │
                     │   approval of    │
                     │   supervisor     │
                     └──────────────────┘
                              │
                              ▼
   ┌──────────────┐   ┌──────────────────┐
   │Receipt copies│   │ Retain copy of   │
   │              │◀──│ the expense      │
   │Expense report│   │ report and       │
   │    copy      │   │ related receipts │
   └──────────────┘   └──────────────────┘
                              │
                              ▼
                     ┌──────────────────┐   ┌──────────────┐
                     │  Send original   │   │   Receipt    │
                     │  documents to    │◀──│   originals  │
                     │accounts payable  │   │Expense report│
                     └──────────────────┘   └──────────────┘
                              │
                              ▼
                     ┌──────────────────┐
                     │ Review expense   │
                     │ report for       │
                     │ accuracy and     │
                     │ compliance with  │
                     │ travel policy    │
                     └──────────────────┘
                              │
                              ▼
                     ┌──────────────────┐
                     │ Generate unique  │
                     │ invoice number   │
                     │ and submit for   │
                     │   processing     │
                     └──────────────────┘
```

The On-Line Expense Report Submission Procedure

Some companies require their employees to use an on-line form to submit their expense reports. This is an efficient way to record and review expenses, since the form typically incorporates the company's travel policy, which automatically rejects any submissions that are not in compliance with the policy. The procedure for completing an on-line expense report form is outlined below:

1. **Enter information in system.** The on-line form prompts the employee to enter the dates and amounts of expenditures, as well as classify them into different expense categories. The system reviews these submissions based on the corporate travel policy and automatically rejects those items prohibited by the policy.
2. **Enter receipts.** The system reviews the expenses submitted and decides which receipts should accompany them. Employees may have the option of scanning in the required receipts, or of mailing them to the payables department.
3. **Obtain approval.** The system routes a digital image of the expense report to the person designated as the supervisor of the employee. The supervisor reviews and approves the document, after which the system routes it to the payables department.
4. **Import expense report.** There should be an interface between the expense reporting system and the accounts payable system, so that expense report submissions are automatically set up for payment. Unlike the manual system, there is no need to devise a unique invoice number for each expense report. Instead, the on-line form automatically assigns a unique number when an expense report has been submitted.

The following exhibit shows a streamlined view of the on-line expense reporting procedure.

On-line Expense Reporting Process Flow

```
[Submit expense as per system prompts]
            ↓
[Expense receipts] → [Submit receipts as requested by the system]
            ↓
[Obtain supervisor approval through workflow management system]
            ↓
[Receipt images]
[Expense report file] → [Import expense report to accounts payable system]
```

The Expense Report Review Procedure

When a company uses a manual submission process for expense reports, there is an enhanced risk of errors in the reports. The following procedure gives direction to the reviewers who examine expense reports prior to issuing payments to the submitting employees. We assume that this entire procedure is conducted within the payables department. However, many or all of the investigative aspects of the procedure can be shifted to the internal audit department, if the company prefers to use occasional audits of expense reports. The expense report review procedure is outlined below:

1. **Review for non-reimbursement items.** Review the expense report to see if it contains any of the items noted in the following table. If so, they are to be disallowed and subtracted from the expense report. Send an e-mail to the employee, detailing all disallowed expenses, and copy the message to the employee's supervisor.

Sample List of Non-Reimbursement Items

Adult entertainment	Expenses > 90 days old	Personal reading material
Car washes and cleaning	Finance charges on credit cards	Theft/loss of personal property
Contributions	Health club / spa fees	Toiletries
Child care	Laundry fees on short-duration trips	Traffic fines
Clothing	Lost luggage	Travel insurance
Commuting costs	Movies	Undocumented expenses

2. **Match to receipts.** Compare the expenses claimed on the expense report to the accompanying receipts, and request additional information if some receipts are missing.
3. **Review per diem meals.** Verify from the travel records in the expense report the dates on which travel was conducted, and verify that per diem charges were only applied for during those dates. Also verify that the per diem rates are correct, and that no actual meal expenditures are included in the expense report in addition to per diem charges.
4. **Review mileage claims.** Review the amount of mileage reimbursement claims for reasonableness. This might include running a mileage calculation on an on-line travel site. If the miles claimed figure is within a certain percentage of the calculated amount, accept it.
5. **Verify clerical accuracy.** Re-summarize the totals in the expense report for both rows and columns. If the expense report is based on an electronic spreadsheet, it is particularly likely that someone might have added rows or columns that are not reflected in the grand totals on the report.
6. **Match to advances list.** Compare the expense report to the current list of employees to whom travel advances have been issued. If an advance is not deducted from the expense report, refer the matter to the payables supervisor, who verifies which travel plans are associated with the advance. If the advance should have been deducted from this expense report, do so and issue an e-mail notice to the employee and the employee's supervisor regarding this change in reimbursement.
7. **Update trend analysis** (optional). It may be useful to periodically update a trend analysis of the types of expenses being claimed by those employees who appear to be at higher risk of abusing the company's travel policy. This analysis can extend to a review of receipt copies being used across multiple expense reports, as well as a review of sequential receipt numbers across multiple expense reports (which indicates that an employee purchased a block of receipts and is using them to fraudulently claim fake expenses).

The following exhibit shows a streamlined view of the expense report review procedure, not including the optional trend analysis.

Expense Report Review Process Flow

```
┌─────────────────────────────────────────────────────────────────┐
│  ┌──────────────┐  ┌──────────────┐  ┌──────────────┐  ┌──────────────┐  │
│  │ Review for   │  │ Review for   │  │ Review per   │  │ Verify       │  │
│  │ non-         │  │ missing      │  │ diem and     │  │ clerical     │  │
│  │ reimbursement│  │ receipts     │  │ mileage      │  │ accuracy     │  │
│  │ items        │  │              │  │ claims       │  │              │  │
│  └──────────────┘  └──────────────┘  └──────────────┘  └──────────────┘  │
└─────────────────────────────────────────────────────────────────┘
                                  │
                                  ▼
   ┌──────────────┐            ╱──────────╲
   │ Modify       │           ╱            ╲
   │ expense      │◄── Yes ──│ Adjustments? │
   │ report and   │           ╲            ╱
   │ notify       │            ╲──────────╱
   │ employee and │                  │
   │ supervisor   │                  No
   └──────────────┘                  │
           │                         ▼
           │                  ┌──────────────┐
           └─────────────────►│ Compare to   │
                              │ advances     │
                              │ outstanding  │
                              └──────────────┘
                                     │
                                     ▼
   ┌──────────────┐            ╱──────────╲
   │ Contact      │           ╱            ╲
   │ supervisor   │◄── Yes ──│  Deduction   │
   │ and adjust as│           ╲  needed?   ╱
   │ necessary    │            ╲──────────╱
   └──────────────┘                  │
           │                         No
           │                         │
           │                         ▼
           │                  ┌──────────────┐
           └─────────────────►│ Enter into   │
                              │ accounts     │
                              │ payable      │
                              │ system       │
                              └──────────────┘
```

The Travel and Entertainment Policy

The most significant control over expense reimbursement is the travel and entertainment (T&E) policy. In essence, the T&E policy tells employees which expenses will and will not be reimbursed. The policy also gives guidelines regarding acceptable expenditures. Sample topics for a T&E policy include:

Travel preferences

- States the names of any preferred hotel chains, airlines, and car rental agencies. The company may have bulk purchase discount deals with certain suppliers, so the more volume it can generate with them, the larger the resulting discounts will be.

Expense types

- Describes which expenses will be reimbursed. This section typically includes a discussion of the types of travel arrangements that are considered acceptable, such as:
    - Fly economy for flights having a duration of no more than four hours
    - Fly business class when the trip duration is more than four hours
    - Car rentals must be for intermediate-sized sedans or smaller
    - Hotel rooms cannot be suites
- Notes which expenses will not be reimbursed. This can be a lengthy list, likely including the items in the table in the earlier Expense Report Review Procedure section.

Tip: If certain types of expenditures are prohibited, this will impact the type of purchase receipt evidence to be submitted. For example, if in-room movies are not reimbursed, then employees will need to submit a complete hotel bill itemization. Similarly, if alcoholic drinks are not reimbursed, employees will need to submit complete restaurant bill itemizations.

Evidence

- States when receipts are required. For example, a receipt may be required for all expenditures over $25.
- Describes which documentation to submit. This may include a statement that the most recent expense report form must be submitted, with all relevant receipts attached.

Approvals

- Notes the levels of approval needed prior to submitting a reimbursement request. For example, a minimal reimbursement request may require no approval at all, while all other expense reports must first be signed by the department manager whose budget will be impacted by the reimbursement request.

Direct company payments

- Describes which expenses are to be directly purchased by the company. Some organizations want to pay directly for all airfare and hotel arrangements, thereby greatly reducing the amounts needing to be reimbursed through expense reports.

- Describes who uses mileage points. Employees are usually allowed to retain the mileage points associated with any airfare that they purchase directly. If the company buys the airfare, the points accrue to the business instead.

A bureaucratic payables department could devise an inordinately long T&E policy. However, employees will not read through a lengthy document, so instead try to keep the document both short and relevant. A good way to keep the policy in front of employees is to drop the key policies into a block of text on the face of the expense reimbursement form. Also, include it in the employee manual. A third option is to maintain a current copy of the policy on the company's website.

Tip: Keep track of any requests for clarification of the policy, and include the clarifications in the next iteration of the policy.

The T&E policy will be more closely adhered to if management clearly supports it. This means that senior managers are not seen flying first class in clear contravention of the policy, nor are they claiming reimbursement for country club memberships that are also prohibited. When such behavior occurs, expect other employees to follow suit and claim reimbursement for items that are clearly out of compliance with the policy.

Nearly all employees can be relied upon to submit reimbursement requests that are fully compliant with the company's T&E policy. However, there will be a few employees who routinely violate it. At a minimum, their expense reports should be thoroughly reviewed before any payment is made. If their claims are excessive or fraudulent, it may be necessary to terminate their employment.

Additional Expense Reimbursement Topics

In this section, we address several topics that can improve the efficiency of the expense reimbursement process for all parties, while also reducing the total cost of the reimbursement program.

Form of Documentation

Do employees really need to attach the physical receipts to the expense report for all purchases made? This commonly results in a thick document package that takes up inordinate space in the payables files, and which is likely to fall apart. Also, providing paper-based proof of expenditures means that someone working off-site must mail in this documentation, and so must wait for the mail to be delivered before he or she can expect to receive a payment; this delay can be a real problem if an employee has a short deadline by which a credit card payment must be made.

A possible solution is to allow employees to scan their supporting documents and e-mail them to the payables department, along with a scanned version of the expense report. Doing so eliminates the mail float problem, while also making it optional for the payables staff to print out the receipts or store them electronically.

> **Tip:** If the decision is made to require employees to submit paper receipts, have them tape these documents to a standard-size sheet of paper. Doing so makes it less likely that small receipts will be inadvertently detached from an expense report package.

Cash Advances

A business may find it necessary to issue a cash advance to an employee in order to fund expenditures made during a business trip. The employee is then supposed to deduct the amount of the advance from the expense report resulting from the trip. The trouble is that many employees forget to deduct the advance, resulting in essentially a double payment to them when the company reimburses them for their submitted expense reports.

The traditional approach to this issue has been for the payables staff to manually track all cash advances made, so that they can be deducted from any expense reports submitted thereafter. This approach is time-consuming and subject to error. An alternative approach is to have the company directly pay for a larger proportion of travel costs through a company procurement card, leaving fewer expenses that an employee will likely need to pay for. This step will not completely eliminate the need for cash advances, since some employees have so little cash on hand that they simply cannot support any part of a trip's projected costs.

An additional concern involving cash advances is that an employee may leave the company without ever having paid back an advance. This situation may not be spotted for months, since the payables staff is not usually notified of the departure of employees. One way to avoid this problem is to minimize the use of cash advances, or to have a policy that all advances must be repaid within one month. Another option is to include a notation on the employee termination form, reminding the human resources staff to check with the payables department to see if any cash advances are outstanding; if so, the remaining balance can be deducted from the employee's final paycheck.

Expense Report Auditing

It is very time-consuming to review every reimbursement request on an employee expense report, as well as all attached receipts. The work is not cost-effective, since most employees are always in compliance with a company's T&E policy. Therefore, an excellent alternative is to review expense reports on a more limited basis, while requiring a more intensive level of review for the expense reports submitted by those employees who have had compliance problems with the T&E policy in the past. An example of how this approach can be used is:

- No audits for expense reports totaling less than $100
- Of the expense reports totaling $100 to $1,000, conduct a complete review of ___% of the submitted reports
- Of the expense reports totaling $1,001 or more, conduct a complete review of a higher percentage of the submitted reports
- When a serious policy violation is found, flag the submitting individual for a retroactive review of all prior expense reports submitted in the past year

- In addition, conduct a complete review of the expense reports submitted by the senior management team (mostly to serve notice to the rest of the company that the management team is serious about T&E policy compliance)

Expense Report Outsourcing

An alternative to expense report auditing is to shift the entire expense report data entry and analysis function to a third party. There are several organizations that maintain on-line systems into which employees can enter their expense reports. These systems compare all submissions to the company's travel and entertainment policies, and automatically flag any items that are not in compliance. This approach is comparatively expensive, and so is only effective for larger companies. However, it takes a major labor burden away from the payables staff, and also ensures a high level of compliance with the company's T&E policy.

Spend Management

It can be useful to periodically aggregate the expenditure information in submitted expense reports by the largest suppliers. By doing so, it may be possible to identify a few suppliers who are receiving the bulk of the company's T&E expenditures. This information can be used to strike volume discount deals with the indicated suppliers. This approach goes over well with employees, since the volume discounts are being arranged with those suppliers that employees are already accustomed to using.

Employee Reviews

If an employee persistently displays a tendency to breach the T&E policy, this can be considered a form of attempted fraud. Whether this issue should be included in the performance reviews of employees is an issue that the senior management team should consider. Such behavior may be an indicator of broader problems, and so could be used to develop a more comprehensive view of employee performance. In general, we recommend that the more egregious cases of repeated policy violations be included in performance reviews.

To take the concept a step further, should managers be flagged when they approve expense reports that contain clear T&E policy violations? These managers are probably signing off on the reports without actually reviewing them, rather than actively approving fraudulent requests. Nonetheless, a continual pattern of not reviewing expense reports means a key control point (of having managers review and approve expense reports) is not functioning. Consequently, it *does* make sense for this issue to be noted in the performance reviews of managers who display an ongoing tendency to ignore their reviewing responsibilities.

Summary

The completion and subsequent processing of expense reports is quite time-consuming, and is not even remotely cost-effective when the effort is compared to the (usually) modest sums involved. Because of this issue, consider having the company pay for a larger proportion of expenses, such as air travel and hotels. By doing so, the remaining amount of expense report reimbursements may drop to such a low level that they are less of a concern from a control perspective, and so will require less review time.

The intelligent use of expense report audits should contribute to a gradual decline in the amount of time spent reviewing expense reports. The audits will likely begin by encompassing most expense reports, because some managers are concerned about the potential loss of funds through non-compliant behavior. Then, when the auditing approach is tailored to watch for higher-risk expenditures, managers will likely become more comfortable with the concept of reviewing a smaller percentage of expense reports.

Chapter 5
Procurement Cards

Introduction

A procurement card is essentially a company credit card. Under a procurement card system, the bank managing the card program bills the payer on a monthly basis for all charges made during the month, while remitting funds to the payee within a few days of each charge. If the payer pays the monthly bill late, then the bank charges interest on the open balance. A procurement card program is an excellent tool for any company making payments to its suppliers, since it circumvents the lengthy and expensive process of issuing purchase orders, matching receiving documents to supplier invoices, and making check payments to individual suppliers.

Procurement cards are less commonly used for international payments, because the payer is also charged a fee for any conversions of foreign currencies back into the credit card processor's home currency.

In this chapter, we note the procurement card processes and the forms used within those processes. We provide separate procedures for:

- Procurement card reconciliation
- Lost procurement cards

Procedural improvement tips are provided throughout the text, as well as flowcharts showing a streamlined view of each procedure. A number of additional shorter topics are addressed at the end of the chapter.

When and How to Use Procurement Cards

The general rule of payables processing is that 80% of the invoices comprise 20% of the dollar volume of all invoices processed (which is an application of the Pareto principle). These small-dollar invoices consume the bulk of the time of the payables department, despite their low value. A good way to eliminate this labor is to pay the suppliers whose invoices fall into this classification with procurement cards. By doing so, the department swaps out a large number of inconsequential invoices for a single large procurement card billing.

Tip: A company is not responsible for issuing the annual Form 1099 when payments are made with procurement cards. So, if a supplier is not forthcoming in submitting a Form W-9, pay them with a procurement card to eliminate the Form 1099 reporting obligation. See the Government Reporting chapter for more information.

Procurement Cards

Despite the obvious paperwork reduction advantages of procurement cards, they should not be sprayed throughout the organization. If this were to happen, there would be an increased risk of inappropriate or unauthorized purchases that could increase costs. Consequently, we recommend a multi-step phase-in of procurement cards, using the following steps:

1. *Create a policy.* Develop a procurement card policy that states who can use the cards, and under what circumstances. Possible topics to include in the policy are:

   - *Card user characteristics.* This may include specific job titles within the company that are allowed use of the cards, or perhaps the types of job responsibilities that might warrant being allocated a card.
   - *Usage parameters.* State the circumstances under which a card should and should not be used. For example, all purchases under $250 should be made with a procurement card, with the exception of purchases related to the cost of goods sold. If there are spending limits, either on a per-transaction or per-day basis, state them in the policy. Also prohibit the use of split purchases, where a card user asks a supplier to split an invoice into multiple smaller invoices in order to go under the procurement card purchasing cap; this behavior clearly circumvents the intent of the spending limit.
   - *Preferred suppliers.* The company may have a spend management program, under which it concentrates purchases with a small number of suppliers in order to gain volume discounts. If so, provide a list of these suppliers.
   - *Consequences.* State the consequences of card misuse, which may include the termination of employment.

> **Tip:** Have each card user sign the policy before being issued a procurement card. This indicates that they have read the policy and agree to comply with its contents. This document may prove to be of use if an employee misuses a card.

> **Tip:** A good way to locate potential card users is to comb through the purchasing records and see who is making small-dollar purchases now, irrespective of their job titles or formal responsibilities.

2. *Develop procedures.* Create procedures that state, in detail, exactly how card users are to activate their cards, keep track of receipts, reconcile card statements to those receipts, report lost cards, and so forth.
3. *Conduct training.* Present the procedures to designated users in training sessions. The intent is to reinforce how the cards are to be used. In addition, write down all questions asked and use them to flesh out the procedures in their next iteration, so that they are more understandable to users.

4. *Monitor usage.* Review the level of card usage at regular intervals, by user. The goal is to spot any instances where cards are being used to buy excessively expensive or inappropriate items, and give robust feedback when this occurs. In addition, if a user is under-utilizing a card, either push for more usage or move the card to a different person who is more willing to use it.
5. *Reinforce behavior.* Whenever a supplier invoice is submitted to the payables department that could have been paid locally by a procurement card holder, route the invoice back to the card holder, with a request for that person to pay for it with a card. Though initially time-consuming, this approach eventually reinforces the fact that the company is serious about using its procurement cards.
6. *Examine parameters.* Periodically review the results of the procurement card program, to see if the number of card users is appropriate, and if the targeted usage levels have been met. It is quite possible that the initial results of the program will indicate that a further expansion of the parameters should be used. For example, the maximum purchase might be shifted from $500 to $1,000. If the parameters are changed, be sure to update the card policy and accompanying procedures.

The preceding phase-in steps can be useful for addressing concerns about the control over procurement cards. The initial rollout phase may reveal some control problems, which can then be addressed before a further expansion of the program is initiated. Thus, the initial rollout could be considered a pilot for a more comprehensive card system at a later date.

The Card Reconciliation Procedure

The bank supplying procurement cards to a company issues a statement of card activity once a month. The payables department passes this information along to those employees using procurement cards, who are expected to reconcile the statement to their purchasing records. There may also be a reconciliation checklist that accompanies each card statement, which is a useful tool for reminding card users of the various reconciliation steps. The procedure for reconciling a procurement card statement is outlined below.

1. **Match receipts to statement.** Upon receipt of the monthly card statement and a reconciliation checklist from the payables staff, match all stored receipts to the line items on the statement. A sample reconciliation checklist follows. The checklist shows the key reconciliation steps, which users can check off as they complete each item. The checklist is simply a reminder for card users – it does not have to be returned to the payables staff.

Sample Reconciliation Checklist

Procurement Card Reconciliation Checklist

This checklist shows the steps required to reconcile your procurement card statement. The steps are:

- ☐ Match receipts to card statement
- ☐ Obtain missing receipts
- ☐ Complete the missing receipts form
- ☐ Complete the disputed expenditure form
- ☐ Assign account numbers to statement line items
- ☐ Sign approval block on the statement
- ☐ Make a copy of all documents and retain it for __ years
- ☐ Forward original documents to accounts payable department

Note: All documents must be completed and returned within three business days!

> **Tip:** To speed up the reconciliation process, consider having the payables staff first review all card statements and accept those with small balances for which the account coding is obvious. The card user still receives a copy of the statement, but does not have to complete a reconciliation.

> **Tip:** A high-volume card user might consider logging all purchases made with a procurement card into a transaction log. Otherwise, it may be difficult to sort through what may potentially be several hundred receipts.

2. **Obtain missing receipts.** If the receipts associated with some line items are missing, contact the supplier to see if a replacement receipt can be obtained. If a receipt cannot be obtained (which is likely), fill out a missing receipts form. This form itemizes any statement line item for which there is no receipt and states the purpose of the expense. The card user signs the form to certify that the expenses on the form are valid business expenses. A sample missing receipts form follows.

Sample Missing Receipts Form

Missing Receipts Form			
Employee Contact Information		Statement Date	
		Statement ID Number	
Line Item Date	Supplier Name	Description	Amount
Missing Receipts Detail Block			
I certify that the procurement card expenditures described above are valid business expenses incurred on behalf of the company.			
Signature: [card user]		Date	

> **Tip:** Adopt a cutoff level for the missing receipts form, below which no entries are required. Otherwise, employees may spend an inordinate amount of time documenting insignificant expenditures.

3. **Note disputed charges.** If line item amounts appear to be incorrect or charged in error, circle them on the account statement and note that they are in dispute. Also, complete the disputed expenditure form, which is used by the payables staff to follow up with the card provider. A sample disputed expenditure form follows. There are a number of possible reasons to request a credit, so the form format includes a number of options, as well as space at the bottom to more fully explain the situation. Only one dispute is documented on each of these forms; doing so makes it easier for the payables staff to track each dispute.

Sample Disputed Expenditure Form

Disputed Expenditure Form

| Employee Contact Information | Statement Date |
| | Statement ID Number |

| Line Item Date | Supplier Name | Description | Amount |

Check the box that best states the reason for the disputed expenditure:

☐ Already billed on prior statement
☐ Amount is incorrect
☐ Did not authorize the purchase
☐ Did not receive goods or services
☐ Other (see comments below)

Additional explanatory comments block

Signature: [card user] | Date

Return this form to the accounts payable department as part of the monthly card statement

> **Tip:** Card users are not good at resolving disputed charges, so have them provide the details for each dispute, and then have the person in charge of the procurement card program or the payables staff follow up on the charges.

4. **Assign account numbers.** Write the account number to be charged next to each line item on the statement. A variation is to assign a default account number to each card user, so that they only have to enter an account number if it varies from the default account number.

> **Tip:** Card users may not know which accounts are available for their use, so send each user a list of acceptable account numbers, and issue an updated version whenever there is a change to the chart of accounts.

5. **Sign approval block.** Before forwarding card statements, the payables staff should have stamped an approval block on each statement, in which the card user and the department manager should sign if they approve the expenditures listed in the statement.

Procurement Cards

6. **Forward documents.** Assemble the card statement, missing receipts form, disputed expenditure form, and receipts into a packet. Make a copy of the packet and retain it. Forward the original version of the packet to the payables department.

The following exhibit shows a streamlined view of the card reconciliation procedure.

Card Reconciliation Process Flow

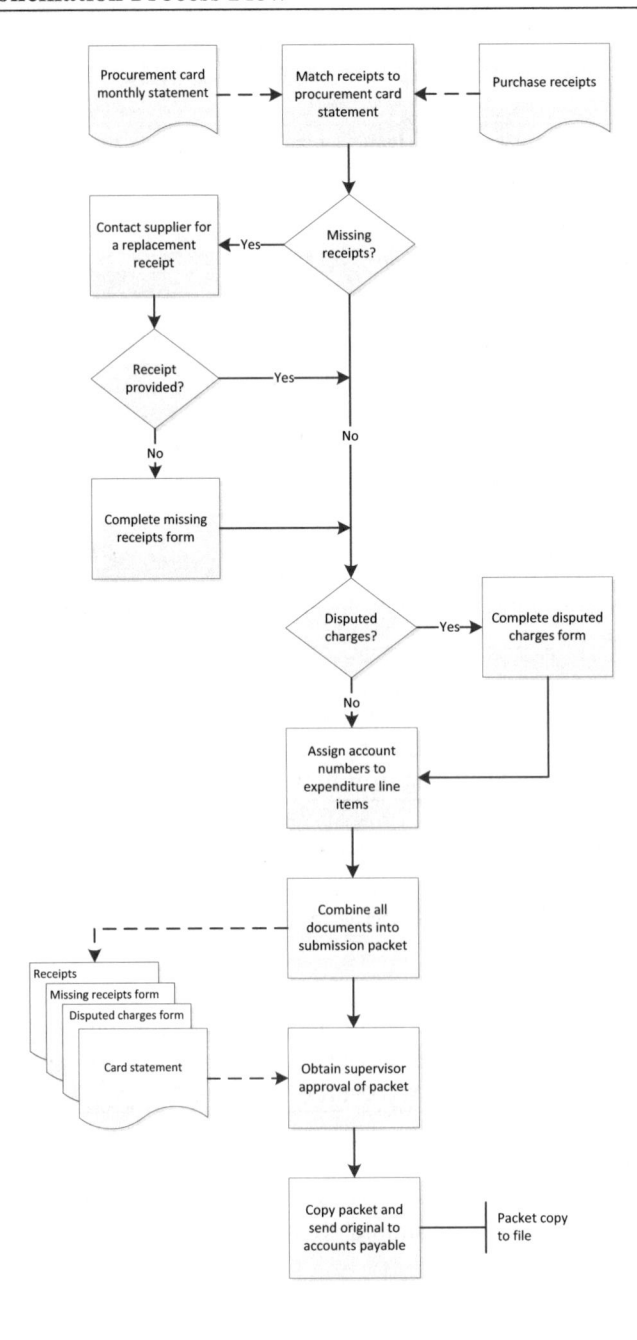

The Lost Card Procedure

There is a significant liability associated with a lost or stolen procurement card, so a company should have a system in place for rapidly notifying its card provider whenever employees become aware that a card is missing. The procedure for lost cards is outlined next.

1. **Complete lost card notification form.** Complete the lost card notification form for the employee name, date, card number, and reason fields. Then forward the form as expeditiously as possible to the procurement card administrator. A sample lost card notification form follows. In the form, the card user completes the information above the solid line. He or she then signs the signature block in the top half of the form and forwards the form to the procurement card administrator. The administrator completes the bottom half of the form and then sends the form to the card provider.

   Sample Lost Card Notification Form

   ### Lost Card Notification

Employee Contact Information	Date
	Procurement Card Number

   Check the box that best states the reason for the card being lost:

   ☐ Lost (describe circumstances): _____
   ☐ Stolen (describe circumstances): _____
   ☐ Other (describe circumstances): _____

Signature: [card user]	Date

Name and address of person contacted at card provider	Date Contacted
	Time Contacted

   ☐ Send replacement by regular mail
   ☐ Send replacement by overnight mail (the company will be billed for this service)

Signature: [card administrator]	Date

   Forward this form to the procurement card administrator at once

> **Tip:** If there is a procurement card user manual, include the lost card notification form in the manual, so that it is easily accessible by card users.

2. **Contact card provider.** Contact the company's contact person at the card provider about the missing card. Note on the form the name of the person contacted, as well as the date and time of notification. This information can be of some importance when determining the respective liabilities of the company and its card provider for any fraudulent charges made after the card was lost or stolen.
3. **Complete form.** Complete the bottom part of the lost card notification form, requesting the speed with which a replacement card should be forwarded by the card provider. Then sign the form and e-mail it to the provider. Retain a copy of the form, in case there are questions later about whether a notification was properly made.
4. **Match to received cards.** As replacement cards arrive from the card provider, match them to the related lost card notification forms. Follow up with the provider if any cards were not received by the expected dates.

The following exhibit shows a streamlined view of the lost card procedure.

Procurement Cards

Lost Procurement Card Process Flow

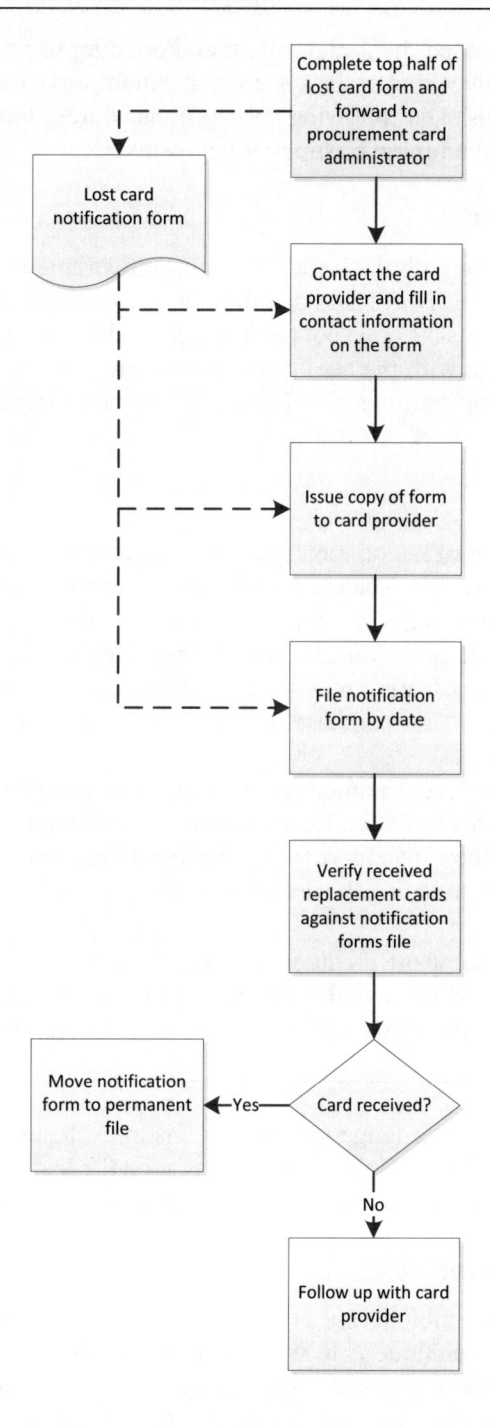

```
                              ┌─────────────────┐
                              │ Complete top half│
                              │ of lost card form│
                   ┌ ─ ─ ─ ─ ─┤ and forward to   │
                   │          │ procurement card │
                   ▼          │ administrator    │
           ╭──────────╮       └─────────────────┘
           │ Lost card │               │
           │notification│              ▼
           │   form    │       ┌─────────────────┐
           ╰──────────╯       │ Contact the card │
                   ├ ─ ─ ─ ─ ─▶│ provider and fill│
                   │          │ in contact info  │
                   │          │ on the form      │
                   │          └─────────────────┘
                   │                   │
                   │                   ▼
                   │          ┌─────────────────┐
                   ├ ─ ─ ─ ─ ─▶│ Issue copy of    │
                   │          │ form to card     │
                   │          │ provider         │
                   │          └─────────────────┘
                   │                   │
                   │                   ▼
                   │          ┌─────────────────┐
                   └ ─ ─ ─ ─ ─▶│ File notification│
                              │ form by date     │
                              └─────────────────┘
                                       │
                                       ▼
                              ┌─────────────────┐
                              │ Verify received │
                              │ replacement cards│
                              │ against notif.   │
                              │ forms file       │
                              └─────────────────┘
                                       │
                                       ▼
     ┌──────────────┐              ◇────────◇
     │Move notification│◀──Yes───│Card received?│
     │form to permanent│           ◇────────◇
     │     file       │                │
     └──────────────┘                 No
                                       ▼
                              ┌─────────────────┐
                              │ Follow up with   │
                              │ card provider    │
                              └─────────────────┘
```

72

Additional Procurement Card Topics

We have thus far discussed the initial rollout and ongoing use of procurement cards, but not the additional tweaking of the system that can improve its financial results and mitigate the risk of loss. The following sub-sections address topics ranging from the use of card rebates to the timing of supplier payments.

Card Issuer Relations

The key point in dealing with the bank that issues procurement cards is to make sure that the card balances are always paid on time. This can be a problem, especially when the corporate treasurer insists upon not paying until as close to the due date as possible. A solution is to arrange with the card provider to extract the funds directly from the company's bank account with an ACH debit. Doing so eliminates the risk of a late payment.

Card Rebates

Given a certain amount of negotiation, procurement card providers may offer monetary rebates when a company spends a large amount through its cards. The discount percentage may increase as the volume of purchases made increases. Given this payback feature, it could be quite valuable for the payables manager to insist on a high level of card usage. This feature may be a good incentive for a business to increase the maximum allowable card purchase, thereby providing an immediate boost to the rebate.

A good way to increase the amount of card usage is to route all card rebates back to the using departments based on their volume of card usage. Once the department managers realize that they have more money to spend, they usually take over from the payables manager in demanding the use of procurement cards.

> **Tip:** Cancel all other company credit cards, such as fuel cards, so that these expenditures will instead be paid for with the mandated procurement card. Doing so concentrates expenditures on the cards and increases the potential amount of rebate to be earned.

The card provider may offer longer payment terms in exchange for no rebate. This is generally a bad idea, since the implicit interest rate on the lost rebate tends to be quite high. Instead, it usually pays to pay sooner in exchange for a higher rebate.

Cash Flow Management

If used adroitly, it is possible to use procurement cards to enhance the cash flows of an organization. The technique is to wait until the due date on an invoice, and then call the supplier and ask to pay with a credit card. Doing so then shifts the payable to the card provider, who may not require payment for several additional weeks.

A certain amount of management is required to maximize cash flows with this method, so it may make sense to reduce the work load by only timing payments for the largest invoices. Timing payments for the smallest supplier invoices will have a minimal positive impact on cash flows.

Card User Relations

The ideal card user is one who keeps his or her card information private, only purchases authorized items, and reconciles the month-end statement to receipts as soon as possible. Unfortunately, the typical card user does not necessarily fit this profile. A common scenario is that a few card users perpetually give the payables staff ulcers by submitting their month-end reports late. It is quite common for these individuals to display the same behavior every month. If so, the payables staff should not be required to backfill for the behavior of these few employees. Instead, pull the card privileges from these individuals and shift the card user responsibility to someone else. Life is too short to continually deal with someone whose work habits are slovenly.

Another issue is cards that are not being used at all. This is an indicator that a card user is not certain about how and when to use the card, or that he or she simply does not need a card. The first issue can be resolved by educating users about proper card usage, while the second issue can only be resolved by shifting the card to a different user.

Departure of Card Users

When holders of procurement cards leave the company, be sure to retrieve the cards from them as part of the exit interview, and cancel the card. Otherwise, there is a risk that the card will be used after the person has left the company.

The retrieval of procurement cards requires coordination between the payables and human resources departments. The human resources staff is responsible for the exit interview, and so must remember to ask for the card at that time. To ensure that this is done, make sure that procurement card retrieval is listed as a standard task on the exit interview checklist.

If the human resources staff forgets to retrieve a procurement card, a backup procedure is to review the procurement card statements at the end of each month, and see if the purchasing activity on any cards have changed or fallen off. If so, contact the human resources department to see if these changes correspond to an employee departure. A variation on this concept is to send the current list of card users to the human resources staff each month, with a request to flag any users who have left the company.

Summary

The managers of the purchasing and payables departments usually want to shift as much purchasing activity as possible to procurement cards, thereby reducing the purchasing workload of their departments. This emphasis on procurement cards can mean that quite a large proportion of all expenditures are made with the cards. If so, it is critical to install a card reconciliation procedure that incorporates an approval process, along with a set of controls over every aspect of card usage. Otherwise, it will be much

Procurement Cards

too easy for employees to make a significant number of purchases that are not in the best interests of the company.

Chapter 6
Use Taxes

Introduction

There are a number of purchases for which a business may be subject to a use tax obligation. If so, the payables staff will be responsible for calculating the amount of use tax to pay. In this chapter, we discuss the nature of the use tax, how to calculate it, use tax audits, and several related issues.

> **Related Podcast Episodes:** Episodes 229 and 230 of the Accounting Best Practices Podcast discuss sales and use taxes, as well as audits of these taxes. They are available at: **accountingtools.com/podcasts** or **iTunes**

Sales and Use Tax Overview

Sales and use taxes are used by governments to derive income from the sale of tangible personal property. These taxes are a common source of revenue by state governments, and sometimes also at the county and city levels. There may also be incremental additions to this tax that are intended to last for a short period of time, until an underlying government expenditure has been paid off. For example, there may be a short-term addition to the sales tax by a city that wants to make a one-time payment for a sports stadium.

The amount of sales and use tax to be paid is calculated by multiplying the amount paid for goods or services by the tax rate; this calculation only applies to sale transactions arising within the jurisdiction governed by the taxing entity.

The application of the sales and use tax to all purchase transactions is by no means comprehensive. Instead, each government jurisdiction has its own rules for which types of purchases may be excluded, such as for the purchase of food. This can make it difficult for a business to keep track of tax inclusions and exclusions on an ongoing basis.

The process flow for a sales tax transaction is for a supplier to charge the sales tax to its customers, which the supplier is then responsible for remitting to the applicable government. This usually means that all sales taxes are sent to the tax division of the state government, which then forwards that portion of the sales tax owed to the county and city governments to those entities.

A business must collect sales taxes if nexus is present. Nexus is the area within which a supplier operates. Nexus is not present if the buyer is located further away from the supplier. A lack of nexus is common when the buyer is located in another state where the supplier has no business presence. A no-nexus situation is increasingly common, since a large proportion of all purchases are made over the Internet, where the buyer could be located many miles away from the supplier.

If there is no nexus, the *buyer* is now liable to the government to pay this tax. However, if the buyer pays the tax, it is now called a use tax, rather than a sales tax. The amount to be paid depends on local regulations. Here are several variations:

- A city may have an ordinance requiring the amount of the use tax to be its own sales tax percentage, irrespective of the rate that would have been charged by the seller if the sale had occurred on its premises.
- A city may require, when a sales tax paid to another government entity is at a tax rate lower than the city's own sales tax rate, and the goods purchased are used within the city's boundaries, that the buyer pay the city the incremental additional amount of the sales tax charged by the city.
- A business leases a machine from a lessor located in another state, and picks up the machine in the other state. The regulations of the city in which the business is located require that the sales tax on the first month's lease be paid to the other state government, and that all subsequent monthly payments are subject to the city's own sales tax rate.

As the examples indicate, use tax regulations can be a tangled affair that requires a close reading of the tax regulations of the government entity within whose boundaries a business is located.

Use Tax Systems

The calculation of the amount of use tax within the payables system can be quite difficult. It involves the following steps:

1. Aggregate all purchases made during the reporting period, with the presence and amount of all sales taxes noted.
2. Separate out for further processing all purchases made for which no sales taxes were paid.
3. Strip away all purchases made for which there is a sales tax exemption certificate (see the Sales Tax Exemption Certificate section).
4. Strip away all purchases to which sales taxes do not apply.
5. For all remaining purchases, apply the applicable use tax percentage.
6. Document the calculation.

There are multiple problems with this process flow. First, the presence of a sales tax must be noted when a supplier invoice is first entered into the payables system. Second, a sales tax exemption flag must be set for those specific purchase transactions to which the exemption applies. And third, any statutory exemptions must also be flagged. Each of these notations must be manually addressed when an invoice is initially entered into the payables system, which greatly reduces the efficiency of the data entry process.

An alternative approach is to treat the calculation of the use tax as an entirely separate project, where the tax is manually compiled. This approach requires the following steps:

1. Determine which supplier billings are subject to the use tax.
2. Pull their files from the archives, sort through the invoices pertaining to the measurement period, and manually compile the total amount of purchases made from them.
3. Calculate the applicable use tax.
4. Document the calculation.

Most organizations prefer the latter approach, since it keeps the primary payables recordation process as simple and clean as possible.

The accounting for use tax is to accrue a use tax liability for each applicable purchase. This amount is also recognized as an expense for the business. Thus, the general format of the journal entry is:

	Debit	Credit
Expense [expense account]	xxx	
Use tax liability [liability account]		xxx

The exact expense account charged when use tax is recognized can vary. If the aggregate amount of use tax recognized per year is small, the easiest approach is to charge it to a miscellaneous expense account. For larger amounts, a unique account can be created for it.

Given the difficulty of calculating the use tax, a further consideration is whether to remit the tax at all, or to wait for a use tax audit and then pay a fine for late payment. The most law-abiding approach is, of course, to determine the use tax as part of the ongoing operations of the department, and remit the tax on a scheduled basis. However, some organizations are so small that there is little likelihood that a use tax audit will ever occur, so they prefer to avoid a remittance until they are forced to do so.

> **Tip:** Depending on local laws, it is possible that nonprofit entities will not have any liability to remit use taxes.

Additional Use Tax Issues

Items purchased for inventory are not subject to sales or use taxation. However, if items are removed from inventory for business or personal use, they have, in effect, been sold to the final user. If this has occurred, the company is now liable to pay use tax on the items removed from stock.

EXAMPLE

A furniture retailer buys furniture from manufacturers and pays no sales tax on these purchases, on the assumption that the furniture will then be sold to customers and sales tax will be charged to the final customers. However, the store manager elects to remove several desks and chairs from stock for use by the staff as office furniture. The retailer owes use tax on these desks and chairs as soon as they are removed from stock.

A business may return goods to a supplier, at which point the supplier issues a credit that reduces or eliminates the amount billed on the original invoice. All credits received should be used to reduce the amount of the use tax accrual, as long as the credits relate to items for which a use tax accrual had originally been made.

A curious issue with use tax payments is that the applicable state's Department of Revenue does not necessarily collect this tax on behalf of counties, cities, or special districts. Instead, it may be necessary to make separate payments to each of these entities. Check with the Department of Revenue to which the company sends payments to determine the local treatment of these remittances.

Use Tax Audits

Since the use tax is one of the main forms of income for many governments, it should be no surprise that they routinely conduct audits of companies to ensure that the correct amounts are remitted. The audits can be conducted by any government in whose territory a buyer is located. Consequently, a multi-location business may be subject to a large number of use tax audits from various city, county, and state governments.

The local government is likely to be aware of a business within its boundaries, since the business would likely have already obtained a sales tax certificate from the government. If so, the government's audit department will then estimate the size of the business' operations, and decide whether there will be a reasonable cost-benefit associated with an audit. This will likely focus the attention of the audit staff on only the larger businesses. Smaller organizations are not usually audited, since any use taxes collected from an audit will not offset the cost of the audit staff employed on the audit. A smaller entity may only receive a use tax reminder letter from the local government, which may cost-effectively dislodge some additional use tax payments.

Some governments issue a combined sales and use tax remittance form to any of their sales tax certificate holders, under the assumption that use taxes will be remitted on a regular basis. If this is not the case, there may be an assumption that use taxes are not being reported, which can then trigger an audit.

Sales Tax Exemption Certificate

Sales taxes are not required when the buyer of goods intends to include them in its own products, which will then be sold to another party. In this case, the buyer must produce a sales tax exemption certificate (sometimes called a resale certificate), to keep the supplier from charging sales taxes. When this approach is taken, only the final party to buy the goods is required to pay the sales or use tax.

However, if the buyer elects to remove purchased items from inventory for its own use, there is no longer an intent to resell the goods, so the buyer must pay the use tax on these items.

Multiple Points of Use Certificate

Sales taxes present a particular problem for those companies that purchase software that is to be concurrently used in multiple tax jurisdictions, since the use tax for this transaction should ideally be remitted to multiple tax jurisdictions.

The issue can be eliminated by obtaining a multiple points of use certificate (MPU) from the state government. By doing so, the buyer of the software is still required to pay a use tax on its software purchase (the seller charges no sales tax). The buyer apportions the amount of the use tax among the applicable tax jurisdictions where the software is to be used. The apportionment method can be based on any reasonable method, as long as it is applied in a consistent and uniform manner, and the method can be justified through supporting records.

A simple apportionment method that should be easy to justify is to base the allocation on the number of software users in each tax jurisdiction.

Several other issues related to the MPU are:

- *Applicability*. The MPU is currently allowed for pre-written software that is delivered by electronic means. The MPU does not apply to software that has been pre-loaded on a computer when the computer is sold.
- *Usage*. The MPU is part of the Streamlined Sales and Use Tax Agreement, so it should become more widely used as the Agreement is gradually accepted among more state governments.
- *Wider use*. A few tax jurisdictions have adopted a more broad interpretation of the MPU, allowing it to be applied to the sale of computer projects or services, usually involving the sale of digital products.

Summary

A reasonable approach to the calculation of use taxes is to begin with a manual calculation of use taxes, and then gradually refine the concept to enhance the accuracy of the resulting tax payment. The additional refinements can be judged sufficient when use tax audits uncover no *substantial* additional liability. If a notable additional liability is found, then only enhance the system again to ensure that the liability found is not missed again in the future. It is not cost-effective to create an absolutely 100% perfect system that uncovers all use tax liabilities, since the cost of such a process is usually prohibitive. Instead, there is a balance between the cost of the tracking system and the results that it produces.

Chapter 7
Finance Issues

Introduction

Payables management is mostly about the timely processing of supplier invoices. There are also several issues related to the finance requirements of a business that may impinge upon the payables manager. In this chapter, we discuss how to determine the effective interest rate on early payment discounts, the ramifications of making late payments, and the concept of supply chain financing.

> **Related Podcast Episode:** Episode 143 of the Accounting Best Practices Podcast discusses supply chain financing. It is available at: **accountingtools.com/podcasts** or **iTunes**

Early Payment Discounts

A key question for the payables manager is whether to take early payment terms offered by suppliers. This is a common offer when a supplier is short on cash.

The early payment terms offered by suppliers need to be sufficiently lucrative for the payables manager to want to pay invoices early, especially when suppliers are offering such generous terms that the company is effectively earning an inordinately high interest rate in exchange for an early payment.

The term structure used for credit terms is to first state the number of days a supplier is giving its customers from the invoice date in which to take advantage of the early payment credit terms. For example, if a customer is supposed to pay within 10 days without a discount, the terms are "net 10 days," whereas if the customer must pay within 10 days to qualify for a 2% discount, the terms are "2/10." Or, if the customer must pay within 10 days to obtain a 2% discount or can make a normal payment in 30 days, then the terms are stated as "2/10 net 30."

The table below shows some of the more common credit terms, explains what they mean, and also notes the effective interest rate being offered to customers with each one.

Sample Credit Terms

Credit Terms	Explanation	Effective Interest
Net 10	Pay in 10 days	None
Net 30	Pay in 30 days	None
Net EOM 10	Pay within 10 days of month-end	None
1/10 net 30	Take a 1% discount if pay in 10 days, otherwise pay in 30 days	18.2%
2/10 net 30	Take a 2% discount if pay in 10 days, otherwise pay in 30 days	36.7%
1/10 net 60	Take a 1% discount if pay in 10 days, otherwise pay in 60 days	7.3%
2/10 net 60	Take a 2% discount if pay in 10 days, otherwise pay in 60 days	14.7%

In case there are terms different from those shown in the preceding table, it helps to be aware of the formula for calculating the effective interest rate associated with early payment discount terms. The calculation steps are:

1. Calculate the difference between the payment date for those taking the early payment discount and the date when payment is normally due, and divide it into 360 days. For example, under "2/10 net 30" terms, one would divide 20 days into 360 to arrive at 18. Use this number to annualize the interest rate calculated in the next step.
2. Subtract the discount percentage from 100% and divide the result into the discount percentage. For example, under "2/10 net 30" terms, divide 2% by 98% to arrive at 0.0204. This is the interest rate being offered through the credit terms.
3. Multiply the result of both calculations together to obtain the annualized interest rate. To conclude the example, multiply 18 by 0.0204 to arrive at an effective annualized interest rate of 36.72%.

Thus, the full calculation for the cost of credit is:

$$(\text{Discount \%} \div (1 - \text{Discount \%})) \times (360 \div (\text{Allowed payment days} - \text{Discount days}))$$

In general, most early payment discounts represent a sufficiently high effective interest rate that the payables staff would be foolish to forego them. However, taking such a discount requires that there be sufficient cash on hand, which may mandate some coordination of discount arrangements with the treasury staff, which invests the company's excess cash.

The simplest way to ensure that all early payment discounts are accepted and paid in a timely manner is to examine every invoice at the point of initial receipt, and set to one side all invoices containing discount offers. This group of invoices containing discounts can then be shifted to a different process flow that emphasizes faster data entry, approval, and payment processing. Where possible, approvals are made using the negative approval system, where payments will be made unless an authorized person protests an invoice. If a positive approval is needed for these invoices, either manually walk them through the approval process or install an automated workflow management system that automatically routes them to a backup approver if an invoice is not approved by a specified date. In short, special handling may be appropriate when it is imperative to accept early payment discounts that have extremely favorable effective interest rates.

> **Tip:** Have suppliers offering early payment discounts send their invoices to a different mailstop number within the company, so that they can receive expedited handling.

If an early payment discount is not taken, be sure to track back through the reasons why the discount was not taken, and adjust the processing system or employee training to ensure that this does not happen again.

> **Tip:** Ask the purchasing manager to negotiate for an early payment discount with the company's larger suppliers. These negotiations should be focused on the 20% of suppliers who comprise 80% of all payments made, so that these discounts can be maximized.

If the company is paying for relatively large amounts through a procurement card, this means that the supplier is being charged a 2% to 3% (or more) fee by the credit card company. In these situations, contact the supplier and offer to make an ACH payment if the supplier is willing to allow an early payment discount. This approach benefits both parties, since the supplier avoids the credit card fee and the company earns the amount of the discount.

Payment Timing

The payables manager may be pressured by the treasurer to make payments to suppliers beyond their normal payment terms. This request may be founded upon a general desire to reduce the overall working capital investment in the business, or perhaps to avoid a forecasted negative cash position.

If the payables manager decides to delay a payment for any reason, it is worthwhile to examine the ramifications of this financing-based decision. If payments are delayed to an inordinate extent, the issue will likely reach the ears of the credit managers of the company's suppliers. If they see a late payment for which no reasonable excuse can be given, they are very likely to reduce the company's credit, or at least put the company on a watch list. The outcome may be cash-in-advance payments in the future. In addition, the following internal issues may arise:

- *Duplicate payments.* When a payment is seriously delayed, a supplier may assume that the original invoice was lost in the mail, and sends a replacement. The company may accidentally pay the replacement invoice, as well as the original invoice.

- *Inquiries*. The payables staff will be forced to field questions from suppliers regarding why payments are being delayed.
- *Tracking*. The payables staff must manually track which payments are being delayed, which is both time-consuming and prone to error.

Given this possible outcome, the delay of payments should be restricted to isolated situations where a delay of just a few days may be necessary. If the treasurer wants to achieve a more significant reduction in working capital, a better approach is to have the purchasing manager negotiate with suppliers for a longer payment period – though this may be at the cost of higher prices imposed by suppliers.

Supply Chain Financing

Supply chain financing occurs when a finance company, such as a bank, interposes itself between a company and its suppliers, and commits to pay the company's invoices to the suppliers at an accelerated rate in exchange for a discount (which is essentially a factoring arrangement). This approach has the following benefits for the entity that is paying its suppliers:

- The company can foster very close links with its core group of suppliers, since this can be a major benefit to them in terms of accelerated cash flow.
- 100% of the invoice value is available for factoring, rather than the discounted amount that is available through a normal factoring arrangement.
- The company no longer has to deal with requests from suppliers for early payment, since they are already being paid as soon as possible.

Supply chain financing has the following benefits for suppliers:

- A cash-strapped supplier can be paid much sooner than normal, in exchange for the finance company's fee.
- The interest rate charged by the finance company should be low, since it is based on the credit standing of the paying company, not the rating of the suppliers (which assumes that the payer has a good rating).

The finance company acting as the intermediary earns interest income on the factoring arrangements that it enters into with the suppliers of the target company. This can represent an excellent source of income over a long period of time, so bankers try to create sole-source supply chain financing arrangements to lock in this source of income.

Supply chain financing is usually begun by large companies that want to improve the cash flow situation for their suppliers. To convince a finance company to be involved in the arrangement requires the expectation of a considerable amount of factoring, which is why this approach is not available to smaller companies.

There are on-line systems available on which a company can post its approved invoices, and which suppliers can access to select which invoices they want to have paid to them earlier than dictated by the standard payment terms.

Summary

Of the three concepts described in this chapter, the one likely having the most impact on the payables manager on a repetitive basis is requests from management to delay payments to suppliers. These requests are unfair to the payables staff, which must field annoyed calls from suppliers, and who may have a difficult time finding reasonable excuses to make. It is much better from a supplier relations perspective for the treasurer to arrange for an adequate line of credit with the local bank, which can be used to fund any projected shortfalls in the company's cash balance.

Chapter 8
Accounting for Payables

Introduction

The accounting for payables is usually quite easy. Invoices are entered through the payables module in the accounting software, which assigns the recorded information to the correct general ledger accounts. In this chapter, we note the entries being made by these automated systems, and also describe a modest range of asset and expense accounts to which expenditures are most commonly applied.

Routine Accounts Payable Entries

The day-to-day accounting for accounts payable is relatively simple. Whenever the company receives an invoice from a supplier, the payables staff enters the vendor number of the supplier into the accounting software, which automatically assigns a default general ledger account number from the vendor master file to the invoice.

EXAMPLE

Milagro Corporation receives an invoice from Maid Marian, which provides the company with janitorial services. In the vendor master file, the payables staff has already assigned general ledger account number 852, Janitorial Expenses, to Maid Marian. Thus, when the payables staff enters the invoice into the accounts payable module of the accounting software, the system automatically assigns the invoice to account 852.

If the invoice is for goods or services other than the predetermined general ledger account number, the payables staff can manually enter a different account number, which is only good for that specific invoice – it does not become the new default account for that supplier. In short, the pre-assignment of account numbers to suppliers greatly simplifies the accounting for payables.

Tip: At the end of each accounting period, print a report that shows the amount of expense charged to each account in each of the past 12 months. Compare the expense balance in the most current period to prior periods; if there is a significant difference, it may be caused by the incorrect assignment of a supplier invoice to an account. If so, investigate the account and see if a different default account should be assigned to the supplier whose invoice caused the discrepancy.

Accounting for Payables

The accounting software should automatically create a credit to the accounts payable account whenever the payables staff records a supplier invoice. Thus, a typical entry might be:

	Debit	Credit
Supplies expense	xxx	
Accounts payable		xxx

Later, when the company pays suppliers, the accounting system eliminates the accounts payable balance with the following entry:

	Debit	Credit
Accounts payable	xxx	
Cash		xxx

It is possible that small debit or credit residual balances may appear in the accounts payable account. These balances may be caused by any number of issues, such as credit memos issued by suppliers which the company does not plan to use, or amounts that the company had valid cause not to pay. The accountant should occasionally run the aged accounts payable report to spot these items. Do not use journal entries to clear them out, since this will not be recognized by the report writing software that generates the aged accounts payable report. Instead, always create debit or credit memo transactions that are recognized by the report writer; this will flush the residual balances from the aged accounts payable report.

There is usually a debit memo or credit memo creation option in the accounting software, which automatically generates the necessary debit memo or credit memo. As an example, a company may have been granted a credit memo by a supplier for $100, to be used to reduce the amount of an outstanding account payable. A payables staff person enters the credit memo screen in the accounting software, enters the name of the supplier and the credit memo amount, and selects the expense account that will be offset. The journal entry that the software automatically generates could be as follows:

	Debit	Credit
Accounts payable	100	
Supplies expense		100

If a supplier offers a discount in exchange for the early payment of an invoice, the company is not paying the full amount of the invoice. Instead, that portion of the invoice related to the discount is charged to a separate account. If an accounting software package is used, the system automatically allocates the appropriate amount to this separate account. For example, an entry to take a 2% early payment discount on a supplier invoice might be:

	Debit	Credit
Accounts payable	100	
Cash		98
Discounts taken		2

This entry flushes out the full amount of the original account payable, so that no residual balance remains in the accounting records to be paid.

Gross and Net Price Methods

The gross price method involves recording a purchase at its gross price when it is first recorded in an organization's payables system. The assumption behind the use of this method is that the payables staff will not take any early payment discounts. When few suppliers offer these discounts, it is more efficient to use the gross price method, since no further entry is required to document a payable. However, if many suppliers offer discounts and those discounts are taken, it makes more sense to use the net price method, where purchases are initially recorded with the related early payment discount. If the entity does not then take advantage of the related discount, a separate entry is needed to add the discount back to the accounting records.

EXAMPLE

A company receives a $500 supplier invoice, which contains within it a $20 discount if payment is made within 10 days of the invoice date. Under the gross price method, the entry is a $500 debit to the appropriate expense or asset account and a $500 credit to accounts payable. If the accountant later decides to take the early payment discount, an additional entry is needed to record the $20 discount.

Under the net price method, the $20 discount would have been recorded when the invoice was initially recorded.

The net price method is the most theoretically correct way to record supplier invoices, since the effects of discounts are taken into account at once, rather than in a later accounting period. However, given the additional complexity of the net price method, the gross price method is used much more frequently.

Period-end Accounts Payable Entries

At month-end, it may be necessary to accrue for expenses when goods or services have been received by the company, but for which no supplier invoice has yet been received. To do so, examine the receiving log just after month-end to see which receipts do not have an associated invoice. Also, consider reviewing the expense accruals for the preceding month; a supplier that issues invoices late will probably do so on a repetitive basis, so the last set of expense accruals typically provides clues to what should be included in the next set of accruals.

When a month-end expense accrual is created, it is done with a reversing journal entry, so that the accounting system automatically reverses the expense at the beginning of the following month. Otherwise, there will be a risk of forgetting that an expense was accrued, so that it is left on the books for a number of months. Also, the accrued expense should be charged to a liability account separate from the accounts payable account, so that all accruals can be tracked separately. A common liability account for this is "accrued accounts payable." Thus, a typical accrued expense entry might be:

	Debit	Credit
Rent expense	xxx	
Accrued accounts payable		xxx

If a period-end accrual is made for income taxes, the tax could be recorded within the accrued accounts payable account. Alternatively, it could be recorded separately, especially if the amount is so large that management wants to report it separately in the balance sheet. An example of such an entry is:

	Debit	Credit
Income tax expense	xxx	
Accrued income taxes		xxx

Applicable Accounts to Charge

In the preceding sections, we have made reference to the account numbers to which expenditures might be charged. The full set of these accounts is listed in the chart of accounts, which is the formal listing of all accounts used in the general ledger, usually sorted in order by account number. The accounts are typically numeric, but can also be alphabetic or alphanumeric. The account numbering system is used by the accounting software to aggregate information into an entity's financial statements.

Accounts are usually listed in order of their appearance in the financial statements, starting with the balance sheet and continuing with the income statement. Thus, the chart of accounts begins with cash, proceeds through liabilities and shareholders' equity, and then continues with accounts for revenues and then expenses. Many organizations structure their chart of accounts so that expense information is separately compiled by department; thus, the sales department, engineering department, and production department all have the same set of expense accounts. Typical expense accounts found in the chart of accounts to which a supplier invoice might be charged are noted in the following table.

Sample Expense Accounts

Account Number	Department	Description
00-700	xxx	Cost of goods sold – Materials
00-710	xxx	Cost of goods sold – Direct labor
00-720	xxx	Cost of goods sold – Manufacturing supplies
00-730	xxx	Cost of goods sold – Applied overhead
10-800	Accounting	Bank charges
10-805	Accounting	Benefits
10-810	Accounting	Depreciation
10-815	Accounting	Insurance
10-825	Accounting	Office supplies
10-830	Accounting	Salaries and wages
10-835	Accounting	Telephones
10-840	Accounting	Training
10-845	Accounting	Travel and entertainment
10-850	Accounting	Utilities
10-855	Accounting	Other expenses
10-860	Accounting	Interest expense
20-800	Production	Bank charges
20-805	Production	Benefits
20-810	Production	Depreciation
20-815	Production	Insurance
20-825	Production	Office supplies
20-830	Production	Salaries and wages
20-835	Production	Telephones
20-840	Production	Training
20-845	Production	Travel and entertainment
20-850	Production	Utilities
20-855	Production	Other expenses
20-860	Production	Interest expense

The sample expense accounts are structured under a five-digit chart of accounts, where a unique department code is used for the first two digits, followed by a three-digit code that represents a particular type of expense. For example, the benefits expense is identified by the code "805" for both the accounting and production departments.

Accounting for Payables

In the table, note how the same expense accounts are automatically replicated for each of the departments. In reality, some accounts would not be applicable to certain departments; for example, the interest expense account for the production department might be blocked from use.

There may be situations in which an expenditure is instead charged to an asset account, indicating that an asset has been acquired that will be consumed over multiple periods. The following table contains a short list of some of the more popular asset accounts. Note how no department code is used – it is more common to assume that asset accounts relate to the entire business.

Sample Asset Accounts

Account Number	Description
100	Fixed assets – Computer equipment
110	Fixed assets – Computer software
120	Fixed assets – Furniture and fixtures
130	Fixed assets – Leasehold improvements
140	Fixed assets – Machinery
200	Other assets

Coding an invoice to an asset account is rather unusual, and may require the approval of the general ledger accountant or controller before such a charge is made. Usually, expenditures are coded to expense accounts.

Summary

When accounting for payables, the main concept is to keep the process flow as simplified as possible. Here are several concepts to which the simplicity goal can be applied:

- *Reduced supplier base.* Once an account has been assigned to a supplier in the vendor master file, it is not usually necessary to alter the account, since the same purchases will likely be made from that supplier in the future. However, what if the purchasing department elects to consolidate suppliers, so that more items or services are provided by each remaining supplier? One alternative is more careful manual coding of each individual invoice, but this approach is prone to error. The easier approach is to shrink the number of accounts to which expenses are being charged, so that a single account can still be used for each supplier. Doing so increases the efficiency of the payables data entry function, and usually has little effect on the overall usability of the financial statements.
- *Specialists – transactions.* What if there are ongoing errors with special entries, such as for credit memos or debit memos? If so, train one senior staff person to be the expert on this type of data entry, and send all of these

transactions to that person. Doing so keeps the bulk of the payables staff concentrating on the basic payables data entry task.
- *Specialists – accruals.* The same concept applies to the generation of accrual journal entries at the end of each accounting period. It is easy to forget an accrual, duplicate an accrual, or not set an accrual to reverse in the next period. To mitigate this risk, authorize only one specialist to create accruals.

Chapter 9
Closing Payables

Introduction

The accounting department as a whole must close the books at the end of each month in order to produce financial statements. This requires many of the functional areas within the department to complete several closing tasks, including the payables area. Payables can require a lengthy closing process, because of the inherent delay involved in waiting for supplier invoices to arrive. In some cases, this single issue can delay the issuance of financial statements by a week or more. In this chapter, we discuss the problems related to closing payables, and the range of solutions available to improve the situation. Major topics include accounts payable accruals, expense reports, suspense items, credit card statements, reconciling accounts payable, and closing the payables ledger.

> **Related Podcast Episode:** Episode 22 of the Accounting Best Practices Podcast discusses accounts payable in relation to closing the books. It is available at: **accountingtools.com/podcasts** or **iTunes**

Accounts Payable Accruals

Payables can be a significant bottleneck in the closing process. The reason is that some suppliers only issue invoices at the end of each month when they are closing *their* books, so their invoices will not be received until several days into the next month. This circumstance usually arises either when a supplier ships something near the end of the month or when it is providing a continuing service. There are several ways to deal with these items:

1. *Do nothing.* Wait a few days for the invoices to arrive in the mail, and then record the invoices and close the books. The advantage of this approach is a high degree of precision and perfect supporting evidence for all expenses. It is probably the best approach at year-end, if the intent is to have the financial statements audited. The downside is that it can significantly delay the issuance of the financial statements.
2. *Accrue continuing service items.* As just noted, suppliers providing continuing services are more likely to issue invoices at month-end. When services are being provided on a continuing basis, it is usually possible to estimate what the expense should be, based on prior invoices, and then accrue an expense. It is likely that the accruals will vary somewhat from the amounts on the actual invoices, but the differences should be immaterial.

3. *Accrue based on purchase orders.* As just noted, suppliers issue invoices at month-end when they ship goods near that date. If the company is using purchase orders to order these items, the supplier is supposed to issue an invoice containing the same price stated on the purchase order. Therefore, if an item is received at the receiving dock but there is no accompanying invoice, use the purchase order to create a reversing journal entry that accrues the expense associated with the received item.

> **Tip:** The last of the preceding options noted that an expense can be accrued for any received item for which there is no supplier invoice. This means that a key step in the closing process is to match the receipts listed on the receiving log to supplier invoices, to see if any invoices are missing. This is crucial, since an expensive item could otherwise be logged into the warehouse as an inventory asset without having any offsetting expense recorded against it.

In short, we strongly recommend using accruals to record expenses for supplier invoices that have not yet arrived. The sole exception is the end of the fiscal year, when the outside auditors may expect a greater degree of precision and supporting evidence, and will expect a firm to wait for actual invoices to arrive before closing its books.

Expense Reports

It can be extremely difficult to obtain expense reports from some employees in a timely manner. Some expense reports are quite large, and so can have a material impact on the financial statements if they are allowed to pile up and then be recorded only a few times per year. Therefore, this issue cannot be ignored. There are two general approaches to handling expense reports, which are:

- *Require company credit cards.* If employees must use company credit cards, this means that the business should receive credit card statements from the credit card company right at month-end, and can then charge these items to the correct department without much trouble. If there is a goal to close the books fast, arrange with the credit card company to close the credit card period a few days early; by doing so, the credit card statement will be received sooner, and the payables staff can have it fully processed before it interferes with other closing activities.
- *Allow personal credit cards.* If employees pay with their own credit cards, they will be quite interested in rapid reimbursement, so that they can pay for their credit cards in a timely manner. This built-in need for payment tends to mitigate the risk of having large overdue expense reports. However, there are usually a few employees who are extraordinarily late in submitting expense reports. Here are some options for dealing with them:
    - *Scheduled reminders.* Issue a general e-mail to all employees a few days before the end of the month, requesting that expense reports be submitted by a certain date.

- o *Performance reviews*. If an employee is persistently very late in submitting expense reports, include it as a discussion point in their performance reviews.
- o *Refuse cash advances*. If an employee is late in submitting expense reports, refuse to process any requests for cash advances until the reports have been submitted.
- o *Refuse payment*. Institute a company policy that expense reports submitted past a certain date will not be paid. However, this is an extreme method for handling the situation, and may result in a very angry employee.

In general, the best solution to keeping expense reports from interfering with the closing process is to require everyone to use company credit cards, and to have the statements for those cards delivered to the company shortly before the end of the month. See the next section for a discussion of an additional issue with company credit cards.

Issues with the Credit Card Close

The divisional controller of a publicly-traded multinational company asked AccountingTools for advice about problems he was having receiving expense reports on a timely basis. His company has a 4-4-5 close, so some months contain four weeks and others have five weeks. His comments are:

> "The killer item is American Express. Currently, AmEx cuts off around the 20th of the month. We get the invoices online on the 21st and send them out electronically to the individual cardholders. That way, they get it via e-mail, even when traveling. Users complete an expense report for their AmEx items and return them to us. This process often takes a week to get everything we need. Due to our odd month-end, a month can end as early as the 23rd or as late as the 31st. I'd prefer not to push back the AmEx statement cutoff, since that means we could be missing a half-month of expenses on the long months, but it creates a crunch in short months. I've looked at online expense processing from vendors like Concur. I'm choking a little on the expense, but beyond that, I'm not sure how much time it would actually save us, since the biggest problem is getting them from people."

> "We finally gave up on the stick approach and moved to a carrot and stick. Everyone who gets their AmEx in on time and complete gets entered for a monthly $50 AmEx gift card giveaway. Everyone not on time gets their name on a list that goes to the CEO."

Here are some possible solutions that we suggested:

- "We find that the carrot does not normally work, unless it is a BIG carrot. Unless you've seen an improvement from the $50 drawing, you might want to drop it, or improve the odds of winning by using multiple gift cards.
- There are usually repeat offenders every month, so target them for special treatment. We assume that they will not submit an expense report, so we immediately start hounding them as soon as they receive the statement. The normal escalation path is a direct e-mail, then a phone call, then the supervisor is contacted, and then the CEO. The total warning period is four days.
- The real problem for us is when people are gone for vacations during this time period, so we have everyone enter their vacation time in a company-wide Outlook calendar, and then ask them in advance who should complete the report if they are not available. Better yet, they can access a partial statement on-line at the AmEx site before they go on vacation, and send us the expense report in advance.
- If we do not receive an expense report, we charge the amounts on credit card statements to default expense accounts, which are then routed back to the department managers for review and correction in the next month. However, this might not work for you if these are re-billable expenses."

Accounts Payable Suspense Items

There are times when a supplier invoice arrives and the payables staff does not know what to do with it; such invoices are stuffed into a payables suspense folder, and the staff researches them when there is time. Examples of such situations are:

- An invoice is for an amount near the company's capitalization limit, which means that the payables staff is not certain whether it should charge the item to expense or record it as a fixed asset.
- It is not clear which department should be charged for the expense.
- The invoice is for an unusual expense, and there is uncertainty about which account should be charged.
- The company has multiple locations, and it is not clear which location should be charged.
- The invoice appears to address multiple accounts or departments, so an allocation is needed for the expense.

The broad range of examples show that there will always be situations that cannot be resolved in advance with a policy or procedure – instead, someone needs to review an invoice and make a decision pertaining to that specific invoice. This involves a certain amount of research time by a senior payables person, who may not have sufficient time available to address the issue. This, in turn, can impact the closing process, for these invoices may be of a sufficiently large dollar amount to impact the reported financial results if they are not recorded within the period.

Here are several possible options for dealing with payables suspense items, particularly in regard to mitigating their impact on closing the books:

- *Scheduled review times*. The payables department tends to have a lower work load at certain times of the month, and those are good times to schedule reviews of all outstanding suspense items. These scheduled reviews should be a formal meeting involving as many people as needed to reach a decision regarding a suspense item. After a few review sessions, it will be apparent how many people are needed to reach a decision, and that group can be scheduled for future sessions.
- *Final review schedule*. There should be a final review of suspense items just *before* the end of the month. By doing so, there should be only a very small number of suspense items remaining *at* the end of the month that must still be addressed.
- *Adjustment policy*. The review group will occasionally make an incorrect decision regarding the disposition of a supplier invoice. If so, create an adjustment policy that allows these invoices to be re-assigned to the correct expense accounts. Doing so makes it easier for a small group to initially disposition suspense items quickly, knowing that they will not get in trouble for an incorrect coding.
- *Immateriality policy*. Create a policy that allows the accounting staff to ignore any payables suspense items still open as of the closing process if they are smaller than a designated amount. These items are immaterial to the results shown in the financial statements, and so can be dealt with after the financial statements have been issued.

In short, dealing with payables suspense items is all about scheduling review meetings in advance of the closing process. By doing so, this becomes a minor issue during the close.

Discrepancy Invoices

There are likely to be a few supplier invoices at the end of the period that have discrepancies between what the company and the supplier believes should be paid. Where these discrepancies are large, put extra effort into resolving them prior to closing the books. Otherwise, there could be a potentially material issue outstanding that could result in inaccurate financial statements. If the amount of a discrepancy is relatively small, there is less of a materiality issue, and final settlement of the issue can wait until the following month.

The settlement of outstanding discrepancies is more of an issue at the end of the fiscal year. In this case, the outside auditors will not want to deal with uncertain expense levels, and may insist upon final settlement of unresolved issues before they certify the financial statements. Again, if the amount of a discrepancy is minor, they will not be overly concerned if settlement has not yet been reached.

> **Tip:** When an invoice has been withheld from entry into the accounts payable system due to a discrepancy and some weeks pass before resolution is reached, be sure to enter it in the correct accounting period. Otherwise, the expense will be incorrectly recognized in a later period.

Uncashed Checks

The end of each month is a good time to examine all outstanding checks that have not been cashed for a long time. Contact the recipients to see if they have lost the checks, and issue replacements as necessary. Doing so will minimize the number of uncashed checks, and also reduces the amount of unclaimed property. This task does not have to be part of the core closing activities – moving it slightly in front of or behind the more crucial closing tasks would be acceptable.

Reconciling Accounts Payable

The payables module in the accounting software automatically populates the accounts payable account in the general ledger with transactions. When the end of the month is reached, it should be possible to print the open accounts payable report and have the grand total on that report match the ending balance in the accounts payable general ledger account. If there is a difference between the two numbers, follow these reconciliation steps to determine the difference:

1. Compare the ending accounts payable account balance in the general ledger for the immediately preceding period to the open accounts payable report as of the end of the same period. If these numbers do not match, it will be necessary to reconcile earlier periods before attempting to reconcile the current period. If the variance is immaterial, it may be acceptable to proceed with the reconciliation for the current period.
2. Review the accounts payable general ledger account to see if any journal entries were made to the account during the current reporting period. If so, document these items in a reconciliation spreadsheet.
3. Print the ending open accounts payable report for the current reporting period. Enter the total amount outstanding from this report on the reconciliation spreadsheet. At this point, the reconciliation should be complete. If there is still a variance, and it is not a variance that occurred in a prior period, consider the following additional reconciliation steps:

    - Verify that the accounts payable journal was properly posted to the general ledger.
    - Verify that the open accounts payable report was printed after all posting was completed.
    - Verify that the general ledger is set to the correct reporting period.

This reconciliation process can be a difficult one when it is being performed for the first time. However, once all errors have been spotted and corrections made, it is usually relatively easy to update the reconciliation document in subsequent reporting periods.

The most common cause of a reconciliation problem is the use of a journal entry that debited or credited the accounts payable account. *Never* create such a journal entry, because there is so much detail in the accounts payable account that it is very time-consuming to wade through it to ascertain the source of the variance.

The one transaction that will be a temptation to record in the accounts payable account is the accrued expense. Instead, create a separate liability account in the general ledger and enter the accruals in that account. By doing so, normal accounts payable transactions are being properly segregated from special month-end accrual transactions.

This differentiation is not a minor one. Accrual transactions require more maintenance than standard accounts payable transactions, because they may linger through multiple accounting periods, and they need to be monitored in order to know when to eliminate them from the general ledger. If one were to lump accrued expenses into the accounts payable account, it would be very difficult to continually monitor the outstanding accruals.

In summary, restrict the accounts payable account to standard payables transactions, which makes it easier to reconcile at month-end. Any transactions related to accounts payable but which are entered via journal entries should be recorded in a separate account.

Additional Year-end Tasks

There are several additional tasks that the payables department should complete as part of the fiscal year-end of the business. These tasks are noted in the following bullet points:

- *Document archiving.* Remove old supplier documents from the files and shift them to long-term storage. It may make sense to shift the files to banker's boxes for long-term storage, but to keep them on the premises until the year-end audit has been completed. Doing so ensures that any documents requested by the auditors can be immediately accessed, rather than having to travel to the long-term storage facility to locate them. An extension of this concept is to temporarily store the boxes in the auditors' work area, to give them optimal access to the files.
- *Expense report submissions.* Few employees travel during the end of the calendar year. If this corresponds to the fiscal year-end, then use this dead period as an opportunity to solicit employees for any last remaining expense reports that have not yet been submitted.

An additional task that occurs at the end of each calendar year is the issuance of the Form 1099. We cover that topic in the Government Reporting chapter.

Closing the Ledger

Depending on the type of accounting system being used, the payables staff may be storing invoice and payment information in a ledger that is separate from the general ledger. This separate ledger may be called the payables ledger or purchases ledger, and its purpose is to keep the large volume of payables activity from cluttering up the company's general ledger. If such a ledger is in use, the final closing task in each period is to go into the administrative settings for the payables system, close the month, and open the following month. This action prevents anyone from inadvertently recording information in the wrong period. This closing step also creates a summary journal entry for the contents of the ledger, which posts the information to the general ledger.

Closing the ledger is an important step, and so should be prominently displayed in the payables manager's calendar of activities.

> **Tip:** Restrict access to the payables ledger's administrative settings with a password, so that no unauthorized person can go into the system, open a period that had been closed, and enter additional transactions. Such an action might be taken to fraudulently shift transactions away from the current period so that expense levels appear to be lower than is really the case.

Not all accounting systems use any ledgers other than the general ledger. If this is the case, there will be no need to post information to the general ledger, though it will still be necessary to close the old period and open the next period for all modules of the entire accounting system.

Summary

The key issue in closing payables is the tradeoff between the relative degree of inaccuracy associated with accruing expenses and the offsetting benefit of closing the books several days sooner. This is a more difficult decision to make if a business does not use purchase orders and regularly receives large amounts of materials, since it is more difficult to accrue an expense for any items received near month-end. Further, a really risk-averse payables manager may not want to take the chance of accruing for an expense that turns out to be substantially different when the invoice eventually arrives, and so will mandate a multi-day waiting period to ensure that all invoices have arrived before closing the books. In these cases, payables may very well be the largest bottleneck interfering with closing the books.

Chapter 10
Department Management

Introduction

If there is one department that responds well to a high level of organizational structure, it is the payables department. This area involves a large number of scheduled activities, procedures, and controls, so the payables manager can take a number of steps to ensure that everything is completed both on-time and without error. In this chapter, we cover several management techniques that a manager can use to improve department operations. We also make note of several alternatives for improving the work environment.

> **Related Podcast Episodes:** Episodes 165 and 180 of the Accounting Best Practices Podcast discuss how to set up an accounting department, and training, respectively. They are available at: **accountingtools.com/podcasts** or **iTunes**

Payables Manager Responsibilities

The issues described in this chapter are mostly of a tactical, day-to-day variety, and so represent responsibilities that are likely to appear regularly in the payables manager's work schedule. Those responsibilities are:

- Monitor and plan for all due dates associated with the department.
- Examine and streamline the flow of accounting information.
- Examine and streamline the physical flow of work in the department.
- Consolidate accounting operations to the extent needed to minimize overall costs.

Schedule of Activities

The payables manager should collect information about when accounting activities must be completed, reports issued, payments made, and so forth, and organize them into a department-wide schedule of activities. It is quite likely that each member of the department is well aware of when their work is supposed to be done, so this may not initially appear to improve the situation in the department. However, there are three good reasons for creating it:

- *Vacations.* Employees leave for vacations and forget to tell their replacements about due dates.
- *Departures.* An experienced employee leaves the company, and the rest of the department has to scramble to figure out when that person's work should be done.

- *MBWA*. This is management by wandering around. The payables manager can use the schedule of activities to chat with the staff about upcoming due dates. This may sometimes detect issues that would otherwise have been forgotten, and is also an excellent excuse to talk to the staff, which may bring up other issues worth investigating.

Error Tracking System

The department handles an enormous number of payables transactions, and some of those transactions will be processed incorrectly. Fixing them requires a large amount of time by an experienced accounting person. Further, if an erroneous transaction is visible outside of the department (such as an unpaid invoice), it gives the department a reputation for substandard work. Thus, one of the first steps for a new payables manager should be to set up an error tracking system.

An error tracking system is a manual one, and involves digging through the accounting records each month for adjusting transactions, such as a special credit memo or debit memo to correct an improper invoice entry. Examples of accounting errors are:

- Not recording a supplier invoice
- Paying a supplier invoice when the amount was not authorized
- Not taking an early payment discount on a supplier invoice
- Recording a supplier invoice in the wrong expense account
- Sending a supplier payment to the wrong address
- Not reversing an expense accrual in the following period

The preceding list of errors makes it clear that the department could be buried under an avalanche of errors. Consequently, it is critical to obtain an understanding of transactional errors.

Once uncovered, compile all errors in a spreadsheet or more formal database. This database should include the following information:

- Type of error
- Description of error
- Date when error occurred
- Person responsible for error

A sample error database appears in the following exhibit.

Sample Error Database

Error Area	Description	Date of Occurrence	Person Responsible for
Payments	Early payment discount not taken (Arnold Distributors)	Mar. 19	K. Dithers
Data entry	Invoice charged to wrong account (Lightspeed invoice)	Mar. 20	Q. Mathers
Data entry	Invoice charged to wrong account (Casey invoice)	Mar. 20	S. Jingle

> **Tip:** A "severity of error" column could be included in the database, which reveals those items causing either a great deal of investigative work to fix or which cost the company money. In the preceding sample error database, not taking an early payment discount might have received a high score for error severity.

By using this format to collect error information, the information can be sorted several ways to see if there are clusters of errors. If a particular payables area is revealing a cluster of errors, there may be a procedural issue that can be readily fixed. Alternatively, if errors appear to be clustering around a specific individual, the solution is likely to be the application of training, though fraud is also a possibility.

> **Tip:** Do not use the error tracking system to fire employees, unless their performance cannot be improved by any reasonable means. Otherwise, the system will be looked upon by employees as the basic tool used for an ongoing witch hunt in the department.

The most effective way to use the error tracking tool is to look for clusters of errors that have a common solution, and then implement that solution in order to eliminate an entire swathe of errors. This is a cost-effective approach, since all of the error correction activities associated with multiple errors can be avoided by implementing just one correcting activity. This approach rapidly reduces the grand total number of errors, which allows the staff to concentrate their attention on a reduced pool of errors.

Process Reviews

Payables processes change periodically to accommodate changes elsewhere in the business. Each incremental change may alter the efficiency with which transactions can be completed, usually making them slower. Over time, a series of these incremental changes can seriously impact the efficiency of the department.

To counteract the ongoing decline in process efficiency, schedule periodic process reviews that are designed to root out inefficiencies and streamline processes. A typical review involves documenting each step in a process, including an examination of all forms, reports, and controls, as well as the movement of paperwork between personnel. The process review team then documents errors created by the system, the time required to complete an average transaction, and the queue time during which a transaction sits between processing activities. Based on this information, the team configures a new process flow that may contain any of the following improvements:

- *Eliminate approvals.* A process may require multiple approvals, where only one is needed.
- *Eliminate data.* A transaction may call for the entry of more data into the payables system than is actually needed.
- *Process moves.* A process may require the movement of paperwork between employees, so concentrate activities with fewer people. By doing so, queue times are eliminated from the process.
- *Automation.* In a few cases, it may be possible to shift manual processing to an automated solution. However, only use this approach when there is a solidly favorable cost-benefit tradeoff. In many cases, an expensive automation solution will not yield much of an overall benefit to the company as a whole.
- *Report reductions.* Are reports really needed? In many cases, a process may result in a variety of reports being issued that are not used by the recipients. Interview recipients to determine which reports can be eliminated, or which information on specific reports can be eliminated.
- *Eliminate controls.* Some controls are redundant, and so only interfere with a process without reducing risk. However, only eliminate controls after having consulted with the auditors, who may have a different opinion.

A process review is a time-consuming activity that involves a number of people both within and outside of the department. For this reason, it is impossible to engage in a continual review of processes. Instead, consider scheduling reviews on a rotating basis, so that a single process is reviewed in detail perhaps every six months to a year. The exact review interval will depend upon the amount of change within a company. If little has changed in the past few years, there may be little reason to invest in a process review. However, if there have been substantial changes, such as acquisitions, it may be necessary to engage in an ongoing series of reviews.

Queue Management

Certain employees may operate with a perpetual backlog of work, or do so at certain times of the month or year. This may not be a problem, as long as these queues do not interfere with cash flow. For example, a payables clerk may have a five-day backlog of supplier invoices to enter into the accounting system, but this is not a problem if payment terms state that the company does not have to pay its suppliers for 30 days. However, if an early payment discount must be taken within five days, this is a much greater concern, since the company may lose the discount. This latter case may call for an alteration in the work load of the payables clerk, or the use of additional staff. Consider using the following techniques to improve the management of work queues:

- Narrowly define the job description of the person who has a persistently large queue, thereby permanently offloading some work. This is a common solution

when transaction volumes gradually increase to the point where an employee is persistently using overtime to complete his or her work.
- Shift work temporarily when the work in a queue is time sensitive. This can involve shifting work to other full-time employees or bringing in part-time help. For example, this works well when processing month-end customer invoices.
- Examine the process flow to see if the activities related to a work queue can be streamlined. This may involve an investment in technology. This approach is more cost-effective when there is a persistent work queue.
- Structure jobs so that some employees are scheduled to have little required work at the same time that there are spikes in the work load elsewhere in the department. This allows employees with low utilization levels to assist those in the reverse situation.
- Compare scheduled vacation times to expected changes in work queue levels. Restrict the use of vacation time during those periods when work queues are expected to be high.
- Delay the performance of routine tasks that have no impact on cash flow, so that staff can concentrate on reducing queues during peak work periods. This is a common solution during the month-end close, when the department stops all other work in order to create financial statements.

Queue management is a nearly daily activity that requires considerable attention to workloads throughout the department, as well as anticipation of queue levels in the near future. Proper scheduling and shifting of personnel among tasks can reduce the most crucial queues and makes the department run more efficiently.

Department Layout

If the department appears to be operating at near-maximum capacity, with employees working furiously throughout the day, then it may be possible to squeeze some extra capacity out of the department by altering its layout. The goals are a combination of improving the workflow within the department and reducing the amount of employee travel time within the building. Here are several layout improvements to consider:

- *Printers*. Provide employees with decent-quality printers that are positioned adjacent to their computers. Doing so eliminates the startling amount of travel time between employee work areas and a central printer; employees may travel back and forth many times during the day. It is still useful to retain the central printer for higher-speed printing jobs.
- *Furniture*. If there is unused furniture or office equipment cluttering the department, then dispose of it. By doing so, it is possible to not only improve the traffic flow within the department, but (better yet) compress the department into a smaller work area, so that total travel times within the department are reduced.

- *Clustering*. Monitor the travel patterns of employees within the department. It is likely that some people must interact with others on the far side of the department, or must access filing cabinets located well away from where they sit. Based on this information, configure the department to cluster together those employees who interact most frequently. This may also result in the central document storage area being broken up and distributed closer to users.
- *Cubicles*. It is difficult to reconfigure the department into clusters when everyone uses cubicles, since they require skilled furniture movers to disassemble and rebuild. Instead, eliminate the cubicles in favor of clusters of desks, which can more easily be moved around in the department.
- *Carts*. An enhancement on the concept of clustering is to issue mobile office carts to employees. They can then shift any documents they need from fixed storage locations into the carts, and roll the carts to where they are working. If employees switch to different workstations during the day, they can just move the carts along with them.
- *Supplies*. Stock an office supplies cabinet, and place it in the middle of the accounting area. Then forbid anyone to keep an excess "stash" of office supplies at their desks. By doing so, significant clutter can be eliminated in employee work areas.

The reconfiguring recommendations just noted do not preclude the use of offices. There is still a need for private meetings from time to time, as well as meeting rooms. However, the proportion of offices to the general work area assigned to the department should be low.

Once the department has been realigned, undertake a formal review of the situation about once a year, which may even involve the use of a consultant who specializes in office workflow. In addition, make minor reconfiguration tweaks to the office layout whenever an opportunity presents itself, possibly at the suggestion of an employee, or as the workload shifts among employees.

> **Tip:** If the business has a highly configurable office where most employees use desk clusters, consider shifting them for each month-end close, so that the closing team is positioned in a group. Then move employees back to their usual positions as soon as the financial statements have been issued. This improves the level of coordination during the closing process.

The improvements outlined in this section will be much less useful in situations where there is clearly excess capacity in the department, since the incremental improvement in efficiency afforded by changing the department's layout will only create a moderate increase in the level of available capacity.

Skills Review and Training

It is common practice to decide which payables employees are deficient in certain skill areas, and then give them training in those areas. However, doing so can involve additional (and expensive) training, much of which may never be used. If a company pays for some portion of an employee's college education, then this cost-benefit effect becomes even more glaring. In short, many training programs result in employees learning skills for which they have no use within the company.

A more prudent view of training is to use the error tracking system described in a preceding section to determine where employees require additional training *in their current jobs*, and apply the exact amount of specific training to reduce the number of errors that they are causing. Or, consider linking training to specific upgrades that are planned for the department's systems. Here are two examples of targeted training:

- The department's error tracking system reveals that the payables staff is not using the automated three-way matching feature in the accounting software, which has resulted in several payments to suppliers that should not have been made. The payables manager has a trainer come to the company's offices to train the payables staff in this feature, as well as to monitor their usage of it over the next few days.
- A company has just upgraded its payables system to a new version of the same software. The payables manager pays the software supplier to send a consultant to the company to give users a training session on the specific changes that were made to system features, and how best to take advantage of them.

In short, avoid broad-based training, such as paying for accounting degrees at the local university, or sending employees to conferences. Instead, expend funds on training that very specifically improves the operations of the department. Also, as you may have noticed in the examples of targeted training, it is more effective if conducted on-site, where employees can use the training immediately. It may be more expensive to bring in consultants to conduct such training, but the results easily offset the costs.

Because of the need to engage in extremely specific training, it is nearly impossible to create a long-term training plan for employees. Instead, training needs are usually uncovered and addressed in the short term. The only case where employees can be involved in a longer-term training plan is when the intent is to promote someone to a different position, and a course of study has been created for them to learn all aspects of their new position.

Measuring the Results of Training

There is no way to directly measure the impact of a training program on a company. That is, one cannot invest a certain amount of money in training and expect to see a specific improvement in profits that directly relates to the training. There are far too many variables impacting a business to prove a direct linkage between training and profits. Instead, it is necessary to monitor several measurements that can give an indication of the effects of training. For example:

- *Turnover by manager.* The employees of certain managers may leave the company at a higher-than-normal rate. If those managers receive training to improve how they oversee employees, it can be useful to conduct before-and-

after turnover measurements to see if the number of employees departing the company declines.
- *Error rates.* If employees receive training in certain technical and clerical skills, their transaction error rates should decline. Error rates can be monitored on a trend line for those employees having received training, to see if the error rate is lower than for a control group.
- *In-house hires.* A company may have a large number of technical positions to fill. If it trains employees for these specific positions, the rate of in-house fulfillment should increase. If so, the cost of advertising outside the company for these positions should decline, since there is less need for external hiring.
- *Employee advancement.* When employees receive executive training, does this correlate to a higher rate of advancement? To measure it, monitor the proportion of employees receiving promotion from a group of employees receiving this training, and for a group not receiving the training. Of course, the result can be skewed, since the most promising employees were probably directed into the executive training in the first place.

All of these measurements must be tracked over a long period of time to discern changes. Consequently, the associated training programs must also be maintained over a long period of time. If a training system is run as a brief pilot project, it is likely that the associated measurements will not change much, since training benefits tend to appear over a longer period of time.

Consolidate Accounting

A business may have a divisional organizational structure, where all business functions are duplicated within an operating division. While this approach works well for localized decision-making, it has the following failings:

- *Cost.* Functional duplication requires headcount duplication, so each division has its own payables manager and payables staff.
- *Procedures.* When there are many divisions, there are many different procedures for handling essentially identical business processes, which can lead to both inefficiencies and control problems.
- *Knowledge.* When there are only a few payables employees at the division level, they are unlikely to be up-to-date on the most recent work efficiencies.

These issues can be eliminated by centralizing the payables function in a single area that services the entire company. Doing so eliminates redundant positions, improves the uniformity of procedures, and results in the most efficient operational practices.

A move to consolidate payables may very well be met with resistance from the division managers, who like to have control over their accounting functions. If so, point out the reduced overall accounting cost that will be assigned to their divisions, since the cost of the entire payables function will decline.

A variation on the consolidation concept is to outsource certain types of accounting work away from the divisions, rather than to a central location. A prime example is employee expense report processing, where employees submit their expense reports to a website that automatically matches submissions against company travel policies, and then sends all approved expenses back to the company's payables system through a custom interface. This approach works well if the corporate payables department does not have the expertise, and the price offered by the supplier is reasonable.

> **Tip:** When acquiring businesses, insist upon moving their entire accounting functions into the corporate accounting group. This is easier to do in an acquisition situation, since the acquiring entity has most of the power; local managers are less likely to resist the change.

Quality of the Work Environment

The work environment in which employees operate needs to be sufficiently permissive and comfortable for them to achieve their best work. Creating such an environment is a balancing act, for a company must still attend to the overriding goal of consistently generating a profit. Consequently, management must find a balance between the pursuit of profit and establishing an environment in which employees can achieve a reasonable work-life balance. If handled correctly, employees are likely to experience less stress, identify more closely with the company, and be less likely to pursue work elsewhere. In this section, we identify a variety of options for creating an excellent work environment.

Flexible Work Hours

Employees may be more productive if they can adjust the hours during which they work, rather than being locked into a regimented set of working hours. Here are several examples:

- *Long commute.* An employee may live many miles from the office, and is stuck in commuter traffic each day. If she can start work an hour later and leave the office an hour later, she can skip much of this traffic.
- *Productive hours.* A software developer working for the payables department finds that he works best late at night, and is nearly non-functional during the morning hours. If his working hours can be shifted well outside of the normal first-shift hours, the company will experience much higher productivity from him.
- *Parents.* A parent needs to be at home to prepare his children for school, after which he can head for the office. This calls for a delayed start to the work day.

In these common situations, it can be difficult to force employees into the straitjacket of the 9-to-5 work day. Instead, consider allowing them to shift their working hours. At a minimum, this can mean allowing the staff to shift their hours slightly around a core set of working hours. For example, all employees are expected to be in the office from the hours of 10 a.m. to 3 p.m. in order to be available for meetings, and can shift their remaining hours as needed. At a more permissive level, employees can work whenever they want, as long as their work products are completed on time.

The concept of flexible work hours is only possible in certain situations. For example, a support person such as a receptionist must be available to answer the department phones during a company's stated work hours. However, if there is no time-specific responsibility, the concept of flexible work hours may be applicable.

Job Sharing

If there is a pool of well-trained job candidates who are only willing to work part-time, consider combining two part-time positions into a single full-time job. By doing so, two people are responsible for the work output of one position. This works well when the two people are responsible, willing to split the normal work week, and compatible with each other. Doing so also reduces the amount of floor space that a company must operate, since the two people typically share the same office or cubicle.

The job sharing concept does not always work out. One party might feel that he or she is shouldering more of the work load, or that the other person's work is substandard. Also, the responsible manager must now keep track of the performance of double the number of people.

A variation on the concept that can achieve more coordination is to have each part-timer work three days per week, with one day designated for them both to be in the office. By doing so, any issues can be ironed out in person, rather than allowing them to fester via e-mail or phone calls.

Permanent Part-Time Work

A company can tap into the large pool of job candidates that are not able to work full-time by offering part-time work arrangements that are permanent. For example, a parent may only be available for a six-hour day, after which he or she must be home to deal with children returning from school. Many of these candidates are highly educated and can be excellent employees, as long as part-time work arrangements can be configured for them.

There are a few issues to consider when creating part-time jobs. First, the company is investing in additional work space that will be unoccupied for a fairly large part of the day. Second, some arrangement must be made regarding benefits – do these employees receive full benefits, or partial benefits, or no benefits at all? And third, how are part-time employees treated when there are promotion opportunities available? There is no perfect answer to any of these issues – management must arrive at solutions that make the most sense for a company's specific circumstances.

Supplier Relations

Proper management of the payables department extends beyond its borders. Having well-defined communication channels in place with suppliers allows for a smoother transaction processing flow, since suppliers know exactly how to submit payment

Department Management

requests that mesh with the department's processes. Accordingly, here are several best practices to consider to enhance supplier relations:

- *Issue a welcome packet.* As soon as the purchasing department issues a purchase order to a new supplier, the payables staff is notified and issues a welcome packet to the supplier's payables department. This packet specifies where invoices should be sent, includes a Form W-9 to be filled out, and a payee direct deposit authorization form. If the company has a sales tax exemption certificate, this should be included in the packet, along with a list of contacts within the payables department.
- *State policies and procedures on website.* State the department's policies and procedures on a company website page, and routinely provide suppliers with a link to it. Doing so provides them with a ready reference for how to deal with the payables department.
- *Provide periodic updates.* Send an annual update notice to all suppliers, noting any changes made to the department's payment processes. This may include changes in contact information, or notations about department policies that are most frequently ignored by suppliers. This may also include reminders to switch to direct deposit payments, along with a form to be filled out with the required bank account information.
- *Document adjustments.* When taking deductions for such matters as early payment discounts, short shipments, penalties, and damaged goods, document them on a standard form and send it to the supplier. Doing so should minimize the number of irate phone calls received in regard to these short pays.
- *Analyze inbound calls.* Make note of all calls received from suppliers (usually regarding late payments), listing the specific reasons for these calls. It behooves the payables manager to minimize these calls, since they waste the time of the staff. Consequently, the contact log should be reviewed to see if there is an underlying procedural issue that can be resolved. It can make sense to contact the more importunate suppliers directly to go over the issues triggering their repeated calls, so that these issues can be eliminated in the future.
- *Prioritize dispute resolution.* When disputes arise with suppliers over payment issues, give them a very high priority, so that the staff is not burdened with an excessive number of contacts related to the same issue. This also improves supplier relations, since they do not have to wait long for issue resolution.
- *Provide on-line payment status.* Set up an on-line interface for suppliers, which they can access to determine the payment status of their submitted invoices. Not only does this take some work away from the department's staff, but it is also more convenient for the suppliers.
- *Create a customer service group.* If the payables department is a large one, it can make sense to create a customer service group within the department, and route all supplier calls to these people. Doing so puts customer service in the hands of a group that is properly trained in how to deal with suppliers, while

keeping these calls away from other employees who will no longer be interrupted.

> **Note:** Settling problems with suppliers sooner also keeps the company from being assessed late fees, and may allow it to take more early payment discounts. In addition, suppliers are less likely to send in an invoice copy on the assumption that the original was lost – this keeps the payables staff from wasting time identifying these invoices.

Some interactions with suppliers can be contentious, sometimes to an extent that appears out of proportion to the amount of money involved. In these cases, it can be helpful for the payables staff to understand the position of the caller. For example, it might be a supplier salesperson who will not receive a commission until payment is received, or a collections person who is being evaluated on how fast she can collect money, or perhaps a business owner who is facing a severe cash crunch. In these cases, the person taking the call can probe a bit more deeply than usual to understand the reason for the caller's vehemence, and perhaps accelerate payment to assist; doing so can generate supplier goodwill that can provide a positive return at some point in the future. This does not mean that *all* payments should be accelerated upon request, only that one should consider what is going on at the supplier to see if this might be an option.

Summary

The payables manager faces a number of opportunities for improving the payables department. Scheduling and work queue analysis can be used to improve the allocation of labor among the various work products that the department must complete, while engaging in workflow improvements, process reviews, and functional consolidations to achieve a substantially higher degree of efficiency. All of the management issues noted in this chapter are not to be treated as one-time events, however. It will be necessary to continually monitor and adjust the condition of the department to achieve a state where the staff is completing its assigned tasks in the most efficient and effective manner possible.

The bulk of this chapter was concerned with ways to improve the efficiency of the department. In addition, be sure to attend to the needs of the employees by constantly inquiring into their needs. This may include certain benefits, alternative work arrangements or job assignments, or other improvements that will lead to greater employee satisfaction with their jobs.

Chapter 11
Payables Controls

Introduction

Accounts payable is an area in which a poorly-controlled department can lose a considerable amount of money, as well as annoy those suppliers who are being paid late. In this chapter, we describe the control systems needed to remediate these issues. Rather than providing a long list of unrelated controls, they are aggregated by the main payables areas, which are:

- Accounts payable processing
- Periodic payables actions
- Expense report processing
- Procurement card reconciliations
- Petty cash activities

> **Related Podcast Episodes:** Episodes 4, 6, 13, and 169 of the Accounting Best Practices Podcast discuss procurement card, expense report, accounts payable, and petty cash controls, respectively. They are available at: **accountingtools.com/podcasts** or **iTunes**

Accounts Payable Processing Controls

In this section, we cover the controls that can be imposed on the core payables processing activities. In addition, refer to the following Additional Payables Controls sections for other controls that are positioned outside of the basic process flow. The following controls are aggregated under each step in the process.

1. Verify Obligation to Pay

The verification of obligation to pay can be accomplished through one of several possible controls. They are:

- *Invoice approval.* The person in a position to authorize payment signifies his or her approval of a supplier invoice. However, this is actually a relatively weak control if the approver only sees the supplier invoice, since there is no way to tell if the goods or services were received, or if the prices being charged were what the company originally agreed to. The approver may also want to know which general ledger account will be charged. Consequently, it is better to have the payables staff first assemble the supplier invoice, authorizing purchase order, and receiving documentation into a packet, then stamp the invoice with a signature block that includes the account number to be charged, and *then* have the approver review it. This approach gives reviewers a *very* complete set of information to work with.

> **Tip:** Approvers are busy, and so have a bad habit of only giving supplier invoices a perfunctory review before approving them. To prevent this, the payables manager can set up appointments with each approver, bring the invoices to them, and discuss the invoices with them. This approach also ensures that every invoice will be returned promptly.

> **Tip:** If invoices are sent out for approvals prior to being entered in the payables system, maintain a log of the invoices that are out for approval, and cross them off when they are eventually returned. This makes it easier to determine which invoices have *not* been returned.

- *Purchase order approval*. The purchasing department must issue a purchase order for every purchase made. By doing so, the purchasing staff is, in essence, approving all expenditures before they have been made, which may prevent some expenditures from ever occurring. Since this control entails a considerable amount of work by the purchasing staff, they will likely ask employees to request items on a formal purchase requisition form.

> **Tip:** In practice, it will be inordinately expensive to enforce the use of purchase orders for everything. Instead, this control is more enforceable for larger purchases, with an automatic exemption for all purchases below a minimum dollar amount.

- *Complete a three-way match*. The payables staff matches the supplier invoice to the related purchase order and proof of receipt before authorizing payment. This approach supersedes the need for individual invoice approval, since approval is based on the purchase order instead. It is also better than approving only based on the purchase order, since it also verifies receipt of the goods. However, it is also painfully slow and can break down if there is missing paperwork.

> **Tip:** Always allow the payables staff some margin for which invoices can be approved under the three-way match. For example, the price on an invoice might be acceptable if it is within 0.5% of the amount on the purchase order, while the received quantity is acceptable if it is within a similar margin. Without these margins, very few invoices would ever be paid. Also, there should be exemptions from three-way matching, such as tax payments, royalty payments, insurance, and benefit payments, where the required paperwork may not be available.

> **Tip:** It seems to be easiest for receiving reports to go astray, so consider having them prenumbered, which helps to determine which reports are missing.

- *Manual duplicate payment search.* As will be described shortly, a computerized payables system conducts an automatic search for duplicate invoice numbers. This is a much more difficult endeavor in an entirely manual accounting system. In this case, the payables clerk can search through the vendor file and unpaid invoices file to see if an invoice just received from a supplier has already been paid. In many situations, the volume of incoming supplier invoices makes this so difficult that the payables staff abandons any attempt to identify duplicate invoices, and simply accepts that it will occasionally pay for such items.
- *Verify purchase order number.* In the evaluated receipts system, there is no supplier invoice. Instead, the company sends a purchase order number to each supplier, which they include on their packing slips when shipping goods to the company. If there is no purchase order number, the delivery is rejected. Thus, verifying an obligation to pay really involves making sure that purchase orders are issued, and that receipts have identifying purchase order numbers that have not expired.

2. Data Entry

There are several ways to ensure that all supplier invoices have been entered into the payables system, though these controls have varying degrees of success. The controls are:

- *Record after approval.* This control forces the payables staff to verify the approval of every invoice before entering it into the system.

> **Tip:** This control can be an expensive one, since some invoices will inevitably not be approved in time to be paid by their due dates. To avoid late penalties, use automatic approvals of smaller and recurring invoices, and have several alternate approvers available if the primary approvers are not available.

- *Record prior to approval.* This control places greater priority on paying suppliers than it does on obtaining authorizations to pay, since every invoice received is recorded in the payables system at once. This control works best where purchase orders have already been used to authorize a purchase.

> **Tip:** When recording supplier invoices in advance, consider using *negative approvals*. This means that approvers receive a copy of each invoice, but only contact the payables staff if they *do not* approve an invoice. This largely eliminates the amount of feedback that the payables staff can expect from authorizers.

- *Adopt an invoice numbering guideline.* Perhaps the largest problem in the area of payables data entry is duplicate payments. This would not appear to be a problem, since most companies use accounting software that automatically detects duplicate invoices and prevents duplicate payments.

  A simple control over the duplicate invoice problem is a one-page description of how invoice numbers are to be recorded, which is to be posted prominently next to the computer of every payables data entry person for easy reference.

3. Payment

The bulk of the controls noted below pertain to payment by check, since that is still the predominant form of payment. Several controls near the bottom of the list are targeted at electronic payments. The controls are:

- *Split check printing and signing.* One person should prepare checks, and a different person should sign them. By doing so, there is a cross-check on the issuance of cash.
- *Store all checks in a locked location.* Unused check stock should *always* be stored in a locked location. Otherwise, checks can be stolen and fraudulently filled out and cashed. This means that any signature plates or stamps should also be stored in a locked location.

> **Tip:** If there is a signature stamp or plate, store it in a different locked location from the check stock, and keep the keys to the two locations in different spots. Ideally, different people should be responsible for the check stock and the signature plate. This makes it more difficult for someone to obtain both and generate valid-looking check payments.

- *Secure check-printing equipment.* Some printers are only used for check printing. If so, keep them in a locked location so that no one can print checks and have the integrated signature plate automatically sign the checks.
- *Track the sequence of check numbers used.* Maintain a log in which are listed the range of check numbers used during a check run. This is useful for determining if any checks in storage might be missing. This log should not be kept with the stored checks, since someone could steal the log at the same time they steal checks.
- *Issue checks in numerical order.* This is not actually a control, but rather a means of ensuring that there are few gaps in the sequence of check numbers that need to be investigated. From a practical perspective, checks are nearly always used in batches, so they will always be issued in numerical order.
- *Require manual check signing.* A company can require that all checks be signed. This is a relatively weak control, since few check signers delve into why checks are being issued, and rarely question the amounts paid. If a company chooses to use a signature plate or stamp instead, it is much more

important to have a strong purchase order system; the purchasing staff becomes the de facto approvers of invoices by issuing purchase orders earlier in the payables process flow.

> **Tip:** If the company requires manual check signing, do everything possible to strengthen the control. This means assembling a voucher package for each check that the check signer can review, and having a payables person sit with the check signer to answer questions during signing sessions.

- *Require an additional check signer.* If the amount of a check exceeds a certain amount, require a second check signer. This control supposedly gives multiple senior-level people the chance to stop making a payment. In reality, it is more likely to only introduce another step into the payment process without really strengthening the control environment.
- *Stamp invoices "paid".* In a purely manual payables environment, there is a risk of paying an invoice more than once, so a reasonable control is to stamp each paid invoice, or even perforate it with a "paid" stamp. This control is less necessary (if at all) in a computerized system, which automatically tracks which invoices have been paid.

> **Tip:** If the choice is made not to use a "paid" stamp in a computerized environment, be sure to install a consistent procedure for assigning an invoice number to those invoices that are not numbered. Otherwise, the copies of the same invoice could be assigned different invoice numbers and then be paid.

- *Lock up undistributed checks.* If the company does not distribute checks at once, they should be stored in a locked location. Otherwise, there is a risk of theft, with the person stealing the checks modifying them sufficiently to cash them.
- *Use positive pay.* Positive pay is a program under which a company sends a file containing its check payment information to its bank; if a check is presented for payment and it is not on the list of checks issued by the company, the bank rejects it. This can eliminate check fraud, though there is some question of whether it is more beneficial to the bank (which could be liable for accepting fraudulent checks) or the company.

> **Tip:** It is easy to forget to notify the bank of check payments, especially manual checks that are created outside of the normal check printing process. Therefore, have an iron-clad bank notification system in place before enacting positive pay. It may help to run positive pay on a test basis for a few months to see how many check notifications were not made, and what caused them.

- *Initiate banking transactions from a dedicated computer.* It is possible for someone to use keystroke logging software to detect the user identification

and password information that a business uses to authorize direct deposit and wire transfer information. To reduce the risk, set up a separate computer that is only used to initiate transactions with the bank. This reduces the risk that keystroke logging software might be inadvertently downloaded onto the machine from an e-mail or other transaction.
- *Pay from a separate account.* There is a risk that someone could use an ACH debit transaction to move funds out of a company's bank account. To reduce this risk, only shift sufficient funds into a checking account to cover the amount of outstanding checks, ACH payments, and wire transfers that have not yet cleared the bank.
- *Password-protect the direct deposit file.* Some companies accumulate bank account information for their supplier payments in a computer file, while others may access it online in their bank's systems. In either case, the file should be password protected to prevent tampering with the accounts. Also, the password should be changed regularly, and certainly after anyone with access to the file has left the company.
- *Different person verifies or approves wire transfers.* When a company authorizes a wire transfer, one person issues the instructions to the bank, and a different person verifies or approves the transaction.

Tip: If a different person is to verify or approve each wire transfer, set up the e-mail address of the verifying person in the confirmation contact list in the bank's records, so that notifications are automatically sent to that person.

Tip: Direct deposit and wire transfer payments are frequently made outside of the payables system, which means that someone has to manually record these payments in the payables system. If they forget to do so, there is a risk that these items will be paid again, or paid by check. Consequently, be sure to set up a default payment type for each supplier in the vendor master file, and stick to that payment type. Treat any request for a different type of payment as a policy violation, which requires extra approvals.

Alternative Accounts Payable Control Systems

In this section, we assemble a selection of the controls just described and apply them to different accounts payable scenarios involving a manual system, a computerized system, electronic payments, and an evaluated receipts system. While there are certain similarities in the controls used for each system, there are also crucial differences to consider when constructing a system of controls.

Control System for Manual Accounts Payable

In a manual accounts payable system, it is theoretically possible to use any of the three approval methods – by invoice, purchase order, or three-way match. Realistically, a company running a manual system probably is not using purchase orders, so the most likely control over verifying the obligation to pay is invoice approval. In the data entry area, invoices can be recorded in the system before or after invoice approval. Generally, recording invoices before approval makes more sense, since invoices can be lost on the desks of those supervisors assigned to approve them.

In a manual system, it certainly makes sense to lock up all unused checks. It is a good idea to track the sequence of check numbers, but if there are few people who could potentially steal checks, this control could be avoided. It is very likely that manual check signing will be needed in this environment, especially if purchase orders are not being generated. Finally, in the absence of a computer system that can determine when invoices have been paid, stamp or perforate all paid invoices with the word "paid".

Control System for Computerized Accounts Payable

When accounts payable transactions are recorded in a computer system, it is easier to match invoices to the authorizing purchase orders, as well as to conduct three-way matching. Thus, all three verification to pay methods are available to the user.

The chief difference between the data entry for manual and computerized environments is that an invoice numbering guideline is much more necessary in a computerized system, where the software can automatically detect duplicate supplier invoices.

The payment step changes somewhat in a computerized system. We assume that the business is larger, so it is more likely that there are enough people in the payables department to justify splitting the check printing and signing activities, thereby providing a cross-check. Also, with the software generating a list of checks issued, it is easier to subscribe to the bank's positive pay system (though it is not necessary to do so). Finally, it is less necessary to stamp invoices as "paid," since this information is tracked by the software.

Additional Payables Controls – Trend Analysis

Some controls are not directly related to any of the process flows noted earlier. Instead, they are more of the investigative variety, and so are used to spot possible control problems after the fact. These controls include:

- *Review expense trends.* There may be an unusual blip in an expense line item in a particular month that was not caught by any of the in-process controls. Once investigated, the system can be modified to catch similar offending transactions in the future.

> **Tip:** Formulate a trailing 12-month income statement that shows the monthly results for each of the preceding 12 months for every expense account. This is the best source of information for conducting an expense trend analysis.

- *Review supplier trends.* As just noted for the review of expense trends, create the same report at the supplier level for each of the past 12 months. It may

reveal billings from suppliers who had otherwise been inactive. This can indicate that an employee used one of the inactive accounts to fabricate an invoice and submit it to the company for payment.
- *Hire a payment analysis firm.* Some consulting firms specialize in finding duplicate payments. Hire one of these firms occasionally to look for such payments. The key point in these reviews is to determine the reasons why such payments were made, and install controls that will keep them from happening again. See the Cost Recovery chapter for more information.

While these controls may be useful for spotting larger anomalies, they are not of much use if there are discerning perpetrators on the premises. Knowing that these controls exist, someone could hide a series of improper payments by recording them in accounts having large expense balances, or by incurring relatively small charges over a long period of time.

Additional Payables Controls – Fraud Related

There is a reasonable chance that fraud will occur in the payables area, since it involves the disbursement of cash. Accordingly, consider implementing the following controls to prevent or at least detect fraud:

- *Run a credit report on new suppliers.* Someone within the payables department could create a vendor record in order to pay fraudulent invoices to it, with the payments being routed back to the employee. It is possible to detect this by running a credit report on all new suppliers to verify their existence. From a practical perspective, this is an expensive way to locate potentially fraudulent activity.
- *Search for purchase authorization avoidance.* Run a search through the payables records to see if the company received multiple invoices from a supplier during a period. If so, investigate to see if the invoices should have been aggregated into a single invoice for a large-dollar item that would otherwise have required a higher level of purchase authorization. This indicates possible chicanery within the company to obtain assets.
- *Match supplier addresses to employee addresses.* An employee may be directing supplier payments to his or her home address, or may own a supplier that does business with the company. To detect these payments, periodically run a comparison of employee addresses to supplier addresses to see if there are any matches. From a practical perspective, a reasonably knowledgeable employee will simply set up a post office box and have payments sent there, so this is not an overly productive control.
- *Review vendor master file change log.* An employee could access the vendor master file, change a payment address to his or her home address, then cut a check that is mailed to that address, and then re-enter the file and switch the address back to the supplier's real address. This can be detected by

periodically reviewing the change log for the vendor master file. Less expensive accounting systems may not have this feature.
- *Review direct deposit change log.* Some high-end accounting systems store supplier direct deposit information in a separate file. If so, conduct a periodic review to see if anyone has altered the direct deposit information. This is one of the easier ways to route money into an account owned by an employee.
- *Set check printing to avoid blanks.* Set the check printing methodology in the accounting software to insert characters into the blank spaces on the amount and payee lines of checks. This makes it more difficult for someone to fraudulently alter checks.
- *Make check reproduction difficult.* There are a large number of anti-fraud features built into check stock that make them more difficult to reproduce. This can hardly be called a control anymore, since many of the features are provided automatically by check stock printers.
- *Destroy check stock for inactive accounts.* If a checking account is no longer being used, shift out any residual funds, close the account, and shred any remaining check stock. Otherwise, someone could clear out any remaining funds with one of the unused checks.

> **Tip:** It is especially common to eliminate bank accounts following an acquisition, so include a work step in the acquisition integration procedure to close the accounts and shred the related check stock.

- *Reconcile the checking account daily.* It is extremely useful to conduct a complete account reconciliation of the checking account every day. By doing so, any problems with fraudulent checks will be immediately apparent.

> **Tip:** Daily reconciliations are possible as long as the bank makes detailed account information available on-line. If so, the procedure is identical to the month-end bank reconciliation.

- *Install a debit block.* Someone can create an ACH debit transaction that removes funds from the company's bank account. It is possible to set up a debit block with the bank that prevents ACH debits from being enacted. Under this approach, the company must notify the bank when it authorizes a debit from a specific supplier. Also, it may make sense to set a daily cumulative limit for ACH debits; this keeps even an approved supplier from withdrawing an inordinate amount from the bank account.

Additional Payables Controls – Periodic Actions

The following controls are useful for keeping costs down or making payables operations more efficient. They are not necessarily part of a specific process; instead, the payables staff schedules them as separate tasks. These controls are:

- *Investigate credits.* The aged accounts payable report almost always contains a plethora of residual supplier credits or credits caused by overpayments. The payables staff should periodically review and resolve these items, either by offsetting them against payables not yet paid, or by obtaining reimbursement from suppliers. This can be considered a control, since it involves the prevention of funds being lost through inaction.
- *Investigate old unpaid payables.* The payables manager and controller should conduct a monthly review of the aged accounts payable report to determine the nature of any clearly overdue supplier invoices, and decide what to do with them.
- *Match aged payables report to general ledger.* The total of the aged accounts payable report should match the related account balance at the end of the month. A reasonable control is to see if there is a difference between these two numbers, and to reconcile the difference.
- *Investigate missing matching documents.* If a company is using three-way matching and some of the supporting documentation has not appeared, a periodic investigation should be focused on finding these documents or finding a way around the situation, in order to pay suppliers on a timely basis.
- *Match returns log to credits.* If the company routinely returns goods to its suppliers, maintain a log of returned items, and match it against credits received from the suppliers. This will likely call for follow-up with those suppliers that are laggards in providing credits.
- *Investigate early payment discounts.* There should be an occasional review of early payment discounts to see if the cost-effective ones were taken. If a number of early payment discounts are being missed, this may call for an examination of the underlying system that brings discounts to the attention of the payables staff.
- *Maintain a voided checks log.* By documenting every check that has been voided, it is easier to determine which checks are still outstanding for bank reconciliation purposes, as well as to track down missing checks. This control is not necessary in a computerized environment, since the accounting system keeps track of voided checks.

> **Tip:** A check that has been voided in the accounting system could still be stolen and cashed. Accordingly, buy a "void" or "cancelled" stamp and use it to mark every voided check.

- *Review for duplicate supplier records.* It is very easy to accidentally create multiple records for the same supplier, which causes problems in linking

invoices to the correct supplier record. Consequently, there should be a periodic review of the vendor master file for duplicate supplier records. Any duplicates should be merged into a single supplier record.
- *Assign inactive status to suppliers.* When suppliers are no longer used, set their status in the vendor master file to "inactive." In most accounting systems, this will prevent any additional payments from being made to them.
- *Audit recurring payments.* The payables system may be set up to continually issue the same payment amount to the same supplier on the same date of every month. To guard against paying these recurring amounts for an excessive period of time, conduct an occasional review of all recurring payments to verify that they should still be paid.

Expense Report Processing Controls

In this section, we cover the controls that can be imposed on the core expense report processing activities. In addition, refer to the Additional Expense Report Controls sections for other controls that are positioned outside of the core expense report transactions. The following controls are aggregated under each step in the process.

1. Expense Report Submission

The proper submission of expense reports can be accomplished through several possible controls. They are:

- *Use a standard report format.* The payables staff cannot reasonably be expected to sort through a pile of receipts to determine how much to pay an employee. Consequently, employees should be forced to use a reporting form to organize their submissions.
- *Issue reporting guidelines.* Employees may rightfully take the position that they are being denied reimbursement because of a company rule of which they had no knowledge. Accordingly, issue a brief document to the staff, detailing expense submission guidelines. See the Expense Reimbursement chapter for more information.
- *Require approval for all expense reports.* The intent of this control is to notify supervisors of the expenses that are about to be charged against their departments. The control can be mitigated to skip approval for very small expense reports.
- *Adopt an invoice numbering method.* If the payables staff is entering expense reports into the accounting system, the software will not accept the entry unless there is an invoice number. Consequently, there needs to be an invoice numbering procedure in place to reliably derive invoice numbers.

2. Expense Report Examination

The examination of expense reports can range from a cursory review to a startling amount of in-depth analysis. The most basic controls are noted here, with a number of additional controls listed later in the Additional Expense Report Controls sections. The basic controls are:

- *Compare expenditures to company policy.* Claimed expenditures should fall within the parameters set by the company's travel and entertainment policy. The payables staff likely has this policy memorized, and so can review expense reports in search of any non-reimbursement items.
- *Verify receipts.* There should be a receipt for every item listed on an expense report. Ideally, a credit card statement can be used in place of some receipts, while handwritten receipts can be used to document cash payments.
- *Examine non-receipt expenditures.* In many expense report systems, employees are exempted from supplying receipts for items below a certain dollar limit, perhaps in the belief that doing so would be cruel and unusual punishment. Employees may take advantage of this rule by claiming a number of reimbursement requests that are just under the exemption level. Consider tracking the total dollar amount of these claims by employee, to see if anyone is taking an unusual number of them.

Alternative Expense Report Control Systems

In this section, we assemble a selection of the controls just described and apply them to different expense report scenarios involving manual and automated expense reporting. While there are certain similarities in the controls used for each system, there are also crucial differences to consider when constructing a system of controls.

Control System for Manual Expense Reporting

A manual expense reporting system requires a complete set of controls, since there is no automated review process to take some of the work load away from the payables staff. This means that a standard reporting form and associated guidelines should be issued, and that an invoice numbering scheme be deployed to mitigate the risk of having the system reject a unique expense report as having already been entered. A complete suite of examination controls should also be considered.

Control System for Computerized Expense Reporting

A computerized expense reporting system where employees enter their own information into an on-line form requires substantially fewer controls during the submission phase. First, there is no need for a standard printed form, since the on-line entry form takes its place. Second, it can be argued that reporting guidelines are no longer needed, since they are incorporated into the rules used to examine submissions in the automated system. Third, there is no need for an invoice numbering method, since there are no longer any invoice numbers. The examination phase still requires the same controls enumerated for a manual system, but they are usually handled automatically by the system; comparing expenditures to company policy is relatively easy to automate, while the remaining two controls (regarding receipt verification and non-receipt expenditures) may still call for human intervention.

Additional Expense Report Controls – Fraud Related

There is a very good chance that fraud will occur in the expense reporting area, since it delivers cash directly into the hands of employees. Accordingly, consider implementing the following controls to prevent or at least detect fraud:

- *Restrict access to the vendor master file.* Many accounting systems require that employees be set up in the vendor master file in order to pay them. If so, make sure that a password is required to restrict access to the file; this is particularly important if the file contains the employee bank account information needed for direct deposit payments.
- *Review employee expense trends.* There may be an unusual blip in the expenses charged by an employee in a particular month that was not caught by any of the in-process controls. Once investigated, the system can be modified to catch similar offending transactions in the future.

> **Tip:** Formulate a trailing 12-month expense report for each employee, detailing the expense accounts charged in each month from their expense reports. This is the best source of information for conducting an expense trend analysis.

- *Review for multiple flight bookings.* An employee could book several flights for the same trip, submit the highest-priced flight on his or her expense report, and obtain refunds for the remaining flights. To guard against this, trace airline travel to the credit card statement.
- *Review detailed hotel billings.* Employees can pile a number of additional expenditures onto their room charges, such as meals and in-room movies and games, so have employees submit the detailed hotel bills for examination.
- *Review for excessive miles.* Given the high mileage reimbursement rate, someone might take advantage of the situation by reporting an excessive number of miles. When there seems to be a clear overage, use an Internet search engine to estimate the miles that should have been driven, and point out the issue to the employee.

> **Tip:** If the company has common travel destinations, such as from the company headquarters to specific customers or suppliers, create a table that lists the miles that will be reimbursed for these standard trips, and issue it to employees.

- *Review actual receipts.* Many expense reporting systems allow employees to submit scanned copies of their expense receipts. If so, consider adding a requirement that they retain the original receipts for a few months following the expense report date, so that you can request to see the originals. This may reveal that some of the receipts were doctored to show larger expense amounts.

> **Tip:** What if a request is made to see the original receipt and the employee does not have it? Do not automatically assume that someone is hiding nefarious deeds – it is quite likely that they simply threw it away. However, make a note of the incident, and if repeated requests result in the same answer, it may be time to engage in a more detailed examination of that person's submissions.

- *Look for sequential receipt numbers.* An employee may have purchased a block of blank receipts from an office supply store and is using them to create fake receipts for fraudulent claims. If so, the receipts may be consecutively numbered, so look for the numbering across several consecutive expense reports. This control is a manual one, since no expense report systems track receipt numbers.

> **Tip:** A possible solution to the use of questionable receipts by employees would appear to be that all purchases must be made with a credit card, and that the credit card statement be submitted along with the expense report. Unfortunately, this does not work well for tips or other cash payments. One possibility is to require a credit card statement for nearly all expense submissions, with receipts allowed for only a small subset of expenses.

Additional Expense Report Controls – Periodic Actions

The following controls are useful for updating records related to expense reports. They are not necessarily part of a specific process; instead, the payables staff schedules them as separate tasks. These controls are:

- *Set employee vendor records to inactive after departure.* Many accounting systems require that employees be set up as suppliers in the vendor master file in order to process their expense report reimbursements. If so, periodically set these records to inactive status for any employees who have left the company. This prevents the accounting system from making additional payments to them.
- *Set employee status in automated system to inactive after departure.* If a company uses an on-line form and automated back end to process expense reports, it should set employees to inactive status in this system once they have left the company. Doing so prevents the system from letting them submit additional expenses for reimbursement.
- *Issue a new expense reporting form and guidelines once a year.* Update the standard reporting template once a year with the new mileage reimbursement rate, as well as any other information (such as reporting guidelines) that the company wishes to change on the form.

In-Process Procurement Card Controls

In this section, we cover the controls that can be imposed on the core procurement card processes. In addition, refer to the Additional Procurement Card Controls sections for other controls that are positioned outside of the basic procurement card transactions. The following controls are aggregated under each step in the process.

1. Purchasing

There are few controls at the purchasing stage of procurement card usage, since the bulk of the controls are detective, and so appear later in the process. The main control is to have any number of restrictions built into the procurement cards, so that employees are limited from making incorrect or excessively large purchases.

> **Tip:** Have the procurement card provider send a warning e-mail to the procurement card administrator whenever a purchasing rule is breached, so the administrator can investigate the situation before more purchases are made.

2. Reconcile Card Statements

Once the bank has sent month-end statements to the company for each procurement card, the card users should at least examine the statements, assign account codes to each line item, and see if any expenditures appear to be incorrect. At a more advanced level, they can maintain their own transaction log and compare it to the summary shown on the statement; this latter approach is much more time-consuming, but is also the best way to spot potential problems with a statement. The following controls may apply to one or both of these approaches:

- *Issue a standard account code list.* Given the large number of items typically purchased with procurement cards each month, it is common to find a substantial amount of coding to incorrect accounts. This problem can be mitigated by issuing a standard account code list to card users, possibly alongside each monthly statement.
- *Maintain a transaction log.* It is possible for infrequent card users to simply scan through their month-end card statements, assign account numbers to each line item, and be comfortable in signing off on them. However, a heavy card user who may make dozens or even hundreds of purchases per month should take a more detailed view of the situation, and so should track each purchase in a log and then reconcile this log to the card statement.
- *Reconcile transaction log to card statement.* The person responsible for each procurement card should match his or her transaction log to the month-end card statement. The reason for this review is not only to verify that all charges are correct, but also to use the usage notations in the transaction log to code the expenditures on the card statement into the most appropriate accounts. Examples of problems that a card user may find include charges altered by the supplier, duplicate charges, and unexplained credits.

- *Complete missing receipts form.* There will inevitably be cases where card users lose receipts. When this happens, they should fill out a one-page missing receipt form that describes the nature of each expenditure on the card statement for which there is no receipt. This is later used for a formal review and approval of missing receipts.
- *Complete expenditure protest form.* Card users should fill out a one-page form that details all the line items on the card statement that they are protesting, and the reasons for their recommendations not to pay. This information is used to remove items from the card statements.
- *Retain a copy.* Heavy card users might consider retaining their own copies of procurement card reconciliation packages for future reference purposes. Doing so can be of assistance from a control perspective, since the copies make it easier for them to research possible card-related issues.

Once all of the preceding controls have been completed, each card user assembles the card statement, transaction log, all receipts, the missing receipts form, and the protest form into a reconciliation package, and forwards it to the department manager for approval. Or, if the "no log" control version is used, only an adjusted card statement may be forwarded, along with receipts.

3. Approve Card Reconciliations

The department manager should review each procurement card reconciliation package in detail, since the expenditures involved can be substantial. This may require a discussion with the card user, as well as consideration of whether any expenses can be shifted to another department or into an asset account.

Then, the manager approves the packages and forwards them to the payables department for data entry and payment.

Alternative Procurement Card Control Systems

In this section, we assemble a selection of the controls just described and apply them to different procurement card scenarios involving either no transaction log or the use of a transaction log. A transaction log provides a useful cross-check against any errors that might appear in the card statement, but is time-consuming to maintain. Thus, neither approach is necessarily better than the other.

Procurement Card Control System without a Transaction Log

The lack of a transaction log reduces the core group of procurement card controls to a very small number. There will likely be built-in preventive controls to keep excessive purchases from being made, while card users are required to review the card statements, and supervisors must approve them.

Procurement Card Control System with a Transaction Log

When a transaction log is required, the set of associated controls becomes much more extensive. The card user compares it to the card statement, notes any exceptions, and notes any items for which there are no receipts. The department manager then reviews and approves the packet of information, and forwards it to the payables department.

Additional Procurement Card Controls – Fraud Related

There is a reasonable chance that fraud will occur in the procurement card area, since it can be quite tempting to use a card to make a purchase unrelated to company business. Accordingly, consider implementing the following controls to prevent or at least detect fraud:

- *Separation of duties.* One person should order procurement cards from the bank, while a different person receives them from the bank and distributes them to employees. This separation of duties keeps someone from ordering a card for a fake employee and then using it for personal reasons.
- *Conduct employee background checks.* It would be foolish to issue procurement cards to all employees, since some are more capable of handling them than others. One way to determine their capability is to conduct a background check on anyone who is targeted to receive a card.

> **Tip:** Many companies conduct background checks on employees when they are hired, so this information may already be available from the human resources department. Also, it may be prudent to gradually roll out the procurement card program, to see how the initial group fares with the added responsibility.

- *Cross-reference procurement card receipts to expense reports.* An employee could retain the receipts associated with procurement card purchases and use them to claim reimbursement on his or her expense report. This can be found by cross-checking the expenses on the procurement card statement and the expense report.
- *Review expense trends.* There may be an unusual blip in an expense line item in a particular month that was not caught by any of the in-process controls. Once investigated, the system can be modified to catch similar offending transactions in the future.

> **Tip:** Formulate a trailing 12-month report that shows the monthly results for each of the preceding 12 months for every expense account, by procurement card. This is the best source of information for conducting an expense trend analysis.

While this control may be useful for spotting larger anomalies, they are not of much use if there are discerning perpetrators on the premises. Knowing

that these controls exist, someone could hide a series of improper payments by incurring relatively small charges over a long period of time.
- *Terminate lost cards at once.* The company should mitigate its liability by having a system in place to terminate lost procurement cards as soon as possible. The easiest method is to plaster the contact information for the procurement card administrator on every document sent to card users, so that they know who to call.
- *Retrieve procurement cards as part of terminations.* The human resources staff should have an item on its employee termination checklist to retrieve any procurement cards held by terminated employees, to prevent them from making purchases after they have left.
- *Cancel the procurement cards of terminated employees.* The person responsible for procurement cards should cancel the card of any person who leaves the company, even if they have turned in their cards. The problem is that the terminated employees may still have access to the card numbers, and so can still pay for items without the physical cards (for example, using Internet stores).

> **Tip:** The person responsible for the procurement card program may not be aware of employee departures, especially if there are many employees. Accordingly, the human resources staff should have an item on their terminated employee checklist to notify the procurement card manager of all departures.

Additional Procurement Card Controls – Periodic Actions

The following controls are useful for keeping costs down or making operations more efficient. They are not necessarily part of a specific process; instead, these are separate tasks. The controls are:

- *Require users to sign a contract.* The company should prepare a procurement card usage agreement that states the responsibilities of the user, and what happens if cards are misused. This agreement not only makes responsibilities very clear to the user, but may also be of assistance in obtaining repayment from card users if they buy unauthorized goods or services.
- *Issue an approved supplier list.* The company may have a spend management program under which it directs its purchasing activity at certain suppliers in order to obtain volume discounts. A good control over this program is to issue a list of approved suppliers to procurement card users.

> **Tip:** If procurement card volumes are sufficiently high to improve the company's volume discounts with suppliers, it may be cost-effective to review the Level III data (see next) to ensure that only approved suppliers are being used. Purchases from unapproved suppliers can then be discussed with the card users.

- *Review Level III data.* Procurement card providers can send a company more information than is available for a typical consumer credit card. This additional information is known as Level III data, and includes the items purchased, item descriptions, quantities purchased, prices paid, sales taxes, freight charges, and purchase order numbers. This information may be useful for delving into exactly what is being purchased.

> **Tip:** If you elect to receive Level III data, obtain it as a download, so that the information can be re-sorted on a spreadsheet. Also, it may not be cost-effective to review this level of detail for all procurement cards; instead, consider only using it when there have been questionable purchases.

- *Investigate bill of materials purchases.* If the company has a computerized manufacturing planning system, that system should automatically notify suppliers of purchasing requirements, usually as releases under a blanket purchase order. Thus, any items listed on a bill of materials (the official list of the components of a product) should never appear in the Level III data for a procurement card.

> **Tip:** If someone buys a bill of materials item with a procurement card, this is strong evidence that the manufacturing procurement process has broken down, since someone probably had to buy parts on a rush basis, and outside of the normal purchasing process. This requires investigation to locate the cause of the problem and correct it. Sample causes are incorrect inventory records, incorrect bills of material, and unusually high scrap levels.

Petty Cash Controls

In this section, we cover the controls that can be imposed on the core petty cash activities. In addition, refer to the Additional Petty Cash Controls section for other controls that are positioned outside of the basic petty cash transactions. The following controls are aggregated under each petty cash activity.

<u>1. Fund Petty Cash</u>

It is of moderate importance to keep some cash in the various petty cash boxes; otherwise, employees may badger the payables staff to cut manual checks for small expenditures. The following control addresses this situation:

- *Require a monthly petty cash funding review.* There should not be so much cash in the petty cash box that it represents a serious temptation for someone to steal it. Instead, schedule a monthly review to see if more cash is needed, and set the petty cash amount to a level that should have the remaining cash balance running low by about the time of the review.

2. Disburse Petty Cash

The core of the petty cash process is the disbursement of cash. The following controls are needed to ensure that there is sufficient documentation of each disbursement:

- *Require receipts for all cash withdrawals.* When employees request funds from petty cash, they should always submit a receipt in exchange. This receipt may be a receipt from a supplier whom the employee has just paid out of his own pocket, or it may be a form filled out by the employee, stating the purpose of the payout. The amount on the receipt should always match the exact amount paid out, so that the sum of the cash and the receipts in the petty cash box at any time always equal the designated funding level for the box.
- *Employees sign for cash received.* Whenever an employee takes petty cash, he or she must sign a "Received of Petty Cash" form which states the amount paid out. The petty cash custodian then staples the receipt submitted by the employee to the Received of Petty Cash form. This information packet remains within the petty cash box, providing evidence that cash was paid out for a certain purpose and that a specific person received the cash. It is later extracted and attached to a journal entry documenting the use of cash.
- *Fill out receipts in ink.* An employee could submit a receipt or Received of Petty Cash form in exchange for cash from the petty cash box, after which the petty cash custodian could increase the amount on the receipt or form and remove the related amount of extra cash. To make it more difficult to alter receipts and forms in this way, require employees to complete them in ink, not pencil.

3. Document Petty Cash Expenditures

It is common for the petty cash custodian to make mistakes in properly documenting payments from the petty cash box. The following controls are designed to locate these problems, as well as to aggregate expenditures into the proper accounts in the general ledger:

- *Use a standard expense form.* Though there are usually many petty cash expenditures, they tend to fall into a small number of expenditure categories, such as office supplies. To ensure that petty cash is always consistently charged to the same accounts, construct a form for recording petty cash expenditures that incorporates a standard set of the most common accounts used.
- *Reconcile petty cash.* An essential step in petty cash processing is to periodically reconcile the account. This involves adding up the amount of cash and receipts in the petty cash box, matching it to the designated petty cash balance, and researching any differences. Petty cash is an area in which errors are common, so a periodic reconciliation is needed to keep the petty cash records close to reality.

Additional Petty Cash Controls – Fraud Related

There is an excellent chance that fraud will occur in the petty cash area, since it involves the disbursement of cash. Accordingly, consider implementing the following controls to prevent or at least detect fraud:

- *Eliminate petty cash.* The best control over petty cash is to not have petty cash. This completely eliminates the risk of loss. A reasonable replacement for a petty cash system is a combination of company procurement cards (see the Procurement Cards chapter) and requiring employees to pay for items themselves and then request reimbursement from the company by check or direct deposit. If there is a continuing need for petty cash, then at least consider reducing the number of petty cash boxes in use.
- *Conduct random audits.* It is fairly common for the petty cash custodian to use petty cash as a bank, pulling out funds for personal use from time to time. This issue and others can be spotted by conducting a series of random audits. Even if no issues are ever found, the mere presence of these reviews will encourage the custodian to keep a tightly-run petty cash box.
- *Track reimbursements by person on a trend line.* It is entirely possible that a few employees will figure out that they can falsify receipts and obtain a small amount of cash by making submissions to the petty cash custodian at relatively long intervals. If reimbursements are tracked by person over time, it may be possible to detect these submissions. However, the cost of detecting the problem may not be worth the savings generated by putting a stop to it.
- *Bolt down the petty cash box.* One of the easier ways to steal from the petty cash box is to steal the entire box. This risk can be eliminated by bolting down the box. A variation on the concept is to install a contact alarm under the petty cash box that is triggered as soon as the box is lifted out of direct contact with the alarm device.
- *Require receipts to spell out sums issued.* If employees are required to fill out receipts with fully spelled-out amounts, it is less likely that someone can later alter the amounts. Thus, a $30.00 receipt would be submitted as "Thirty Dollars."

Payables Policies

Quite a large number of policies can be implemented that are intended to bolster the controls noted in this chapter. Though many policies are presented in this section, it is not necessary to install all of them. Only focus on those that will clearly assist the control environment. All other policies simply add so much verbiage to the employee manual that the staff will not spend any time reviewing them.

Payables Policies

- *The payables staff shall be independent of the purchasing and receiving departments.* This policy is needed to prevent collusion in the creation and payment of fraudulent supplier invoices.
- *Payments from invoice copies require manager approval.* When a payment does not arrive on time, the supplier typically makes a photocopy of its copy of an invoice and forwards it for payment. Thus, a request to pay from a copy is a near-certain sign that there are at least two copies of the invoice floating around in the company, which increases the risk of a duplicate payment. By requiring manager approval for such invoices, it is hoped that the manager will examine the payables records to see if the original version was already paid.
- *No payments shall be made from supplier statements.* A statement of unpaid invoices does not provide sufficient information for a payment, so the underlying supplier invoice must be obtained before there is sufficient evidence to justify a payment.
- *Do not make checks payable to "bearer" or "cash".* This policy may occasionally be breached in cases where a supplier actually asks for this type of payee on a check. Nonetheless, allowable situations should be extremely rare.
- *Do not sign blank checks.* It is easy for a fraud-minded employee to get around this policy if the company uses a signature plate or stamp, so it tends to serve more as a general admonition to check signers. It could, for example, be included in a short training class given to new check signers.
- *Early payment discounts shall be taken when the effective interest rate exceeds the corporate cost of capital.* This policy may be too strict if a company has little excess cash, in which case the payables manager should be allowed to override it.
- *Manual checks are only to be used in emergencies.* It is much more time-consuming to create checks manually. In addition, the payables staff may forget to record these checks in the accounting system, or make a positive pay notification to the bank. Consequently, all check printing should be channeled through the check printing function of the accounting software. This policy can be enforced by charging requesters an inter-company fee for creating a manual check.

> **Tip:** An additional problem with manual checks is that they are sometimes for entities that are not even listed as approved suppliers in the company's payment system. A policy to only issue manual checks to approved suppliers will further reduce the number of manual check issuances.

- *Payment terms shall be followed.* This policy is less about an overly obvious mandate to pay as per the terms negotiated with suppliers, and more about requiring controller approval in order to accelerate a payment.

- *A stop payment shall be issued when there is no physical evidence of a voided check.* This policy is useful in situations where the company is intent on keeping a complete record of all voided checks, such as a file containing every voided check. In cases where the checks were sent to suppliers and then voided, a copy of the bank's stop payment confirmation could be filed.
- *Check signers shall be disallowed immediately following departure.* As soon as an employee who is authorized to sign checks leaves the firm, contact the bank to remove them from the authorized check signer list. This also applies to the wire transfer approval list.

Expense Report Policies

- *All airline travel shall be booked and paid for by the company.* By having the company pay for airline travel, there is no way for an employee to commit fraud in relation to airline travel. This has the side benefit of possibly giving the company a volume discount on travel.
- *Hotel bills shall be submitted with expense reports.* Employees may have added extra charges to their hotel accounts, so require them to submit the hotel bills for perusal.
- *Commuting mileage will not be reimbursed.* This policy is fairly obvious, but is needed for those rare cases where an employee persists in attempting to be reimbursed for commuting.
- *All cash payments must be justified with a receipt.* This policy is intended to close one of the worst loopholes in the expense report system, which is reimbursing people for cash payments that may never have happened.
- *Employees will be reimbursed within __ days of expense report submission.* The number of days until payment should be quite short, since employees may need the cash to pay their credit card statements. This policy is designed to force the payables staff to make rapid payments.

In addition, there should be a policy related to meals. Management needs to make a decision about reimbursing the entire amount of meals or reimbursing on a per diem basis. Either approach works, though the sales staff is more likely to take clients out for meals, and so will not be able to work within the restrictions of a per diem system. The advantages and disadvantages of the two approaches are:

- *Per diem.* This reduces the paperwork included in an expense report. Also, it tends to force employees to purchase less expensive meals. There may be some gaming of the system, where employees purchase very inexpensive meals that cost less than the per diem, and pocket the difference.
- *Reimbursement.* There is more paperwork included in expense reports, but this is essentially a required method when taking business partners out for meals. A few employees will take advantage of this approach to buy inordinately expensive meals.

Procurement Card Policies

- *Cash advances shall be prohibited for procurement cards.* This policy is a rather obvious restriction on the cards, so that they cannot be used to withdraw cash from an ATM. There should be no valid business reason for a cash withdrawal.
- *Only the procurement card manager is authorized to alter card spending limits.* This policy mandates that the bank be notified that only one person is allowed to change card spending limits, thereby reducing the risk of someone altering their own card limits and overspending.

Petty Cash Policies

- *The petty cash box shall be locked in the absence of the petty cash custodian.* The policy is essentially stating that the petty cash box is to be locked unless it is in use. The box contains cash, so it would otherwise be too easy for someone to enter the area, reach into the box, and extract cash.
- *Petty cash cannot be used to pay for invoices of more than $__.* There is a chance that supplier invoices can be paid twice – once through petty cash, and again as a direct submission to the payables system. This policy should reduce the number of invoice payments being run through the petty cash box, thereby reducing the risk of duplicate payments. A variation on this policy is stated next.
- *Individual petty cash reimbursements shall not exceed $__.* This policy is designed to restrict petty cash usage to very small incidental items. All other payments must therefore be routed through the payables system.
- *Employee advances and traffic citations cannot be reimbursed from petty cash.* Certain types of payments, such as employee advances and traffic citations, require approval from someone higher in the company than the petty cash custodian, so this policy prevents the custodian from making such payments. The policy can be expanded to encompass other types of expenditures, such as payments for gifts.

Summary

Clearly, there are many controls that can be applied to the various payables processes. However, an overly cautious payables manager may implement every possible control, only to see the efficiency of the department decline precipitously. The solution is a combination of two items:

- *Exclusions.* Adopt a reduced set of controls for lower-cost purchases. This usually means shifting to procurement cards for low-cost items.
- *Controls based on risk and probability.* Examine the payables process from the perspective of reducing high-risk and high-probability issues, and only implement controls for those items. Conversely, it usually does not make

much sense to install controls to mitigate potential problems that are not only unlikely, but which will only result in small losses.

Procurement cards require no prior purchase order authorization, and there may not be any evidence of receipt at the receiving dock, so several of the primary controls used for more typical accounts payable cannot be applied to it. Instead, the controls involve a few preventive ones (mostly spending limits) and a larger number of detective ones. Thus, it is entirely possible that there will be an ongoing flow of smaller expenditures that would not have been made under a traditional payables system. If these expenditures become large in aggregate, it may make sense to shift some purchases away from procurement cards and back to the traditional purchase order system.

Petty cash is a relatively small part of a company's system of handling expenditures, but it requires a surprisingly large number of controls. This is because it involves the relatively insecure storage of loose cash within a business. Though the theft or misuse of petty cash in a single event may not result in a large loss for a business, its long-term pilfering can add up to quite a significant amount. Consequently, given the large number of controls and prospects for long-term losses, it may be worthwhile not to operate a petty cash system at all.

Chapter 12
Payables Fraud

Introduction

The last chapter contained a large number of controls, some of which could deter fraudulent behavior. What types of fraud were those controls intended to mitigate? In this chapter, we cover a number of fraudulent activities that impact the payables function, and briefly note the controls that are most likely to prevent or detect them.

> **Related Podcast Episode:** Episode 247 of the Accounting Best Practices Podcast discusses payables fraud schemes. It is available at: **accountingtools.com/podcasts** or **iTunes**

Personal Purchases

An employee uses company credit to purchase goods or services for himself. This is most easily accomplished by including a smaller expenditure on an expense report that is unlikely to be questioned. Or, if a flaw in the control system allows a manager to approve his own expense reports, larger purchases can be passed through to the company. Managers may also make purchases through suppliers, and then approve the invoices when the payables department routes the invoices to them for approval.

Personal purchases fraud can be mitigated by the use of detailed expense report audits and mandatory approvals for all expense reports. Larger supplier invoices should be verified against the receiving log and an authorizing purchase order. It is still possible for smaller personal purchases to be made with only a minor risk of detection.

Refunds of Personal Purchases

An employee may make a reasonable and fully authorized purchase and be reimbursed for it through his expense report – and then obtain a refund from the supplier. For example, an employee may gain approval to take a class at a local community college, and the company reimburses the employee for the course – after which the employee cancels the class and obtains a refund. Similarly, the company could reimburse an employee for an airline ticket, after which the employee skips the flight and obtains a refund.

A company can avoid this type of fraud by only reimbursing employees (for example) when they present proof of having completed a course or a flight.

Fake Suppliers

A payables employee could create a vendor master file record for a fake supplier, and then submit fake invoices to the company that are supposedly submitted by the supplier. Once entered, the payables system will generate payments to the fake supplier as part of its normal check runs or ACH payments. To achieve this level of fraud properly, the same person must have access to the vendor master file and the payables data entry system. Such a thorough level of fraud is much more committing for an employee than the personal purchases and refunds frauds noted in previous sections. Given the level of commitment to this type of fraud, expect the employee to engage in additional activities to cover his or her tracks, such as only submitting smaller invoice amounts at irregular intervals, or closing down one fake supplier record and replacing it with another. These actions can make it quite difficult to spot fake suppliers.

Fake supplier fraud can be reduced by restricting access to the vendor master file, setting up a change log for the vendor master file and perusing it regularly, and by monitoring the trend line of expenses over time.

Supplier Overbillings

A supplier may elect to overbill the company. For example, a legal billing could be inflated or a billing is for an amount greater than the number of goods shipped. This can be an especially pernicious problem when the amount of the overbilling is only somewhat greater than the expected amount, so that the excess could be ascribed to a clerical error or an incorrect receiving report. If so, a continuing series of overbillings could eventually result in significant losses.

This issue can be mitigated by the use of three-way matching. However, it can be inordinately difficult to detect overbilling for services, since there is no physical cross-check. In this case, trend line analysis can be used to detect excessive billings, while purchase orders can put a cap on the amount paid.

Unauthorized Shipments

A common form of fraud is for someone in the company to take a phone call from an outside party that is offering an uncommonly good deal on copier toner, or some other office supplies. Any agreement is considered a verbal purchase order, which is used as the basis for a delivery of substandard goods to the company's receiving dock a short time later. The seller then bills the company, referencing the name of the person who gave verbal approval.

While the amounts lost to this type of fraud are not great, they can be annoying. Unauthorized shipment fraud can be reduced through proper training of employees in regard to why verbal authorizations are not to be used.

Supplier-Staff Collusion

A supplier may contact one of the payables employees with an offer to split the proceeds from fraudulent billings to the company. This may involve sending inflated invoices to the company, which the employee approves and processes for payment. Once payment is made to the supplier, a kickback is paid by the supplier to the assisting employee.

This can be a difficult type of fraud to detect, since more than one person is conspiring to sidestep the company's controls. One option is to require purchase orders for larger purchases, and to enforce the matching of supplier invoices to these purchase orders to ensure that the correct amounts are paid. Another option is to rotate the payables staff, so that they deal with different suppliers each year, and so have less time to build relationships that could become harmful to the company.

Authorization Limit Avoidance

Employees outside of the payables department may want to make a purchase, but are not sure that it will be authorized. If the company has a threshold below which authorizations are not needed, these employees may advise suppliers to present several invoices, rather than one invoice, with each invoice total set somewhat below the authorization threshold. This is active authorization avoidance, which many suppliers are more than happy to assist with in order to make a sale.

This issue can be detected by examining expenditures just below the authorization threshold. However, if the supplier billings are spaced across several months, authorization avoidance may be difficult to detect.

Petty Cash Theft

One of the easier types of fraud is to either steal cash from the petty cash box, or to steal the entire box. Since the cash is not traceable, petty cash theft can be a nearly perfect crime. Also, since the amount kept in a petty cash box is relatively minor, management does not spend additional funds on video surveillance or other types of monitoring equipment that might otherwise detect a theft.

A simple prevention technique is to install a lock on all petty cash boxes, as well as to bolt down the boxes. Better yet, eliminate all petty cash, and instead require all purchases to flow through the normal payables system, expense reports, and/or procurement cards.

Redirected Payments

An outsider could contact the company and request that all future payments made to a particular supplier be made to a new bank account or mailing address. Once these payments are made, the individual absconds with the funds, leaving the company still having an obligation to pay its suppliers. This type of fraud is becoming increasingly difficult to spot, since requests to redirect payments can be included in quite convincing-looking e-mails or letters.

This fraud can be reduced by contacting suppliers upon receipt of these requests, to obtain confirmation that a new bank account or address actually pertains to the supplier. To add an extra level of security, ask the contact at the supplier for the supplier's old bank account information as well, which is information that an outsider is unlikely to have.

Check Fraud

One of the older types of fraud is for someone either within or outside of a company to alter the stated payment amount or the payee name (or both) on a check, and then cash the check. A more sophisticated person may attempt to chemically erase certain information on a check, or create a copy using a color copier. If the paying company is inattentive in reviewing cashed checks through its bank reconciliation process, this likely means that someone could get away with an excessively large payment, or a payment intended for someone else.

There are several methods available for reducing the risk of check fraud, including positive pay, completely filling all fields on each check, and conducting daily bank reconciliations. There are a number of preprinted features that can be added to check stock that can assist in identifying copied or modified checks, such as watermarks and paper that reacts to chemical alterations.

Check Theft

An employee may gain access to the company's check stock, and extract a blank check. The person then forges a payment amount on the check. If the company uses a check stamp and the employee has access to this stamp, it is then an easy matter to sign the check and present it to a bank for payment. Since the check looks entirely official, even a substantial amount is likely to be paid.

This fraud can be mitigated by locking up the check stock and signature stamp in different locations, and with different lock combinations. In addition, a daily bank reconciliation may spot these checks shortly after they are presented for payment, while a check log may spot instances when a check is missing.

ACH Debits

An outside party that knows a company's bank account information can set up an ACH debit, which extracts money from the account through an ACH transaction. This approach is most likely to succeed if the amount is relatively small, thereby passing under any threshold that the company may have imposed that requires the bank to first contact the company to verify that such a debit is authorized. If someone were to use an ACH debit to extract a small sum from a bank account on a monthly basis, this could add up to quite a substantial amount over time.

The fraudulent use of ACH debits can be avoided by imposing a debit block on the company bank account. These blocks may only allow ACH debits from certain suppliers, and only for specific amounts. Alternatively, they may block all ACH debits.

Keystroke Logging

Someone outside of a company may want to learn the user identifications and passwords of employees operating the payables software. With this information, they can access the system, create false suppliers, and enter fake invoices that are to be paid to those suppliers. The company then sends a payment in the ordinary course of business. If this person continues to have access to the system, he can continue to access the system and enter additional invoices, all of which will be paid.

One of the methods used to learn user login information is to send e-mail messages to employees that contain attached files. If an employee accesses one of these files, it downloads keystroke logging software onto his or her computer. From that point onward, a complete record of all keystrokes made on that computer is sent to the outsider, which can be sifted for login information.

This approach is a particular problem when a company sends wire transfers over the Internet by accessing its bank account on-line. If a hacker obtains this login information, large payments can be sent out of the country, which will probably not be recoverable.

Keystroke logging fraud can be reduced by employing a firewall and spam filter for e-mail, as well as by requiring that the computer used to set up wire transfers not be used for any other purpose.

The Need for Controls Reviews

Some of the fraud schemes noted in this chapter are made possible by ongoing changes in the payables department. There may be process changes, acquisitions, or new software installations that result in altered controls (or no controls at all). A canny employee may note these changes and take advantage of them. Consequently, it is particularly useful to conduct a controls review after one of these major events occurs, or just at regular intervals. Controls reviews can be conducted by the internal audit staff, but also consider bringing in an outside expert to conduct the review. These people have seen many systems and so are more aware of potential controls flaws that could result in fraud. The worst controls review is by the accounting staff, because they are *too* familiar with the system – they may ignore a glaringly obvious control problem, simply because they work with the system every day.

Summary

It is difficult to point at one of the preceding fraud types as being the most prevalent, and recommend that this particular item be guarded against, above all others. Instead, the type of fraud to which a business is susceptible will likely vary, depending on the nature of the industry, the level of rigor used to hire employees, the example set by senior management, the quality of the system of controls currently in place, and so on. A better approach is to hire a fraud and controls expert, who examines the company and notes which types of fraud are best guarded against, which are still viable risks, and the levels of monetary risk involved. This type of analysis will give management a better idea of the types of control systems and other changes that must be made in order to mitigate the risk of payables fraud.

Though more than a dozen general types of payables fraud were outlined in this chapter, the list is probably not conclusive – there are always new approaches being created by fraud-minded individuals. Consequently, keep an open mind regarding the nature of irregular payments, and be willing to dig deep to determine the underlying causes of suspicious expenditures.

Chapter 13
Payables Technology

Introduction

The basic accounts payable system is assumed to comprise a payables module that is part of the larger accounting system, and perhaps an ACH payment feature that is accessed through the web site of the company's bank. These elements are sufficient for the operation of a reasonably efficient payables department. But what if management wants to attain an industry-leading standard of performance? This may require the acquisition of additional payables technology. In this chapter, we explore several additional systems that can drastically reduce the cost of payables processing.

The Payment Factory

When a company has a number of subsidiaries, it may allow each of them to operate separate payables processes. If so, the company as a whole is likely to incur more administrative costs to operate payables, since the payables infrastructure is duplicated several times over.

The situation can be improved considerably by installing a payment factory. This is a payables function that has been centralized for an entire organization. Such a system may have the following features:

- Robust software to handle large transaction volumes
- Ability to accept incoming payment information in many formats
- Inbound document digitization
- Online form for supplier entry of invoices
- Workflow management system to handle document approvals

The system has the following benefits:

- Better prediction of cash outflows for centralized cash forecasting
- More efficient payables processing; it is easier to install best practices in a single location
- Can realize greater returns from acquisitions, since an acquiree's payables function can be shifted to the centralized system
- Higher volume with fewer banks, resulting in lower transaction fees
- More control over when cash outflows occur
- Netting of payments between subsidiaries
- Route payments through in-country accounts to avoid foreign transaction fees to suppliers located outside the country

However, a payment factory also has the following problems, which must be explored before installing the system:

- Expensive software and related systems
- Takes payment control away from subsidiaries
- Terminates some banking relationships that may have been in place for years
- Workflow management of approvals must be accessible in all participating subsidiaries (if approvals are required)

Automated Expense Report Submissions

There are several suppliers of automated expense reporting systems that operate Internet-based portals. An organization pays these suppliers to have employees access their portals and enter their expense reports on-line, along with supporting documentation. The underlying software compares these submissions to the company's travel and entertainment policy, checks the mileage claimed by employees, and automatically makes determinations regarding which claims are valid. The resulting payables are routed into the company's payables system via a custom interface, and so are scheduled for payment.

The great advantage of these automated systems is that each expense report is subjected to some level of review, so that the most egregious claims are flagged and denied. The systems also take the reviewing burden away from the payables staff. There is also no software that the company must maintain – it is all serviced on-line by the provider. However, these systems have a significant setup charge, as well as a charge per expense report processed. Consequently, their cost places them out of reach for smaller organizations.

Automated Payables Matching

The classic approach to managing the accounts payable paper flow is to match three documents against each other, as follows:

- Compare the supplier's invoice to the company's authorizing purchase order to ensure that the pricing terms are correct
- Compare the purchase order to the receiving documents to ensure that the quantities received match the authorized amount

This comparison process is slow, so many companies try to avoid it by shifting small-dollar payments to procurement cards, or by waiving the matching requirement if the amount of a supplier invoice is small. Yet another alternative is to pay based on the quantity received, and not bother with any supplier invoices.

If, despite taking these alternative steps, a company still has a fair number of purchases requiring three-way matching, it can consider doing so through an automated process. This requires that the following system components be present:

- A document management system into which all supplier invoices are scanned as they are received.

- An automated matching system, as is found in some enterprise resource planning (ERP) systems.
- A data capture system that extracts information from scanned documents and stores this information in a database for use by the automated matching system. Data capture requires that a number of rules be loaded in advance, detailing such issues as where information is located on a supplier invoice, for each supplier invoice template.

Ideally, this combination of systems should scan all incoming invoices, extract information from them, load it into the ERP system for matching purposes, and schedule the invoices for payment.

A large amount of customization is required before these systems can be relied upon to consistently conduct three-way matching with minimal operator intervention. Typically, the system begins with a low success rate, which gradually increases as the data capture rules are improved to match the requirements of each supplier's invoice.

Given the cost of the systems themselves and the time required to customize them, this solution is only cost-effective in environments that must handle large quantities of supplier invoices.

The Reverse Lockbox

A common treasury practice for a business is to instruct customers to mail their payments to a mailbox operated by the company's bank, in order to cash their checks more quickly. This is known as a lockbox. The reverse concept, called a reverse lockbox, is also offered by a few of the largest banks. Under a reverse lockbox arrangement, suppliers are instructed to send their invoices to the company's bank, which digitizes the invoices and forwards them to the company's accounts payable system through an online interface.

The company then flags the approval status of each invoice and transmits this information back to the bank, which pays the invoices when their payment terms indicate that they are due for payment. The bank then sends payment information back to the company's accounts payable system, indicating which invoices have been paid.

The bank can take on some of the payment approval process by working through a set of automated decision rules, such as paying all invoices below a certain threshold amount, and all invoices from a list of pre-approved suppliers. It may even be possible for the bank to access the company's purchasing and receiving systems, and conduct a three-way match based on the information in these files.

Using a bank to process some aspects of a company's accounts payable transactions shifts some control issues to the bank, which makes it easier for a publicly-held company to comply with the control requirements of the Sarbanes-Oxley Act.

In short, banks can use their high-speed document management systems that are normally applied to the handling of incoming checks to the handling of incoming invoices, thereby taking some accounts payable tasks away from client companies. This also makes it less likely that bank customers will shift their business to a different bank, given the high level of customized integration needed to install a reverse lockbox system.

Supplier Portals

The payables staff can spend an inordinate amount of time dealing with suppliers on a number of issues, such as the status of payments, inquiries about deductions taken, and the proper address and bank account to which payments are to be made. A better approach is to set up a supplier Internet portal, which suppliers can log into to access, load, and update information. A portal could be used for the following purposes:

- Suppliers can enter their invoices directly into the company's payables system, along with any supporting documentation.
- Suppliers can access the current payment status of their invoices, as well as the details of any deductions being taken from payments.
- Suppliers can update their Form W-9 information.
- Suppliers can update their pay-to address information and/or bank account information.

Portals are available from the suppliers of the more expensive accounting packages, or can be custom-designed with interfaces that connect into the current accounts payable system.

Automated W-9 Forms

Following the end of each calendar year, the payables staff must evaluate whether to issue a Form 1099 to suppliers. The evaluation is based in part on the information provided by suppliers on the Form W-9, which is the Request for Taxpayer Identification Number and Certification. If there is no form on file for a supplier, then the payables staff must badger suppliers to obtain one.

Rather than issuing printed W-9 forms to suppliers, the IRS permits an alternative, which is to allow them to submit an electronic version of the form. When this approach is used, the IRS requires that:

- An electronic signature be used that authenticates and verifies the submitted form; and
- The company has made reasonably certain that the person submitting the online form is actually the person identified on the form.

Here are several ways to set up an electronic Form W-9 submission process:

- Post an online form on the company's website that suppliers can access. Issue a password to users to access the form, which is a reasonable way to assure that an authorized person is accessing the form. This is the best approach, but also requires the most custom programming.
- Integrate the form into an online credit application.

- Create a form using Adobe Acrobat and e-mail it to suppliers to be completed.
- Download the IRS' version of the Form W-9 in PDF format, and e-mail it to suppliers.

Of these options, only the first can require that certain fields be filled in. All of the other variations could result in the submission of a partially completed form.

Summary

Of the additional types of technology covered in this chapter, supplier portals and automated Form W-9 systems can provide a modest level of improvement, while the automated matching system is used to improve upon a fundamentally inefficient manual process. The real leaps in department performance can be gained by using a reverse lockbox to outsource the initial data entry of payables, or the payment factory to create a super-department that can use efficiencies of scale to process payables at the lowest possible cost per transaction. Unfortunately, these latter two alternatives, as well as automated expense report submissions, are expensive, and so are realistic options only for larger entities. A smaller business may find that there are no "great leap forward" technologies that will trigger a notable reduction in the cost of the payables department.

Chapter 14
Payables Record Keeping

Introduction

The payables staff engages in some of the highest-volume record keeping in a company. It must set up standardized information about each supplier, record and store incoming supplier invoices, purchase orders, and receiving documentation, and monitor how this information is stored and eventually disposed of. In this chapter, we describe the uses and contents of the vendor master file, how to maintain it, the nature of the payables filing system, and how technology can be used to improve record keeping.

The Vendor Master File

The vendor master file is the central repository of information about each supplier with which a company deals. The file is stored within the accounts payable software, and typically contains the following minimum set of information:

- *Supplier identification number*. This is the unique identification number assigned to each supplier by the company, and which is used to identify the supplier's record in the payables system.
- *Taxpayer identification number*. This is the identification number assigned to a business by the United States government. This information is needed by the company when completing the year-end Form 1099.
- *Supplier name*. This is the legal name of the supplier, and is commonly used as the pay-to name on check payments to suppliers.
- *Supplier DBA name*. In some cases, a company may have a legal name and a different "doing business as" (or DBA) name by which it is more generally known. This name may instead be used as the pay-to name.
- *Supplier address*. This is the administrative address of the supplier, usually where its billing department is located. This address is used to communicate with the billing department of a supplier.
- *Remit to address*. This is the address to which payments are sent to a supplier.
- *Contact phone number*. This is the phone number of the payables department's contact in the billing department of a supplier, to be used if there are questions about a received billing.
- *Early payment discount code*. If a supplier offers a discount for early payments, enter the terms in this field.
- *1099 flag*. If the company is required to issue a year-end Form 1099 to a supplier, click on this flag. Doing so will include a supplier in the year-end print run for the Form 1099.

- *Default account.* This is the default expense account to which payments made to the supplier are charged.
- *ACH information.* Separate fields contain room for the supplier's bank routing number and bank account number, as well as the name on the supplier's bank account.

Vendor Master File Usage

The vendor master file is a central component of many payables activities, which is why a high level of record accuracy is needed. Here are several examples of situations in which the file is used:

- *Invoice receipt.* The payables department receives an invoice from a supplier. To enter the invoice in the accounting system for payment, a payables clerk first does a lookup of supplier names in the vendor master file, to find the correct record. Once this record is selected, the system automatically links the new invoice record with the supplier address and early payment discount information (if any) in the vendor master file. The only information that enters the invoice record from the invoice is the invoice date, invoice number, and total amount payable.
- *Supplier payment.* When it is time to pay suppliers, the accounting system draws the amount payable from the invoice record, and the pay-to name and address from the vendor master file. If an ACH payment is being made, the supplier's bank account information is also drawn from the vendor master file.
- *1099 reporting.* At year-end, the company may have to issue a completed Form 1099 for certain suppliers. The program in the accounting system that generates these reports uses the 1099 flag in the vendor master file to decide whether a report should be issued at all, and uses the supplier address information and taxpayer identification number in the file to populate the report.

In short, the vendor master file contains a large amount of information about suppliers that is central to the efficient functioning of the payables department.

A supplier may not necessarily be set up with a record in the vendor master file. This is most likely to be the case when there is an expectation that a supplier will only be used once. In this case, it may be more efficient to enter all necessary payment information in a separate data entry form in the payables software. The result will be a single invoice record that contains all information needed to pay a supplier. If such an entity were to become a more frequent supplier with regular billings, it would then make more sense to create a unique record for it in the vendor master file.

> **Tip:** It might be tempting to create a vendor master file record for every supplier, no matter how infrequently the company uses the supplier. However, this creates an inordinate number of records in the file, which makes it more difficult to manage.

If the company is a large one, it may be able to afford an online supplier portal, which is a web page that suppliers use to access their vendor master file records. Suppliers can update their information in the file, which takes this chore away from the payables department. However, this approach is more applicable to larger organizations; a smaller one does not have the purchasing clout to force its suppliers to engage in this additional activity.

Supplier Naming Conventions

It is important to avoid creating a new record in the vendor master file for suppliers that already have an existing record. Otherwise, the payables staff will assign some supplier invoices to one version of a master file record, and some invoices to a different version. This can lead to the following situations:

- *Duplicate payment.* An invoice is initially submitted and recorded under one version of the supplier record; the invoice payment is late in arriving, so the supplier sends a duplicate invoice, which is recorded under a different version of the supplier record. The result is that the second invoice is not flagged by the software as being a duplicate invoice, so the company pays the supplier twice.
- *Incomplete records.* The accounting system reveals an incomplete list of billings from a supplier, since some billings are linked to a different supplier record.
- *Incorrect 1099.* A year-end Form 1099 is completed that does not contain the total amount paid to a supplier, since the payments are split among different records.
- *Missing address update.* A supplier submits an address change, but the change is only updated on one of its record versions, resulting in some old invoices being paid to an old pay-to address.

To avoid these problems, it is necessary to create and follow a rigidly-defined naming convention. A naming convention sets forth rules for how to create a supplier identification number. For example, the name of a new supplier for a restaurant chain is The Scot's Guard Brewery. When developing an identification number, the following problems arise:

- Should the identification number start with "The" or with "Scot's"?
- Should the identification number include the apostrophe in the "Scot's" part of the name?
- How much of this long supplier name should be included in the identification number?

The usual naming convention would drop "The" and the apostrophe from the identification number, and probably truncate the name after five or six characters. By employing these rules, the supplier identification number would become either SCOTS (five characters) or SCOTSG (six characters).

How should a naming convention deal with several suppliers whose names begin with the same characters? The convention usually allows for the sequential numbering of these additional suppliers. For example, the first supplier that the restaurant chain has is The Scot's Guard Brewery, so the preceding naming convention indicates that the supplier identification number should be SCOTS001. A year later, the restaurant chain takes on a supplier with the somewhat similar name of Scot's Yard Service. Under the terms of the naming convention, the identification number assigned to this supplier will be SCOTS002.

There may be a need for a number of additional naming conventions to deal with unusual supplier names, such as:

- Eliminate all spaces from supplier names. For example, Jones and Smith could be interpreted as JONESAN001.
- Drop all periods from a name. For example, I.D.C. Corporation could be interpreted as IDCCO001.
- Use an ampersand (&) instead of "and" in a name. To return to the preceding Jones and Smith supplier name, it could be interpreted as JONES&S. Doing so leaves more room to introduce additional characters that could uniquely identify a supplier.
- Use the last name of an individual. The company pays a private contractor named John Arbuckle. There are many contractors named John, so the identification number instead uses the last name to derive ARBUC001.

Vendor Master File Errors

When a business has even a relatively small number of suppliers, many errors will gradually creep into the vendor master file. Here are a number of ways to clean the file:

- *Missing information*. On a regular basis, print a report for each supplier that shows every field being used in the vendor master file. Scan the report for missing information in the more important fields, such as taxpayer identification numbers (TINs).
- *Duplicate records*. Print a list of suppliers, sorted by name, and look for duplicate names that indicate the presence of duplicate records. Determine which of these records to archive and flag them as not to be used again. See the Duplicate Record Detection and Prevention section for more information.
- *Inactive records*. Print a report that shows payments to suppliers over the past two years. If there has been no activity during that time period, flag the related vendor master file records as archived.
- *TIN matching*. Compare the recorded taxpayer identification numbers (TINS) for the newest suppliers to the TIN matching program (see the TIN Matching section) on the IRS website to verify that the recorded numbers are correct. Update any information that is incorrect.

The cleanup tasks noted in the preceding list are called "scrubbing accounts payable," which refers to the review of payables records to see if any records should be purged or enhanced. By scrubbing accounts payable, a business is reducing the risk of having different records for the same supplier, each with potentially different payment terms, addresses, and so forth. It also allows the payables staff to more easily organize its record keeping for each supplier, so that the purchasing department can more easily approach them about volume discounts (which would otherwise be dispersed across multiple supplier records).

Duplicate Record Detection and Prevention

The typical vendor master file contains a large number of duplicate supplier records. Though an occasional review can eliminate many of these records, a more efficient approach is to install controls over the creation of supplier records that make it more difficult to initially generate a duplicate record (a preventive control), as well as to regularly scan the file for duplications (a detective control). Several control possibilities that can limit record duplication are:

- *Centralize changes.* Lock down the vendor master file with password access, and only allow a small number of people access to the file. Then enforce a rigid set of standards for creating identification numbers and entering information into supplier records. Doing so can reduce the incidence of duplicate or incorrect information in the file. See the preceding Supplier Naming Conventions section for more information.
- *Vendor ID match.* When creating a new supplier identification number, scan through adjacent entries for existing suppliers to see if the entity is already listed. This is a very rough control, and may only prevent a few duplicate records from being created.
- *Spreadsheet matching.* Extract the name, address, and tax identification number fields from each supplier record, and copy them into an electronic spreadsheet. Then use any of the following sorts to locate duplicate information:
    - First: Sort the column for the tax identification number, and see if any numbers are duplicated. This only works if identification numbers have already been entered for suppliers.
    - Second: Sort the column for supplier name. This may not yield many duplicate records, since some supplier locations are listed under different names.
    - Third: Sort the column for the address, and see if any addresses are duplicated. Since street numbers appear first, matching fields should readily appear next to each other in the sort.
- *Error review.* Whenever a duplicate record is found, question how the duplication occurred, and whether the imposition of a new control could prevent it from happening again.

A concern with any of these preventive or detective controls is that they introduce more work into the payables process. Consequently, it is worthwhile to examine the cost-effectiveness of each possible control, and decide whether it should be used.

> **Tip:** Error checking of the vendor master file should be conducted by a senior payables clerk with deep knowledge of suppliers. Someone with this level of experience is more likely to spot errors, and cares enough about the information to ensure that it is corrected properly.

The error detection and correction process is a time-consuming and painstaking one. It should be addressed at least once a year. In order to give the staff sufficient time to engage in a thorough review, schedule it for a time of the year when there are no period-end closing activities, training, or other events that might interfere.

> **Tip:** Send an e-mail to each supplier at annual intervals, stating the contents of their vendor master file record, and asking if the information is correct. This can be set up as an automated bulk mailing, requiring little staff time.

TIN Matching

The taxpayer identification number that each supplier provides to the company is used to identify suppliers on the annual Form 1099 that the company is required to prepare for certain suppliers. If the TIN is incorrect, then the Internal Revenue Service (IRS) will reject a submitted 1099. To mitigate the risk of rejection, go to the TIN Matching program in the ww.irs.gov website. The site allows for the entry of up to 25 supplier TIN/Name combinations on-screen, or the submission of up to 100,000 such combinations through a text file submission. The program is intended to match the supplier name and TIN with IRS records. Doing so flags faulty TIN information in advance of preparing the Form 1099.

The Payables Filing System

The payables function is one of the largest generators of paperwork in the accounting department. It should be organized to meet the following two goals:

- To make documents easily accessible for payment purposes
- To make documents easily accessible for auditors

The second requirement, to have paperwork available for auditors, does not just refer to the auditors who examine the company's financial statements at year-end. In addition, the local government may send use tax auditors who will also review the records. Consider maintaining the following systems of records to meet the preceding needs:

- *Supplier files*. There should be one file for each supplier that has been paid within the past year. Within each file, staple all paid invoices and related

documents to the remittance advice for each paid check. These checks should be filed by date, with the most recent payment in front.
- *Unpaid invoices file*. There should be a separate file of unpaid invoices, which is usually sorted alphabetically by the name of the supplier. If there is more than one unpaid invoice for a supplier, sort them by date for each supplier.
- *Unmatched documents file*. If the company is using three-way matching, have separate files for unmatched invoices, purchase orders, and receiving documentation.

> **Tip:** It is not necessary to maintain a separate supplier folder for every supplier. If a supplier only issues invoices a few times a year, include them in an "Other" folder that applies to a letter range of suppliers. For example, there may be an "Other A-C" folder, followed by an "Other D-F" folder, and so forth. Review these "Other" folders periodically, extract the invoices of any suppliers that are generating an increasing volume of invoices, and prepare separate folders for these suppliers.

It is useful to maintain supplier files on the premises of the department for at least the current year, if not for the preceding year. The needs of the department are likely going to be met by just maintaining records for the past few months, but auditors may also want these records for a longer period of time. Older records can be stored elsewhere.

Off-site Storage

Office space is quite expensive to own or rent. If the payables manager insists on storing multiple years of documents on site, this represents a waste of expensive office space. A better alternative by far is to shift older documents into the least expensive space available, which usually means off-site storage space. The location should have adequate fire protection, but certainly does not need all of the expensive amenities found in an office.

> **Tip:** The proper location for off-site storage should represent a combination of low cost, document safety, and a reasonable distance from where the payables staff is located. After all, there will still be situations where archived documents must be reviewed, so the off-site location should not be at an inordinate distance.

The payables staff usually does quite a good job of labeling the current files that are located on-site. However, this discipline typically breaks down when the files are moved to long-term storage. They have a disturbing habit of throwing files into boxes, palletizing the boxes, and sticking them on a distant shelf in the warehouse – and probably under a sprinkler head. Instead, consider the following storage improvements:

- *Consistent contents*. Do not jumble documents into a storage box. Instead, ensure that material is consistently filed. This may require the use of additional boxes.

- *Detailed content labeling.* Carefully identify everything in a box and state the contents clearly on the outside of the box.
- *Accessible storage.* Reserve a storage room in which storage racks are set up at no more than head height, and with readily accessible tables on which storage boxes can be opened.
- *Labels face outward.* Store all boxes in the storage racks so that the labeled end of each box is facing outward, with no additional boxes hidden behind them.
- *Functional storage layout.* Cluster together storage boxes containing similar document types, and in alphabetical order within these clusters.

> **Tip:** Be sure to segregate permanent files (such as legal documents and property title documents) from those files that will eventually be destroyed. Keep the permanent files in an entirely separate location, in fireproof and locked cabinets.

Though these steps certainly take more time to complete, and may require additional storage boxes and storage space, the result should be vastly less research time to locate documents that have been placed in long-term storage.

Document Imaging

There may be situations where a business must deal with massive amounts of paperwork, or where documents cannot be stored near the payables staff, or where several clerks may need access to the same document at the same time. A document imaging system can resolve these problems.

Document imaging involves scanning documents as they arrive at the company, assigning an index number to the images, and storing them in a high-volume storage device. Some higher-end accounting systems can link to these images, so that anyone researching a transaction in the on-line accounting records also has immediate access to the scanned images. The source documents are then sent to long-term storage. With document imaging in place, there is no need for any document storage in higher-cost office space. Also, many people can access the same image at the same time on their computer terminals. Thus, document imaging can be an excellent technology solution to the old problem of dealing with too much paper.

However, there are a number of issues with document imaging that make it an effective solution only in certain situations. First, there needs to be a system in place for scanning documents, which will require additional clerical help. Alternatively, there are suppliers to which paperwork can be routed, who will digitize documents on the company's behalf. Also, if documents are not properly indexed in the imaging system, they can be difficult to find. And third, the cost of the system's software and hardware can be excessive for a smaller business.

Document imaging is least practical when the payables staff is relatively small, and is already centrally located with the relevant accounting documents nearby. Conversely, it may be an excellent solution if there are many documents, the department is large, and there is an ongoing need to access a large number of documents.

Document Destruction

In some businesses, documents may be retained until there is no more storage room, after which the oldest documents are thrown out to make room for the most recent arrivals. Alternatively, all documents may be eliminated after a short time, on the grounds that minimal records make it more difficult to find evidence against the company in court (!). In reality, the only approach that works is to consult with the company's legal counsel regarding the mandated time period over which documents are to be retained, and to follow those time periods religiously.

The payables manager should adhere to a document destruction policy. The goal of the department should be to eliminate only those documents allowed by the document destruction policy, but to do so as soon as permitted by the policy. Thus, there should be at least an annual, if not a quarterly, comparison of the document destruction timelines to the documents that are being maintained in long-term storage. As soon as anything is eligible for destruction, do so by the method mandated in the policy.

Realistically, this is a minor issue, since the amount of storage space being opened up through document destruction is relatively minor. The key issue is the reverse – to keep from incurring a legal liability by destroying documents too soon.

Summary

Of particular importance in the record keeping arena is the completeness and accuracy of the information stored in the vendor master file. To that end, we recommend tightening access to the file, as well as periodic cleanup operations to examine and update its contents.

The filing requirements of the payables area are so significant that the payables manager could consider obtaining extra training in document storage systems and processes, and becoming the company expert in this area. This is because the payables staff needs to have ready access to supplier billings, while also finding a way to shunt these voluminous documents off-site as soon as the need for them declines.

Chapter 15
Government Reporting

Introduction

The key government reporting requirement of the payables department is the provision of the Form 1099 to the government following the end of each calendar year. In this chapter, we describe the contents of this form, the use of the Form W-9 to obtain the identification information used on the Form 1099, and several offshoots of these forms – the verification of taxpayer identification numbers (TINs) and the issuance of "B" notices to suppliers who have provided incorrect information to the payables staff.

> **Related Podcast Episode:** Episode 283 of the Accounting Best Practices Podcast discusses Form 1099 compliance. It is available at: **accountingtools.com/podcasts** or **iTunes**

The Form 1099-MISC

The Form 1099-MISC, "Miscellaneous Income," contains the aggregate amount of cash payments made to a supplier in the preceding calendar year. The IRS uses this document to confirm the amount of income that each supplier reports on its annual tax return. Depending on the type of payment made, it is usually not necessary to issue the form if the cumulative cash payments to a supplier for the full calendar year are less than $600. The form must also be filed for any person from whom you withheld any federal income tax under the backup withholding rules, no matter how small the amount may be.

> **Note:** Personal payments are not reported on the Form 1099-MISC, only payments made in the course of your trade or business (which includes payments by government agencies).

The form is to be sent to the payee by January 31 and filed with the Internal Revenue Service (IRS) by February 28 (or by March 31 if filing electronically[1]). The filing period can be extended 30 days by requesting an extension on IRS Form 8809 (which is available as an on-line form). The form copies are distributed as follows:

- Copy A to the IRS
- Copy B to the recipient (supplier)
- Copy C to be retained by the company

---

[1] Electronic filing is required when filing 100 or more 1099 forms. See IRS Publication 1220 for more information about electronic filing.

Government Reporting

- Copy 1 to the state tax department
- Copy 2 to the recipient (supplier) to file with its state income tax return

There are several exceptions to the requirement to issue a Form 1099-MISC. All of the following do *not* require reporting:

- Payments made to corporations, including S corporations
- Payments for merchandise, telegrams, telephone, freight, and storage
- Payments of rent to real estate agents or property managers
- Wages paid to employees
- Business travel allowances paid to employees
- The cost of life insurance protection
- Payments to a tax-exempt organization
- Payments to the United States, a state, a U.S. possession, or a foreign government
- Payments made to homeowners from the HFA Hardest Hit Fund or a similar state program
- Compensation for injuries or sickness by the Department of Justice as a public safety officer disability or survivor's benefit, or under a similar state program
- Compensation for wrongful incarceration
- Fees paid to informers, if made by a nonprofit or a federal, state or local government agency
- Scholarship or fellowship grants, except grants that are taxable because they are considered wages

The following additional issues may apply when preparing a Form 1099-MISC:

- *Attorney payments.* The exception noted earlier for reporting payments to corporations does not apply to payments for legal services. Attorney's fees are reported either in Box 1 of the Form 1099-NEC (as described later in this course) or in Box 10 of the Form 1099-MISC (to corporations that provide legal services).
- *Employee business expense reimbursements.* Do not report reimbursements made to employees for their business expenses on the Form 1099-MISC.
- *Reporting to recipient.* Every Form 1099-MISC must also be furnished to the payee.

A sample Form 1099-MISC appears in the following exhibit.

Sample Form 1099-MISC

[Sample IRS Form 1099-MISC for 2020, Miscellaneous Income]

Explanations of the key boxes on the form are noted in the following table.

Contents of Key 1099-MISC Fields

Box ID	Description
2nd TIN	2nd TIN notification – Check this box if you were notified by the IRS twice within the last three calendar years that the payee provided an incorrect taxpayer identification number. By marking this box, the IRS will send no further notices about this account.
Box 1	Rent – Includes real estate rentals paid for office space, unless they were paid to a real estate agent. Also includes machine rentals and pasture rentals. The minimum reporting threshold is $600.
Box 2	Royalties – Includes gross royalty payments, such as from oil, gas, and other mineral properties, as well as from patents, copyrights, trade names, and trademarks. The minimum reporting threshold is $10.
Box 3	Other income – Includes other income of at least $600 that is not reportable under any of the other boxes on the form. Includes the fair market value of merchandise won on game shows, as well as payments to individuals for participating in a medical research study and punitive damage payments.

Box ID	Description
Box 4	Federal income tax withheld – Includes any backup withholdings made on payments to suppliers. This is most likely when suppliers have not furnished you with taxpayer identification numbers.
Box 5	Fishing boat proceeds – Includes an individual's share of all proceeds from the sale of a catch, or the fair market value of a distribution in kind to each crew member of a boat with fewer than 10 crew members. Also includes cash payments of up to $100 per trip that are contingent on a minimum catch and which are paid solely for additional duties performed, such as engineer.
Box 6	Medical and health care payments – Includes payments to each physician or other provider of medical or health care services. The minimum reporting threshold is $600. Typical payments include charges for injections, drugs, dentures, and similar items. This does not include payments made to a tax-exempt hospital or an extended care facility.
Box 7	Payer made direct sales of $5,000 or more – Check the box to indicate sales by the firm of $5,000 or more of consumer products to a person on a buy-sell, deposit-commission, or other commission basis for resale anywhere other than in a retail location.
Box 8	Substitute payments in lieu of dividends or interest – Includes aggregate payments of at least $10 of substitute payments received by a broker for a customer in lieu of dividends or tax-exempt interest as a result of a loan of a customer's securities.
Box 9	Crop insurance proceeds – Includes payments made by insurance companies to farmers. The minimum reporting threshold is $600.
Box 10	Gross proceeds paid to an attorney – Includes amounts paid to an attorney for legal services. The minimum reporting threshold is $600.
Box 12	Section 409A deferrals – Includes the total amount deferred during the year of at least $600 for a non-employee under all nonqualified plans. Entries in this box are optional.
Box 13	Excess golden parachute payments – The excess amount of a golden parachute payment to be included here is the excess amount over the average annual compensation in a person's gross income over the most recent five tax years.

When submitting 1099 forms to the federal government, also include a Form 1096 transmittal return, which is essentially a cover letter that identifies the entity providing the forms. A sample Form 1096 follows. This form is not required when submitting an electronic filing.

Sample Form 1096

[Form 1096: Annual Summary and Transmittal of U.S. Information Returns, 2020]

The Form 1099-NEC

The Form 1099-NEC, "Nonemployee Compensation," is to be filed for compensation paid to anyone classified as a non-employee. The form should be filed when:

- At least $600 was paid; and
- Services were performed by someone who is not an employee; or
- Cash was paid for fish purchased from anyone engaged in the business of catching fish; or
- Payments were made to an attorney.

In all of the preceding cases, a Form 1099-NEC is required even when the payee is a corporation.

Examples of payments that would be reportable on a Form 1099-NEC are:

- Director's fees
- Commissions paid to lottery ticket sales agents
- Payments made on behalf of another person
- Payments to accountants, attorneys, architects, contractors, and engineers
- Fees paid by one professional to another, such as fee-splitting or referral fees
- Payments by attorneys to witnesses or experts in legal adjudication
- Payments to nonemployee salespersons that are subject to repayment but not repaid during the calendar year

- A fee paid to a nonemployee for which the individual did not account to the payer
- Payments to nonemployee entertainers for services
- Gross oil and gas payments for a working interest

A Form 1099-NEC must also be filed for any person from whom you have withheld federal income taxes under the backup withholding rules; there is no minimum reporting threshold for this reporting.

There are some exceptions that are not to be reported on the Form 1099-NEC. These are:

- Payments to corporations (except for those already noted earlier in this section)
- Payments for merchandise, telegrams, telephone, freight, storage, and similar items
- Payments of rent to real estate agents or property managers
- Wages paid to employees
- Military differential wage payments made to employees while on active duty
- Business travel allowances paid to employees
- The cost of current life insurance protection
- Payments to a tax-exempt organization
- Payments made to homeowners from the HFA Hardest Hit Fund or a similar state program
- Compensation for injuries or sickness by the Department of Justice as a public safety officer disability or survivor's benefit, or under a similar state program
- Compensation for wrongful incarceration
- Fees paid to informers
- Scholarship or fellowship grants
- Difficulty of care payments that are excludable from the recipient's gross income
- Cancelled debt
- Expense reimbursements paid to volunteers of nonprofit organizations
- Deceased employee wages paid in the year after death
- Payments for rent
- The cost of group-term life insurance paid on behalf of a former employee

The following additional issues may apply when preparing a Form 1099-NEC:

- *Reporting to recipients.* Every Form 1099-NEC must also be furnished to the payment recipient.
- *TIN truncation.* A filer of a Form 1099-NEC is allowed to truncate the taxpayer identification number on any statements sent to the borrower. However, truncation is not allowed on any documents filed with the IRS.

Government Reporting

Explanations of the key boxes on the form are noted in the following table. A sample Form 1099-NEC appears in the second exhibit.

Contents of Key 1099-NEC Fields

Box ID	Description
2nd TIN	2nd TIN notification – Check this box if you were notified by the IRS twice within the last three calendar years that the payee provided an incorrect taxpayer identification number. By marking this box, the IRS will send no further notices about this account.
Box 1	Nonemployee compensation – Includes all nonemployee compensation of $600 or more, subject to the limitations noted earlier in this section.
Box 4	Federal income tax withheld – Includes all backup withholding amounts. This typically involves individuals who have not furnished their taxpayer identification numbers to you, which makes them subject to withholding.

Boxes 5-7 in the form are provided for your convenience and do not have to be filled out. They provide space for state-specific withholding and related information.

Sample Form 1099-NEC

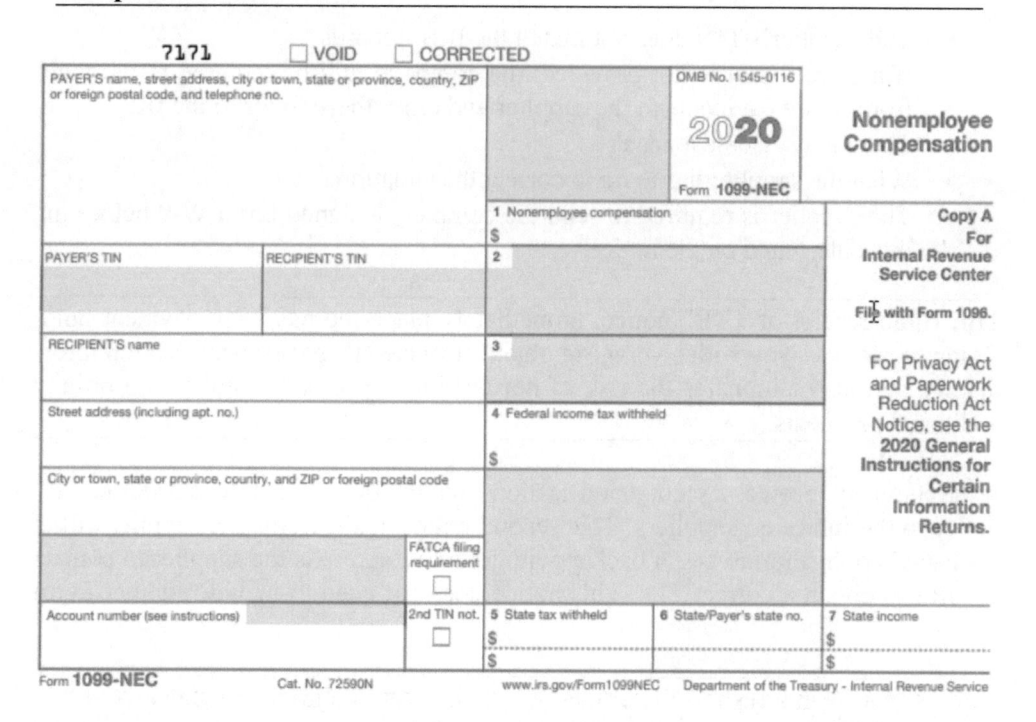

The due date for filing a Form 1099-NEC is January 31 of the following calendar year.

Treatment of Incorrect Filings

It is unfortunately common for a Form 1099 to contain incorrect information. In this section, we describe how to provide corrected information to the IRS, as well as how to deal with recalcitrant suppliers who do not provide correct identification information to the company.

If the amount paid or payee name information on a Form 1099 is found to be incorrect, create a replacement form, check the "Corrected" box at the top of the form, and enter the correct information.

If the TIN number on a Form 1099 is found to be incorrect, create a replacement form, check the "Corrected" box at the top of the form, and enter the payer, recipient, and account number information as it appeared on the original incorrect return, with the amount paid set at zero; this deletes the original filing. Then prepare and submit a new Form 1099 with the correct TIN included, which will replace the original filing.

If 1099s are sent to the IRS and the IRS finds that one or more of the TINs on these forms are incorrect, it will send a notification to the company, detailing which TINs are incorrect. Upon receipt of this document, the company must send a "B" notice and a Form W-9 to each indicated supplier within the later of the next 15 business days or the date of the IRS notice. A "B" notice is a backup withholding notice. The first of these notices contains the following statements:

- The supplier's TIN does not match the IRS' records
- If a correct TIN is not provided, the company will be required to withhold from future payments to the supplier and remit these funds to the IRS
- There may also be a penalty
- What the supplier has to do to correct the situation
- The supplier is required to send the company a signed Form W-9 before the due date stated on the notice

Tip: Upon receipt of a "B" notice, immediately place the payee on payment hold. Doing so provides you with leverage to obtain corrected taxpayer identification information, and also eliminates the risk of not conducting backup withholding on any additional payments.

If the company receives a second notification from the IRS, it must send a second "B" notice to the indicated suppliers. This second notice again warns the supplier of the company's obligation to begin backup withholdings, and tells the supplier to contact the IRS to obtain a correct TIN. This notice does not need to include another Form W-9.

Tip: Do not be in a rush to file any Form 1099, given the grief associated with "B" notices and 1099 correction filings. Instead, take the time to review all expected 1099 amounts. Compare them to the amounts filed for the prior year, and investigate any that are unusually high or low.

Tip: Taxpayer identification numbers are issued for a legal business name, not a "doing business as" (dba) name. Consequently, make sure that 1099 forms are issued using the legal business names of payees, or else the IRS will likely issue a "B" notice for these filings.

The Form W-9

A company needs accurate identification information about each of its suppliers before it can submit the Form 1099 to the government. To collect this information, have all suppliers submit a Form W-9, Request for Taxpayer Identification Number and Certification. A sample Form W-9 follows.

Sample Form W-9

It is a good practice to have the Form W-9 updated on an annual basis, in order to have the most recent mailing address on file for each supplier. Doing so also warns of any organizational changes in a supplier. However, this can be difficult if there are many suppliers. Usually, a simple e-mail notice to each supplier to ask for a revised Form W-9 if there have been any informational changes is considered sufficient.

It is acceptable for a business to develop its own Form W-9, as long as the contents of the substitute form are substantially similar to the contents of the most recent official version issued by the IRS. It may be useful to take this approach when you want to incorporate a customized form into some other business forms currently in use. However, if the W-9 contents are included in another business form, it is not acceptable to use the merged document to force suppliers to agree to provisions unrelated to the W-9 information. Further, the following statement must be presented so that it stands out on the page, and must appear immediately above the signature line:

> "The Internal Revenue Service does not require your consent to any provision of this document other than the certifications required to avoid backup withholding."

Automated W-9 forms are described in the Payables Technology chapter.

The Backup Withholding Rule

Backup withholding requires a payer to withhold tax from payments not otherwise subject to withholding. It is applied when the payee does not provide a correct taxpayer identification number on a Form W-9 to the reporting entity. Backup withholding can apply to most payment types reported on a Form 1099, including the following:

- Interest payments
- Dividends
- Rents, profits, or other income
- Commissions, fees, or other payments for work performed as an independent contractor
- Payments made by brokers
- Payments made by fishing boat operators that represent a share of the proceeds from a catch
- Payment card and third-party network transactions
- Royalty payments

The reporting entity is required to withhold a flat 24% rate from payments made to the payee under the following circumstances:

- The payee does not provide the reporting entity with a taxpayer identification number.
- The IRS notifies the reporting entity that the taxpayer identification number given is incorrect.
- The IRS notifies the reporting entity to start withholding on interest or dividends, because the payee underreported these amounts on his or her income tax return.
- The payee fails to certify that he or she is not subject to backup withholding for the underreporting of interest and dividends.

> **Tip:** Rather than actually withholding the 24% rate, first contact the payee and explain that this withholding will commence unless they provide you with a correct taxpayer identification number. Doing so will usually extract the necessary information.

Form 1099 Administrative Issues

The issuance of the Form 1099 calls for several administrative activities at various times of the year, which are as follows:

- *Eliminate duplicate records.* A common problem with the issuance of the Form 1099 is that some suppliers will receive more than one, because the company has multiple master vendor file records for them. To prevent this from happening, review the master vendor file for duplicate records, and deactivate any excess records. This will likely mean that any payables transactions related to the deactivated records must be shifted over to the remaining record pertaining to each supplier, which can be a substantial chore.
- *Order forms.* The Form 1099 prominently lists the calendar date to which it pertains, and so must be ordered fresh each year – old forms from a prior year cannot be used. Be sure to order these forms well in advance of the date on which they are scheduled to be printed, and order somewhat more than are expected to be used, just to ensure that a complete print run can be accomplished.

Form W-9 Administrative Issues

The collection of the Form W-9 is an ongoing task that must be monitored throughout the year. We suggest engaging in the following administrative activities:

- *New supplier monitoring.* Ensure that a notice is sent to each new supplier, requesting that a Form W-9 be sent to the payables department. This can be a mailed notice with an attached Form W-9, or perhaps an e-mail with an attached PDF version of the form. Whatever the form of distribution may be, have a system for verifying that the forms are actually received. Once a form arrives in the mail, check it for completeness and then set a W-9 flag in the master vendor file to indicate that the form has been received.
- *Old supplier updates.* Compare the file of received Forms W-9 to the list of current suppliers, and contact any suppliers for which there is no W-9 on file. Contact these suppliers at once with a request for a Form W-9. Also, a supplier needs to send a replacement Form W-9 if any of the information on the last form has changed.
- *Document management.* Maintain a log of all Forms W-9 received, sorted by supplier name. This can be in a binder or digitized in an on-line database, with the supporting paper records stored elsewhere. The main point is to keep the forms sufficiently organized that they can be readily accessed if a supplier complains that a form was already sent.
- *Verify taxpayer identification numbers.* The TIN that a supplier includes on a Form W-9 must be correct, or else the resulting Form 1099 that a company submits to the IRS will be rejected. To verify that these TINs are correct, go to the TIN on-line matching page on the IRS website. The interactive TIN matching function on the site accepts up to 25 supplier TIN/name

combinations on-screen. If there are many more TINs to be verified, the site has a bulk TIN matching option that allows for the automated review of up to 100,000 supplier TIN/name combinations that are submitted through a text file submission. If the site rejects a TIN, contact the supplier for a replacement number.

> **Tip:** Consider developing a TIN verification stamp that can be placed on all W-9 forms for which the TIN has been verified. Alternatively, set up a field in the vendor master file that can be checked off to indicate verification.

It can be very difficult to persuade some suppliers to issue a complete and signed Form W-9. An excellent way to overcome their reluctance is to require that a complete Form W-9 be received before any payments are made to a supplier.

The payables department may not receive much support from management in obtaining the Form W-9 from suppliers, on the grounds that this is a bureaucratic paperwork issue. If so, there may be a number of Form 1099 rejections by the IRS, along with penalties. The amount of these fines should be presented to management in order to build a case for more support in obtaining correct W-9s in the future. The penalties levied by the IRS are noted in the following exhibits.

Penalties for Large Business with Gross Receipts Exceeding $5 Million

Not More than 30 Days Late	31 Days Late to August 1	After August 1 or not at all	Intentional Disregard
$50 per return or statement, $556,500 maximum	$110 per return or statement, $1,669,500 maximum	$270 per return or statement, $3,339,000 maximum	$550 per return or statement, no maximum

Penalties for Small Business with Gross Receipts Less Than $5 Million

Not More than 30 Days Late	31 Days Late to August 1	After August 1 or not at all	Intentional Disregard
$50 per return or statement, $194,500 maximum	$110 per return or statement, $556,500 maximum	$270 per return or statement, $1,113,000 maximum	$550 per return or statement, no maximum

A good way to keep track of the status of requests for the Form W-9 and subsequent TIN verification is to set up three date fields in the vendor master file. These fields are for the date on which a Form W-9 was first sent to a supplier, the date on which it was received back from the supplier, and the date on which the TIN was verified. By collecting status information at this level of detail, the payables manager can run reports that specify which suppliers are late in supplying necessary information, or which have supplied incorrect information.

Summary

The most labor-intensive and pervasive issue related to the Form 1099 issuance is tracking down those suppliers that have not submitted a Form W-9. The best way to deal with this situation is to require a Form W-9 before any payments will be issued to suppliers. Otherwise, suppliers have no incentive to supply a completed form.

An additional concern is the extraordinary amount of work associated with incorrect TINs, since the company must scramble at year-end to replace incorrect TIN/name combinations and deal with "B" notices, withholdings, and possibly even penalties. To reduce this level of grief, the payables staff should engage in TIN matching on the IRS website throughout the year, so that immediate feedback can be given to suppliers if there is a problem with their Form W-9 information. To enforce this high level of attention to the issue, develop a formal policy that mandates rapid TIN matching, include it in the department's calendar of activities, and state it specifically in the job descriptions of those employees assigned to this task.

Chapter 16
Unclaimed Property

Introduction

The state governments have unclaimed property laws, under which unclaimed property belonging to third parties must be turned over to the state government. The government then holds onto the property and advertises the existence of the assets on a website, which can then be reviewed by prospective claimants to see if there is any property they can claim from the government. Eventually, the government keeps all remaining unclaimed property, which can represent a notable portion of their annual budgets. Some state governments even charge administrative fees to claimants, thereby further increasing their income.

Each state has unique laws governing unclaimed property, so rather than delving into the details for each individual state, we will only address in this chapter the more common concepts of unclaimed property, with particular attention to the involvement of the payables department.

The Unclaimed Property Liability

The state government that is to be paid any unclaimed property is the state at which the owner of the property last had an address. Or, if there is no record of the owner's address, the property is to be sent to the company's state of incorporation. This means that a broad-based company with many business partners could theoretically be required to forward unclaimed property to all of the state governments, along with the appropriate forms mandated by each government.

EXAMPLE

An employee of Billabong Machining Company, David Emerson, leaves the company's facility in Goodland, Kansas, so the payroll department sends his final check to his last known address, which was also in Goodland. However, by the time the check arrives in the mail, Mr. Emerson has moved and not left a forwarding address. After the required dormancy period has passed (see the Dormancy Period section), the company must instead remit the funds to the state of Colorado, where the business is incorporated. The government of Kansas, which is the state in which Mr. Emerson worked and lived, does not receive any funds.

The issue of which government to pay becomes more interesting in the event of an acquisition. In an acquisition, it is quite common for the acquiring entity to impose its accounting systems on those of the acquiree. During the process of converting to the acquirer's accounting system, it is entirely possible that the addresses associated with old unclaimed property records will not be added to the acquirer's system, and so are effectively lost. In this situation, unclaimed property would revert to the government of the state in which the acquired entity is incorporated. However, if the acquired entity is dissolved, then the remaining entity is the acquirer, and the property would then revert to the government of the state in which the acquiring entity is located.

Uncashed Checks

When completing the monthly bank reconciliation, a common occurrence is to find that some check payments have not been cashed by their recipients. These uncashed checks are unclaimed property. There are several possible causes, such as lax check cashing procedures at suppliers, checks lost in the mail, or checks sent to the wrong address. To keep these uncashed checks from piling up, the payables staff should make inquiries with suppliers about them. If a check has been lost for any reason, the payables staff should void the old check in the accounting system, also notify the bank that the check is void (for which there is a stop payment charge), and then issue a new check. In a larger business, it is reasonable to expect that a few checks will need to be replaced in this manner every month.

The same uncashed check problem can occur in the payroll system, where a few employees are dilatory in cashing their checks. While less of a concern than with suppliers, it is quite possible that a small number of employees delay in cashing their checks for so long that they misplace the checks, which must then be replaced. Another cause for an unclaimed payroll check is when an employee leaves to work in another state and does not leave a forwarding address, so his final check is returned to the company by the postal service.

> **Tip:** A good way to locate former employees who have moved is to look them up on the LinkedIn website, and send them a message through this site to ask for a forwarding address.

The best way to avoid badgering suppliers and employees about uncashed checks (and to avoid the bank fees for stop payments) is to switch to electronic payments. This means setting up suppliers with ACH payments. The range of choices is somewhat broader for employees, where both direct deposit and payroll debit cards can be used.

> **Tip:** If a supplier or employee persistently requests that check payments be replaced, consider charging them the stop payment bank fee for the checks to be replaced, and also use each request as an opportunity to pester them about switching to electronic payments.

Treatment of Credits

A common state of affairs is for a company to issue a credit to a customer for a damaged shipment, or perhaps as a refund for a volume purchase discount. Whatever the reason may be, these credits are not always used by customers. After a certain period of time, perhaps a year, the collections staff decides to clean up the aged accounts receivable report by writing these credits off to miscellaneous income.

This is a problem from the perspective of unclaimed property, since state governments consider these unused credits to be abandoned property that must be turned over to them. To root out these credits, their audit teams will ask for the detail on the miscellaneous income account, and ask for justification for all of the items listed in it.

To avoid having stray credits linger on the books and eventually having to send the funds to the government, consider the following alternative actions:

- Charge interest on late customer payments (which customers rarely pay) and then use the credits to pay down the interest charges.
- Send monthly statements to customers that clearly state all open credits, perhaps with a cover letter pointing out the existence of these credits.
- Adopt a policy that all credits will be paid back to customers in cash if they have not been used by a certain date.

The last recommendation, of paying customers for unused credits, might seem extreme. However, since the funds will otherwise be paid to the state government as unclaimed property, doesn't it seem better from a customer relations standpoint to instead route the cash back to customers?

Due Diligence Letters

Some states require that companies mail due diligence letters to the owners of unclaimed property prior to listing the property on a report to those governments. These letters notify the owners of the presence of unclaimed assets. Doing so reduces the possibility that a state will receive funds from a reporting entity and then have to turn around and pay out the funds shortly thereafter. Instead, they would rather have companies settle as many of these situations as possible, so that only the most intractable cases are forwarded to the government.

The use of due diligence letters is actually quite a good idea, since they can indeed result in assets being properly distributed to owners. We suggest accelerating the process, however, rather than waiting several years before issuing a letter. Instead, consider issuing these mailings once every few months as scheduled activities, so that owners are as well-informed as possible regarding the existence of unclaimed property.

The Dormancy Period

The dormancy period is the amount of time that a business is allowed to retain unclaimed property before it must be turned over to the applicable state government. The dormancy period pertains to the underlying liability of a business, rather than the existence of a specific payment. For example, if the dormancy period for a supplier check is one year, and an uncashed check was replaced after four months, this does not mean that the check re-issuance has now extended the dormancy period for another year. Instead, the dormancy clock is still ticking, and has now declined to eight months. The company must still find a way for the recipient to cash the check before the end of the one-year period, or else it must remit the funds to the applicable state government.

The dormancy period may vary, depending on the type of property. For example, the dormancy period for uncashed payroll checks may be shorter than for uncashed checks paid to suppliers. Also, there are differing definitions of when the dormancy period begins; it could be the date when an uncashed check was issued, or the date when the company last corresponded with an owner regarding unclaimed property. There is an ongoing trend for state governments to reduce the dormancy period, so that they receive funds sooner. This can be a problem in the first year of a dormancy period reduction, since the company must report several years of unclaimed property and submit a larger payment to the government than normal. Generally, the mandated dormancy period is in the range of three to five years, though the period is much shorter for certain assets.

It helps to be aware of the dormancy period, so monitor state publications and websites related to unclaimed property to see if the period is being altered. This can modify the company's planning regarding when to remit payments to the state.

The Unclaimed Property Audit

A state government may decide to conduct an audit of an organization to see if there is any unclaimed property that the business should have been forwarding to the government. These audits cover the period from the last such audit; if no prior audit ever occurred, then the audit team may require the company to dig back through its records for a large number of years.

> **Note:** there is no statute of limitations pertaining to unclaimed property records, so a company that uses the usual seven-year document retention policy may find that it has no records for some of the years that an audit team wants to see, which may be in the range of the last 10 to 15 years.

The auditors may request a broad range of information, including the following:

- Bank reconciliations and bank statements
- Credit memos listing
- Detail for the miscellaneous income account
- Payables check registers
- Payroll check registers
- Voided checks

> **Note:** If the company outsources its payroll processing, payables, or cafeteria plan administration, any checks issued on the company's behalf by these organizations are also subject to an unclaimed property audit. Consequently, it helps to understand the efforts (if any) that these parties are undertaking to ensure that checks are cashed.

Responding to audit requests represents an extraordinary waste of time for all employees in the accounting department, who must interrupt work schedules to locate the required files and respond to auditor questions.

If the company's accounting records are incomplete, the audit team will likely extrapolate the number of unclaimed property issues found to cover the periods for which there are no records, and add on an interest charge for the periods during which the company has held the property when it should have been in the care of the government. Once the company controller sees the size of this prospective charge to the company, he will likely initiate a frantic effort to dig even deeper through the records to mitigate the proposed fee, which could bring department operations to a halt for the remainder of the audit.

> **Tip:** To estimate the possible liability arising from an audit, estimate the amount of unclaimed property generated in the past year, and multiply it by ten to cover the 10-year period that an audit might claim to cover. This would be the prospective liability of the company, plus penalties and interest.

An additional concern with one of these audits is that the audit team may be empowered to look for other problems while they are on-site. For example, they could ask for the company's state income tax or sales tax returns for the past few years and audit those documents, too. Given this additional risk, unclaimed property audits should certainly be avoided whenever possible.

The worst case scenario is when a state government contracts with a third party audit firm to conduct the audit on their behalf. These firms are typically paid a percentage of the amount that they recover, and so have a strong incentive to root through the company's books as deeply as possible. Furthermore, they may represent several dozen state governments at the same time, in order to maximize the amount of unclaimed property that they can find, and the amount they will be paid. And finally, these firms have a propensity to use estimation techniques that maximize the amount of unclaimed property to be recovered, so that they can claim the largest possible percentage payment.

Document Retention Policy

The standard document retention period for a business is seven years, and yet the typical period covered by an unclaimed property audit can cover ten years – or more. How can we reconcile these differing periods? There are several alternatives available:

- *Keep as is.* Continue with the current policy of retaining most documents for seven years, and accept that an unclaimed property payment will have to be extrapolated into any additional years for which information is not available.
- *Extend slightly.* A reasonable midway accommodation is to retain all documents for a period of ten years, which will cover the bulk of the time periods

that most audits will address. If they cover an even longer period, then an additional extrapolation of the unclaimed property liability must be made.
- *Pick and choose*. Retain for an extended period those documents that auditors are most likely to request, such as check registers, and continue to scrap all other records in accordance with the existing record retention policy.

Any of these alternatives are acceptable, as long as management is aware of the advantages and limitations of each one.

Filing Unclaimed Property Reports

The preceding discussion of unclaimed property audits and fees should make it clear that these events are to be avoided. A good way to do so is to make regularly-scheduled unclaimed property reports to the applicable state governments, which are usually due on November 1. These reports should be filed even if there is no unclaimed property to report. However, before doing so, consider the following factors:

- Is it worthwhile to do so if the amount of unclaimed property is minimal or there is none at all?
- Is there a chance that certain governments use these reports as triggers to schedule audits?
- What condition is the company's record keeping currently in? Would it make more sense to begin filing reports after the record keeping system has been cleaned up?
- Does the government routinely offer amnesty programs, where no penalties or interest are charged to late filers? If so, does it make sense to wait for the next such program to be offered?
- There may be a charge for late filing in subsequent years, so can you commit to reliably filing on a timely basis in each subsequent year?
- Are there disgruntled current or former employees? If so, expect them to notify the state government about unclaimed property issues in order to collect a whistleblower fee. This means becoming compliant and filing reports as soon as possible.

When in doubt about how to proceed, consult with a qualified attorney who specializes in unclaimed property compliance.

Note: Beginning to file unclaimed property reports does not create a statute of limitations that will limit a company's exposure; an audit team can still request financial records for periods prior to the filing date of the first report.

As a defensive measure, consider working with corporate counsel to contact each applicable state government regarding a voluntary disclosure agreement (VDA). This is an agreement under which the company audits its own books and self-reports any past-due unclaimed property. This approach usually forgives any penalties that would otherwise be payable. Besides the forgiven penalties, this approach can result in a limitation on the period covered by future audits, and also allows the company to conduct its own audit at its own pace – preferably during a slow period in the accounting department.

> **Tip:** When applying for a VDA, consider doing so through an attorney or consultant, so that the state government does not know the identity of the company.

If the decision is made to begin making annual unclaimed property reports, a good place to start is with the state in which the company is incorporated. This is likely to be the state with the largest claim on the company's unclaimed property, since it is the default remit-to entity. Once relations with this state government have been normalized, the company can work through those states in which it has facilities, and then consider reporting to additional governments.

Claiming Unclaimed Property

Thus far, our concern has been with the avoidance of sending funds to the government for unclaimed property. The concept can also be reversed. Assign someone on the payables staff with the task of reviewing the government's unclaimed property database to see if the company is entitled to receive any of this property. If so, file a claim with the government for the funds. However, be aware that the state government may check all incoming claim forms to see if the entity filing a claim has itself been sending in unclaimed property funds for the past few years. If not, the government might schedule an audit of the claimant's accounting records to see if any unclaimed property has been improperly retained. Consequently, it can be less expensive to *not* pursue unclaimed property.

Summary

The best way to avoid an unclaimed property liability is to have no unclaimed property. Achieving this goal is not easy, and requires the cooperation of more than just the payables staff. The collections team needs to pester customers to use any outstanding credits, the general ledger clerk needs to review the bank reconciliation for uncashed checks, the payroll staff must beg employees to cash their checks, and the payables staff must work with suppliers to switch to electronic payments. To provide some additional structure to the minimization of unclaimed property, create an internal report that itemizes all unclaimed property currently on the books, and schedule a quarterly review of this report to determine what additional steps can be taken to get payments into the hands of the owners of the property. If attended to persistently, this should result in an extremely minimal amount of unclaimed property to be forwarded to the government.

Chapter 17
Cost Recovery

Introduction

No organization has perfect systems that protect it from excessive expenditures. Even a business with systems that are 99.9% accurate still incurs extra costs during that remaining 0.1% of the time. When multiplied by the total costs incurred by a business, even a tiny error rate can lead to notable excess expenditures. The role of cost recovery efforts is to identify these excess costs and obtain repayment from suppliers for these amounts, as well as to keep these costs from being incurred again in the future.

In this chapter, we explore the types of cost recovery activities that a business may engage in with its own staff, as well as the additional contribution to the effort that can be made by hiring an outside group of recovery auditors.

> **Related Podcast Episodes:** Episodes 35, 48, 52, and 60 of the Accounting Best Practices Podcast discuss cost recovery, while Episode 257 addresses the presentation of cost control information. They are available at: **accountingtools.com/podcasts** or **iTunes**

Internal Cost Recovery Targets

The cost recovery field can be considered a target-rich environment, for there are many ways in which a business can overpay. In the following subsections, we present a sampling of the areas in which cost recovery efforts can yield a notable positive return.

Advertising Expenditures

Businesses routinely spend enormous sums on advertising, but do not follow up to see if their expenditures were actually directed as intended. Someone should routinely verify that ad placements were actually made, that they were positioned as contractually agreed, and that they ran for the predetermined time period or for the designated number of page views (depending on the situation). It may also be useful to peruse the billings for the production of advertisements, to see if all billings complied with the terms of the contract, and that no excessive administrative or other overhead charges were billed.

Allowances

Suppliers may grant a company an array of allowances, many of which are never used. For example, a supplier may offer allowances that can be applied against supplier-specific advertising, or freight paybacks, or for limited-duration promotional periods.

Announcements about these allowances may never reach the payables department, so the payables staff never has any idea of the range of possible allowances that it could be taking. By exploring the allowances that have been offered in the past, it is possible to apply for a number of credits from suppliers. Also, better coordination between all parts of the company can ensure that allowances are used more effectively in the future.

Contracts

The purchasing department may have negotiated excellent terms in a contract with a supplier, but this does not prevent poor contract management that results in a supplier not observing the terms of the contract. Consequently, each contract must be examined on a regular basis to ensure that volume discounts are being granted at the appropriate times and are calculated correctly, and that scheduled price reductions are being billed to the company. It is also entirely possible that contracts have terminated, but suppliers are continuing to bill the company after the expiration date. This monitoring does not have to be limited to contracts related to the cost of goods sold. Excess costs may be incurred in relation to all types of contracts, including those for maintenance activities, facility leases, and services. Facility leases can be a particularly rich source of cost recoveries, since landlords may incorrectly bill for parking, real estate taxes, weekend utilities usage, inflation-based rate adjustments, and the company's share of general building operating expenses.

Duplicate Payments

Any accounting software package will immediately flag a duplicate supplier invoice as already being in the system – but only as long as the invoice numbers of the first and second versions of the invoice are identical, and the invoices are being charged to the same supplier account number. Also, if a supplier payment was made by wire transfer or ACH, instead of by check, it is possible that no one logged the entry into the accounting system, so that a duplicate payment is then made by check. A routine search can be conducted at regular intervals that looks for duplicate invoice numbers, duplicate invoice amounts, and duplicate payments.

Freight Billings

Freight companies routinely negotiate customized agreements with their larger customers, setting specific rates and volume discounts. If these agreements are not properly loaded into the billing systems of the freight companies, a business may continue to be billed at the rates noted under an older agreement, or perhaps at the higher default rates accorded to smaller customers. It requires a detailed review of freight billings to determine whether the most recent rates and discounts have been properly billed to the company.

> **Tip:** It makes considerable sense to conduct audits of freight invoices *before* paying them, so that an organization does not have to argue with freight companies to obtain refunds of overbillings. Such an audit can involve price verifications and matching to company shipment documentation.

Health Plan Enrollment

The dependents of health plan participants will no longer be covered once they reach a certain age. However, it is in the interests of employees to keep their dependents on the company medical plan for as long as possible, so there is a strong tendency to continue reporting dependents as plan participants even after their eligibility has expired. This issue can be tracked by auditing the ages of plan dependents.

Legal Billings

Some attorneys will pursue every conceivable lead in a project, tracking down information that is only peripherally necessary to the outcome of the project. In essence, they are working in areas that have marginal value (if any) to the company. This additional work can yield large additional billings to the company. To combat this problem, communicate to the law firm the company's expectations for when a project is considered to be complete, and peruse billings to spot instances of excessive work. This level of detailed examination is only possible if legal billings are submitted in detail, noting exactly which tasks were pursued. If the problem persists, shift legal work to a different firm.

Spend Compliance

The purchasing department may be quite active in requiring that purchases be made only with a small group of pre-selected suppliers. By doing so, the company can maximize its purchasing volume with each one, thereby qualifying it for large volume discounts. However, if employees persist in buying from other companies that are not on the approved list, the volume discounts earned will be reduced. Consequently, it is useful to routinely compare the payables records to the approved supplier list to spot variances, and remonstrate with the responsible employees to ensure that they alter their purchasing activities in the future.

Supplier Credits

Suppliers issue credits to buyers for many reasons, such as for damaged goods, pricing errors, or marketing allowances. Whatever the reason, these credits are worth recovering. Here are two ways to do so:

- Contact suppliers and ask for a full statement of account. Use this approach when there is a chance that the company did not receive a copy of a credit. Review the statement, and either use the indicated credits as offsets to current payables, or ask for a cash refund.
- If there are not currently any payables on the company's books against which a credit can be offset, inquire with the supplier if the credit can be paid to the company in cash.

Telecommunications Billings

A close review of phone company billings can be quite productive, especially since these billings usually include recurring charges that, if no action is taken, will continue in perpetuity. Items to look for include fees for unauthorized services, billings for phone lines or cell phones that are no longer used, and usage plans that do not match the company's actual telecommunications usage levels. In particular, look out for stray billings associated with cell phones that were purchased outside of the corporate plan; the rates associated with these phones are typically much higher than the volume rates applied to the phones in the corporate plan.

Unclaimed Property

As described in the Unclaimed Property chapter, a large number of states maintain control over unclaimed property, which can be claimed from them if you know where to find the information. Much of it is located on the www.missingmoney.com site, which aggregates the unclaimed property files of several dozen states. Consider placing on the department's calendar of activities a periodic task to review this site (and other state government sites, if applicable) to see if the company is entitled to any unclaimed property.

Unreturned Deposits

A company may be required to pay out funds for deposits for a number of reasons, such as for rent, utilities, and bids for government contracts. If the counterparty is operating efficiently, it should send back these deposits when it is no longer contractually required to retain them. But what if they are not efficient? These deposits may be lost for good.

To ensure that deposits are returned is a two-step exercise. First, create a separate deposits (asset) account in the general ledger, and record all deposits in that account. This is done to centralize the record keeping for all deposits. Second, review the contents of this account at regular intervals, and contact counterparties as necessary to see if deposits are due to be returned.

Internal Cost Recovery Staff

It is not sufficient to assign cost recovery activities to whichever payables clerk is not currently busy. Doing so only means that cost recovery activities will proceed in fits and starts, and will dry up entirely during busy periods. Instead, there should be a separate cost recovery staff whose only responsibilities are looking for and following through on cost recoveries. This approach has the following advantages:

- *Familiarity.* A dedicated person can become highly familiar with the corporate accounting system, and can navigate through and extract information from it with ease.
- *Sole focus.* A dedication person will never be pulled away from her cost recovery work – instead, the payables staff will handle ongoing transaction processing activities, while the cost recovery staff focuses on digging up excess costs.
- *Different background.* When there is a position set aside for cost recovery work, the payables manager can hire a specialist into the position whose skill set is different from that of the payables staff. Ideally, the person could have experience with databases, financial analysis, control systems, and supplier negotiations.
- *Specialization.* If a company has a unique area of focus for its costs, such as freight expenditures, the cost recovery staff could hone their skills in this area, gaining the ability to locate cost issues that a part-timer would never have found.

Recovery Auditors

There is an entire industry of audit firms that are willing to comb through a company's records to locate duplicate or excessive costs that can be recovered. They typically work on a contingent basis, taking as a fee a significant amount of the funds recovered (usually in the vicinity of one-third of the recovery amount). Since recovery auditors earn a living from the percentage of savings found, they are going to spend the bulk of their time on cost recovery areas that have historically generated the largest possible return for them. Examples of these areas are:

- Compliance with licensing agreements
- Credit memos not used
- Currency translation errors
- Duplicate payments made to suppliers
- Early payment discounts that were not taken or granted
- Improperly applied taxes
- Incorrect supplier billings
- Rebates not issued

There are additional benefits of using recovery auditors that go beyond the simple recovery of funds. In addition, their explorations through the company's systems may uncover instances of fraud, and they may uncover control weaknesses that have led to excessive costs being incurred in the past. Further, they may find instances of such egregious and long-term overbilling by certain suppliers that the only possible response is to terminate relations with those suppliers.

Recovery auditors tend to be specialists. It is a rare auditor indeed who can review with equal facility freight billings, cell phone records, and facility lease agreements. Consequently, it can make sense to work through a series of recovery auditors, concentrating on those areas of the business where most of the costs are incurred. For example, a telecommunications auditor might be the highest priority to bring in if a company has a massive number of employees who are constantly on the road, using company-provided cell phones. Conversely, a retail chain with a multitude of stores across the country might be more interested in the services of someone with experience in freight charges.

> **Tip:** Require all recovery auditors to provide a final report of their activities that includes any systemic issues found that the company can address. Doing so allows the business to reduce the number of cost "leaks" that are increasing expenses.

The prices charged by auditors can certainly be a concern, since their fees may turn out to be substantial. Here are several concepts to be aware of when discussing pricing with a prospective auditor:

- *Contingency or hourly rates*. If the auditor is willing to work on a contingent basis, expect the bulk of the hours to be put into locating the largest possible recovery items. If the company is willing to pay on an hourly basis, auditors are more likely to search for smaller recoveries, since they have no stake in recoveries of a specific size.
- *Tiered scale*. Will the auditor accept a smaller fee on a large cost recovery? For example, if an auditor uncovers a $1,000,000 savings, should the usual standard contingent fee be charged to the company, or will a smaller percentage apply? This could result in a two-tiered pricing structure, where a high percentage is used on low-dollar amounts (which creates an incentive to search for these items) and a lower percentage on high-dollar amounts.
- *Pricing by area of expertise*. Expect to pay a higher rate if the auditor has an exceptional level of expertise in a certain specialty. It is quite acceptable to pay a higher rate in these situations, since the company will presumably obtain a larger dollar amount of cost recoveries as a result.
- *Second audit pricing*. It can be useful to have a second cost recovery firm examine the accounting records after another firm has made a first pass. Each firm likely has different areas of expertise and different routines for locating cost recovery opportunities, so this is worthwhile for the company. However, the second audit firm may not be so happy about the engagement, since much of the "low hanging fruit" will already have been found. Consequently, it may be necessary to offer a higher contingency percentage to the second group of auditors.

- *Payment timing.* A key issue when settling the terms of a recovery audit is when the audit firm will be paid. If the payment arrangement is on a contingent basis, then payment should only occur after the company has been paid. This means that the recovery firm cannot simply claim it has found a large pile of savings, drop them back onto the accounting department to finalize, and expect to see an immediate payment. However, if auditors are working and being paid on an hourly basis, then the audit firm can reasonably expect to be paid on a monthly basis, since its efforts are not based on the outcome of their review.

When a company enters into an arrangement with a recovery audit firm, expect to provide some level of service to these auditors, though not as much as would be expected for an audit of the financial statements. The recovery auditors may need access to the company's paper records or its accounting database, and may also need on-site office space for its staff.

Cost-Benefit of Cost Recovery Activities

Many payables managers will claim that they do not have sufficient resources to expend on cost recovery efforts. This claim is based on the designation of the payables department as a cost center, where payables are supposed to be processed at the absolute minimum cost. This approach is not necessarily correct, if the amount of funds to be gained from adding additional staff can result in a sufficiently large amount of recovered costs. The concept can be taken somewhat further, as noted in the following bullet points:

- *Incremental analysis.* There will always be certain areas in a business where costs can be identified and recovered with relatively little effort. Once these areas have been addressed, the payables manager must make a determination about whether to pursue more difficult areas that will yield fewer returns. At some point, the incremental cost of hiring one additional internal auditor to address cost recovery issues will no longer be exceeded by the cost recoveries to be gained.
- *Systems effort.* A case can be made that the staff investment should be diverted to the analysis of systems and controls, to arrive at such a robust payables system that there is a reduced need for an internal staff of cost recovery experts.

Both of these viewpoints have merit. The likely outcome of an initial cost recovery effort is that a small staff will be hired to search for cost recovery opportunities, while also working with the company's systems analysts to correct the systemic flaws that caused some of these cost recovery opportunities to arise. The result will be a gradual decline in recoveries from the designated cost recovery areas, at which point the internal staff may be directed into other areas, where they will repeat their systems analysis work. This does not mean that the initial group of cost recovery staff will eventually run out of work – there will always be some level of cost recovery analysis to be performed, no matter how robust a company's systems may be.

A final thought regarding the need for cost recovery activities is that it can have a startling impact on profitability. Consider that one dollar of sales may translate into 10% of before-tax profits, or perhaps much less. Let us assume that the average business is doing fairly well, and is earning 10% before income taxes. What if management decides to double profits? Either it has to double sales or remove 10 cents in costs. While removing the 10 cents in costs may not be easy, doing so is entirely under the control of the company. Conversely, doubling sales requires the agreement of customers, which may not be forthcoming. In short, it is usually easier to improve profits through cost reduction than through sales expansion.

It is useful to understand the formula for the equivalent amount of sales that must be generated to create an additional dollar of profit, since doing so creates a strong argument in favor of a brisk cost recovery effort. The formula is:

$$1 \div \text{Profit percentage} = \text{Equivalent sales volume}$$

EXAMPLE

Excalibur Shaving Company, maker of the world's sharpest razor blades, is under pressure from its investors to increase its dividend. The board of directors is concerned that the business cannot do so on a long-term basis without cutting into its cash reserves, and so asks the CFO to look into ways to increase profits that will help the company meet the demands of investors.

The company's before-tax profit margins are currently 15%, but total before-tax profits must double in order to provide the dividends demanded by investors, who require an extra $1,000,000 of cash per year. One approach would be to double sales. However, the razor blade market is no longer growing, so doubling sales would require a radical drop in prices to lure customers away from competitors, thereby leaving no additional margin. The only alternative is to chop expenses throughout the organization.

If the CFO can find $1,000,000 of cost savings within the business, the amount of additional revenues that the company will not have to generate is $6,666,667, which is calculated as follows:

$$(1 \div 15\% \text{ Profit margin}) \times \$1,000,000 \text{ Required profit increase} = \$6,666,667$$

As an example of the multiplier effect associated with generating additional profits, a company that earns five cents on the dollar can earn an additional five cents either by saving that amount of cost, or by generating 20 times that amount in revenues. Or, to take the case of a *very* profitable organization, a business that earns 25 cents on the dollar can earn an additional amount either by saving 25 cents or by generating four times that amount in revenues. Thus, the multiplier effect makes it much easier to increase profits through proper cost management than through revenue improvements.

In short, increasing profits always presents management with a choice of either reducing costs or increasing revenues by a much larger amount.

Cost Recovery Timing

An essential ingredient of any cost recovery effort is the repetitiveness of the effort. A review for the recovery of costs cannot take place at multi-year intervals, because it is so difficult to prove to a supplier that (for example) an overbilling three years ago must now be repaid. Instead, cost recovery efforts must be ongoing. This could mean that an in-house staff continually cycles through the payables records, or it could mean that recovery auditors are scheduled to arrive once a year – and probably both. Only by paying constant attention to cost recovery can expenditure reductions be maximized.

Fertile Ground for Cost Recovery Efforts

There are certain situations in which a strong cost recovery effort could yield unusually large returns. In any of the following situations, management would be well advised to engage in a vigorous cost recovery effort:

- *Acquisitions*. There is a significant amount of disruption associated with acquisitions, where the acquirer is trying to justify the cost of the acquisition by paring away at expenses with an extremely sharp knife. This can result in an organization with far fewer employees than had been the case prior to the merger of the two entities – and those remaining staff may not be overly willing to work hard for their employer. Furthermore, the acquirer may want to replace the accounting systems of the acquiree with its own systems, resulting in a further level of disruption. In this type of environment, the probability of excess costs being incurred rises significantly.
- *Growth*. When a business grows at an extremely rapid clip, it is difficult to expand the supporting systems at a similar pace. Instead, systems designed for a lower sales volume struggle to keep up with burgeoning sales. Similarly, it can be difficult to provide adequate training to new employees who are being hired faster than the ability of the company's educational systems to train them. In these situations, it is much easier for excessive costs to be incurred.
- *New systems*. Any time a new system is installed, there is a risk that the new system was not properly tested, or that the data in the old system was not properly converted to the new system, or that employees were not properly trained in how to use the new system. In this environment, it is much more likely for excessive costs to go unnoticed.

Summary

We advocate the use of both an internal cost recovery group and an outside group of cost recovery specialists. Only by directing all possible resources toward the examination of expenses will it be possible to reduce costs to the lowest level possible.

Cost recovery efforts are essentially detective in nature – that is, they uncover problems that currently exist, and bring them to the attention of management. This does not mean that an intensive and ongoing cost recovery effort will *stop* excessive costs from being incurred. For that to happen, management must also commit to using the information provided by cost recovery efforts to add layers of preventive controls to the company's systems. Only if this additional effort is made will the amount of excess expenditures made begin to decline over time.

Chapter 18
Payables Measurements

Introduction

The payables manager should calculate measurements to determine how well the department is performing. These are usually ratios, in which case they only provide a high-level view of potential issues, which must then be investigated by drilling deeper into the data to determine underlying causes. In this chapter, we begin with the most heavily-used days payables outstanding measurement, and then proceed to a number of less-common measurements that can be used to detect excessive supplier billings, transaction error rates, cost per person, the success of paperless efforts, and similar issues.

Days Payables Outstanding

The accounts payable days formula measures the number of days that a company takes to pay its suppliers. If the number of days increases from one period to the next, this indicates that the company is paying its suppliers more slowly. A change in the number of payable days can also indicate altered payment terms with suppliers, though this rarely has more than a slight impact on the total number of days. If a company is paying its suppliers very quickly, it may mean that the suppliers are demanding short payment terms because they are suspicious of the company's ability to pay.

To calculate days payables outstanding, summarize all purchases from suppliers during the measurement period, and divide by the average amount of accounts payable during that period. The formula is:

$$\frac{\text{Total supplier purchases}}{(\text{Beginning accounts payable} + \text{Ending accounts payable}) \div 2}$$

This formula reveals the total accounts payable turnover. Then divide the resulting turnover figure into 365 days to arrive at the number of accounts payable days.

The formula can be modified to exclude cash payments to suppliers, since the numerator should include only purchases on credit from suppliers. However, the amount of up-front cash payments to suppliers is normally so small that this modification is not necessary.

As an example, a payables manager wants to determine his company's accounts payable days for the past year. The beginning accounts payable balance was $800,000, and the ending balance was $884,000. Purchases for the last 12 months were $7,500,000. Based on this information, the turnover calculation is:

$$\frac{\$7,500,000 \text{ Purchases}}{(\$800,000 \text{ Beginning payables} + \$884,000 \text{ Ending payables}) \div 2}$$

$$=$$

$$\frac{\$7,500,000 \text{ Purchases}}{\$842,000 \text{ Average accounts payable}}$$

$$= 8.9 \text{ Accounts payable turnover}$$

Thus, the company's accounts payable is turning over at a rate of 8.9 times per year. To calculate the turnover in days, the payables manager divides the 8.9 turns into 365 days, which yields:

$$365 \text{ Days} \div 8.9 \text{ Turns} = 41 \text{ Days}$$

Companies sometimes measure accounts payable days by only using the cost of goods sold in the numerator. This is incorrect, since there may be a large amount of administrative expenses that should also be included. If a company only uses the cost of goods sold in the numerator, this creates an excessively small number of payable days.

A significant failing of the days payables outstanding measurement is that it does not factor in all of the short-term liabilities of a business. There may be substantial liabilities related to payroll, interest, and taxes that exceed the size of payables outstanding. This issue can be eliminated by incorporating all short-term liabilities into the days payable outstanding measurement.

Supplier Billed Price Variance

A high-quality supplier will negotiate the price of goods and services with the buyer up-front, and will not attempt to alter this price in subsequent billings under the related purchase order. In this case, the billed price and purchase order price should always match. A more ethically challenged supplier, or one with severe disconnects between its billing and sales departments may issue invoices that bear little relationship to the prices stated in the original purchase order. In the latter case, the buyer may incur such excessive overbillings that the profitability of the business is seriously eroded. Consequently, management should know which suppliers continually have price variances in their billings.

To calculate the supplier billed price variance, aggregate the amount of excess billings over the amounts stated on purchase orders, divided by the extended prices stated on the purchase orders. The formula is:

$$\frac{\text{Total of excess billings}}{\text{Total of extended prices stated on purchase orders}}$$

This measurement is designed to be calculated for each individual supplier, so it typically takes the form of a report that is sorted in declining order of billed price variance. To save space, the report only lists those variances above a predetermined materiality threshold.

There are cases where a billed price variance is justified. For example, a purchase order may allow the supplier to ship slightly more than the requested amount, in which case the extended price charged by the supplier will be higher than what is noted on the purchase order. This situation usually arises when items are purchased in very large quantities on an ongoing basis, so that slight overages in the units delivered are a standard practice.

EXAMPLE

The purchasing manager of Luminescence Corporation is being paid a bonus if she can restrict the amount the company pays to its LED suppliers for the components used in Luminescence light bulbs. In investigating the company's materials costs, she notes that several suppliers are charging more than the contractual amounts for components. She compiles the following information:

Supplier Name	Extended Price Paid	Purchase Order Price	Billed Price $ Variance	Billed Price % Variance
Dome Ports Ltd.	$52,600	$50,000	$2,600	5.2%
Flange Brothers	40,800	35,000	5,800	16.6%
Glow LED Modules Inc.	21,700	20,000	1,700	8.5%
Totals	$115,100	$105,000	$10,100	9.6%

Based on these results, the purchasing manager meets with the controller and demands tighter three-way matching of supplier invoices, so that these overages will be flagged in the future.

Transaction Error Rate

It is critical to avoid transaction errors, since the cost of correcting them is several multiples of the cost of initially completing them correctly. Consequently, one of the better measurements is to monitor the transaction error rate. The error rate should be monitored in conjunction with the total number of transactions processed by each person, to see if error rates are higher for newer or less-trained employees. The measurement can be further refined by focusing on those transaction errors that require the most time to repair.

To formulate the transaction error rate, add up all transaction-related errors in a reporting period and divide them by the total number of transactions completed within the same reporting period. This calculation should match transactional errors to the pool of the same types of transactions completed, which will result in a separate error rate for each general type of transaction.

EXAMPLE

The senior payables clerk of the Divine Gelato Company wants to reduce the amount of staff time spent correcting transactional errors. She has derived the following information for the last reporting period:

Processes	Number of Errors	Total Number of Transactions	Transaction Error Rate
Supplier ACH payments	28	3,010	0.9%
Supplier address changes	175	1,390	12.6%
Supplier invoice data entry	200	1,720	11.6%

Based on the error rates of the types of transactions measured, it is evident that the clerk should concentrate her attention on the address changes and invoice data entry. Of these two processes, the one requiring the most effort to repair is invoice data entry, so she elects to begin work in this area.

Full-Time Equivalent Measurements

There are several measurements available in which we can compare the headcount in the payables area to various activity levels or costs. The outcome can then be compared to the same measurement for "best in class" companies, to see if the payables function has an appropriate amount of headcount or is paying its employees a reasonable wage. Before discussing these measurements, we must define the concept of the full-time equivalent.

The acronym "FTE" is a contraction of the term "full-time equivalent," and refers to the hours worked by an employee on a full-time basis. On an annual basis, an FTE is considered to be 2,080 hours, which is calculated as:

8	Hours per day
5	× Work days per week
52	× 52 Weeks per year
2,080	= Hours per year

When a business employs a significant number of part-time staff, it can be useful to convert their hours worked into full time equivalents, to see how many full-time staff they equate to.

EXAMPLE

There are 168 working hours in January, and the Big Data Corporation staff works 7,056 hours during the month. When 168 hours are divided into 7,056 hours, the result is 42 FTEs.

There are 8 working hours in the day on Monday, and the Cupertino Beanery staff works 136 hours during that day. When 8 working hours are divided into 136 hours, the result is 17 FTEs.

There are 2,080 working hours in the year, and the Hubble Corporation staff works 22,880 hours during that year. When 2,080 working hours are divided into 22,880 hours, the result is 11 FTEs.

The 2,080 figure can be called into question, since it does not include any deductions for holidays, vacation time, sick time, and so forth. Alternative measures of FTE that incorporate these additional assumptions can place the number of hours for one FTE as low as 1,680 hours per year.

FTEs per $1 Million of Revenue

One way to examine payables headcount is to compare it to the amount of revenue being generated by a business. This could be defined as FTEs per $1 million or $1 billion of revenue. For example, a business has $500 million of revenue, and a payables staff of 15 FTEs. This organization has one payables FTE for every $33.3 million of revenue.

This measurement can be of use when compared to the results of competitors in the same industry, since the competitors will presumably have similar sales environments and suppliers. The measure is of less use when compared to results in other industries, since revenues in some industries can be supported with substantially lower or higher payables volumes.

Staff Cost per FTE

The total labor cost of the payables department can be divided by the number of payables FTEs to arrive at the average staff cost per FTE. For example, a payables department has total labor costs of $2,000,000 and 50 FTEs, which translates into a $40,000 staff cost per FTE.

This measurement can be compared to labor rates in the same industry or geographic region to see if the company is paying an appropriate amount per person. However, there are several factors that can skew labor costs. For example, a company may be located in an unusually high-cost region, such as a major city, where the cost of living is higher. Also, the corporate benefit plan may be unusually rich or poor, which can impact the total cost assigned to labor. Further, a relatively new and inexperienced staff may be paid less, but this does not factor in their reduced level of effectiveness.

Line Items per FTE

One of the better activity measures is to compare the number of FTEs to the number of line items processed in supplier invoices. This approach accounts for the differing amounts of detail included in each invoice received. This calculation only works if the computer system can report on the total number of invoice line items processed in each measurement period. For example, a payables department has entered 120,000 invoice line items in the past month, and the department employs 15 FTEs. This equates to 8,000 line items per FTE.

This measure is more comparable across industry lines, and so can be used to match a company's results to those of a "best in class" organization located elsewhere.

This approach may not work if only invoice totals are entered into the payables system, rather than individual line items. If so, alter the measurement to track invoices entered per FTE.

Paperless Measurements

If there is an efficiency drive to eliminate paperwork from the payables function, it can make sense to track two paperless measurements, which are the percent of paperless invoices and the percent of paperless payments. They are both described in this section.

Percent of Paperless Invoices

If the company uses an electronic data interchange system or an on-line portal into which suppliers can enter their invoices, invoices will be sent directly to the payables software without any data entry. This is to be encouraged, since it reduces payables staff time. For example, a company processes a total of 6,000 invoices in a month, of which 500 were entered through paperless systems. This constitutes an 8.3% paperless invoice percentage.

It is entirely likely that this percentage will reach a certain point and then stall, with no further improvement. The trouble is that some suppliers will continue to send paper invoices, despite all encouragement to the contrary. Only when a company is large enough to really influence the actions of its suppliers can it assume that a high paperless invoice percentage can be achieved.

Percent of Paperless Payments

The payables manager can reduce the cost of check payments by switching to ACH payments instead (see the Types of Payments chapter). Doing so requires that the company obtain bank account information for its suppliers. If they do not provide this information, it will not be possible to issue ACH payments. Suppliers may not provide this information when the relationship is not expected to be long-term, or is only occasional. Consequently, the percent of paperless payments is likely to be close to 100% for the core group of suppliers, and much lower for all other suppliers.

For example, a company has 800 suppliers, of which 160 are considered the core group. The payables manager convinces 152 of this sub-group to accept ACH payments, while only 300 of the remaining suppliers are amenable to the idea. This results in a 95% success rate for the core group, and a 47% rate for the remaining suppliers.

Additional Payables Measurements

There are several additional measurements for the payables area that can have a noticeable impact on the function's operations. The following measurements are intended to be reviewed daily and to trigger immediate corrective action by the accounting staff:

- *Remaining three-way matches.* If a business uses evaluated receipts, pay from receipt, and procurement cards, there should be relatively few remaining supplier invoices that are still being reviewed with the cumbersome three-way matching process. Consider creating a report that itemizes every invoice for which three-way matching was used, with the intent of finding alternative ways to review these invoices.
- *Invoices not mailed to accounts payable.* Whenever an invoice arrives that was mailed to someone other than the accounts payable department, include the supplier name on a contact list. The payables staff should contact these suppliers to request that the contact name be shifted to the payables department. Doing so eliminates a possible bottleneck where invoice recipients might not immediately forward invoices to the accounting staff.
- *Supplier late fees.* Any late payment fee charged by a supplier should be recorded in a separate general ledger account. The information in this account is reviewed regularly to determine what circumstances caused the late fee. The result may be procedural or other changes to keep the issue from occurring again in the future.
- *Manual payments.* Track every manual payment made (including payments by check, ACH, or wire transfer), determine the reasons why manual payments were mandated, and see if they can be converted to the regular payment system in the future.
- *Suppliers with rapid growth rates.* When a supplier or employee is engaging in fraud, there is a tendency for the individual to escalate the fraud at a much more rapid pace than would be considered normal. Consequently, it can make sense to periodically run a report that shows those suppliers with the largest annual growth rate in total dollars, and investigate any amounts that look suspicious.

Note that none of these additional measurements involve ratio analysis. Instead, they mostly require that the payables staff investigate individual transactions in detail, with the objective of locating transactions that either resulted in errors or which required an inordinate amount of effort to complete. The result of these investigations should be a continual improvement in the efficiency of the payables function.

Summary

It is not necessary to maintain a comprehensive set of measurements for the payables function. The payables manager is more likely to adopt a few measurements for the duration of a specific project, such as the rollout of ACH payments, and then stop bothering with the measurements as soon as the project has been completed. These measurements are needed as a feedback loop to determine the success of the project. However, it can be useful to calculate a complete set of measurements once a year, to see if there has been any backsliding in areas that had been considered high-performance when they were originally addressed.

If there is one payables measurement worth monitoring on an ongoing basis, it is the transaction error rate. This is more of a report than a measurement, and is designed to detect and correct errors that creep into the payables system. Consider it an early warning report for issues that can then be corrected before they expand into more wide-ranging problems.

No matter which measurements are used, consider tracking them on a trend line. Doing so gives immediate visual feedback regarding declines in performance, which can trigger an investigation to locate underlying causes.

Glossary

A

Account number. The identifying code assigned to each account in the chart of accounts.

ACH. The Automated Clearing House system, which processes high-volume, low-value electronic payments between payers and payees.

ACH debit. A transaction that allows a payee to initiate a debit of the payer's bank account, with the funds shifting into the payee's bank account.

Accrual. A journal entry that allows an entity to record expenses and revenues for which it expects to expend or receive cash, respectively, in a future period.

B

Bank draft. A check whose payment is guaranteed by a bank.

C

Chart of accounts. A listing of all the accounts used in the general ledger, usually listed in order by account number.

Check. A written order directing a bank to pay the entity indicated on the order a specific sum.

Credit memo. A transaction used to reduce an account payable.

D

Debit block. A limitation imposed on a bank account, not permitting the use of ACH debits to remove funds from the account.

Debit memo. An internal accounting transaction used to offset a stray payables credit balance in an account.

Dormancy period. The amount of time that a business is allowed to retain unclaimed property before it must be turned over to the applicable state government.

E

Evaluated receipts. A system for paying suppliers based on the volume of production completed.

Expense report. A log of expenses incurred, used by an employee to request the reimbursement of funds expended on behalf of a business.

F

Factoring. The use of a borrowing entity's accounts receivable as the basis for a financing arrangement with a lender.

Glossary

Float. The time period during which funds are in transition between the stages in the payment process.

Full-time equivalent. The hours worked by an individual on a full-time basis.

G

General ledger. The master set of accounts that summarize all transactions occurring within an entity.

I

Invoice. A document issued by a seller, stating the amount owed by the buyer for the goods or services stated in the document.

J

Journal entry. A formal accounting entry used to identify a business transaction.

L

Letter of credit. A letter stating that a bank will guarantee a payment from a buyer to a seller; used extensively in international trade.

N

Nexus. A sufficient physical presence in a territory for a seller to be obligated to charge sales taxes to customers located in the same territory.

P

Payables ledger. A subsidiary ledger that stores invoice and payment transactions.

Per diem. A daily allowance for expenses.

Petty cash. A small reserve of cash used to pay for incidental expenses.

Procurement card. A company credit card.

Purchase order. An authorization to purchase a certain amount of goods or services at a stated price.

R

Return merchandise authorization. An authorization granted by the seller to the buyer, authorizing the return of goods.

Reverse lockbox. When suppliers send invoices to the buyer's bank for digitization and possible additional handling.

S

Split purchase. When a supplier is asked to split a billing into multiple invoices so that each individual invoice is less than the buyer's purchasing authorization threshold.

Glossary

T

Three-way matching. The process of comparing receiving documents to a supplier invoice and authorizing purchase order to ensure that a supplier billing can be paid.

TIN matching. The process of verifying taxpayer identification numbers and supplier name combinations on the IRS website.

U

Unclaimed property. Property that has not been claimed by its rightful owner.

Use tax. A sales tax to be paid by the buyer of goods or services.

V

Vendor master file. A file in which is stored information about the suppliers with which a business has ongoing transactions.

Voucher. A business document denoting a liability, used as evidence to authorize a payment.

W

Wire transfer. A low-volume, high-value electronic payment from a payer to a payee, usually within a very short period of time.

Index

Account code list, standard 127
Accounts payable
    Accounting for 86
    Accrual of 93
    Controls, computerized system 119
    Controls, manual system 118
    Credits processing 17
    Measurements 194
    Record keeping 154
    Suspense items 96
ACH advantages 44
ACH debits 141
Adjustment letter 14
Approval escalation 28
Approval minimization 28
Approved supplier list 130
Authorization limit avoidance 140
Automated Clearing House 43
Automated payables matching 145
Automated W-9 forms 147
Availability dates 39
Availability float 41

B notices 165
Bank drafts 42
Bank reconciliation, daily 121
Bill of material purchases 131
Blank checks, signing of 134

Card reconciliation procedure 65
Cash advances 30, 60
Cash advances on procurement cards . 136
Cash payments 34
Centralized processing 27
Chart of accounts 89
Check
    Advantages 42
    Clearing 38
    Clearing, foreign 40
    Disadvantages 42
    Fraud 141
    Issuance procedure 20
    Numbering sequence 116
    Payments 38
    Printing responsibility 116
    Register 22
    Request form 11
    Run frequency 30
    Signer policy 135
    Signer, additional 117
    Signing control 116
    Stock 21
    Stock for inactive accounts 121
    Storage 116
    Theft 141
Commuting mileage policy 135
Consolidate accounting function 108
Cost of credit 82
Cost recovery
    Auditors 182
    Cost-benefit 184
    Targets 178
Credit card close 95
Credit reports for suppliers 120

Days payables outstanding 188
Debit block 121
Deface a check 24
Department layout analysis 105
Direct deposit 24
    Change log 121
    File, protection of 118
Direct invoice delivery 26
Discrepancy invoices 97
Disputed charges analysis 67
Document
    Destruction policy 157
    Imaging 156
    Off-site storage 155
    Retention policy 175
    Storage improvements 155
Dormancy period 173
Due diligence letters 173
Duplicate payment search 115
Duplicate record detection 153

Early payment discount
    Analysis 122
    Calculation 81
    Policy 134
Employee advances 136

Employee background checks 129
Employee reimbursement policy 135
Employee vendor records 126
Entertainment expenses 52
Error tracking 102
Evaluated receipts processing procedure
.... 19
Expenditure protest form 128
Expense report
    Approvals 123
    Auditing.. 60
    Automation...................................... 145
    Controls, computerized system........ 124
    Controls, manual system.................. 124
    Examination controls....................... 123
    Form 50
    Issues 94
    Numbering method.......................... 123
    Outsourcing 61
    Receipt verification 124
    Review procedure.............................. 55
    Submission controls........................ 123
    Submission procedure 50
    Trend analysis.................................. 125
Expense trend analysis 119, 129

Fake suppliers...................................... 139
Financing cycle... 1
Flexible work hours............................. 109
Flight bookings, analysis of................. 125
Float.. 41
Form 1096 161
Form 1099-MISC 158
Form 1099-NEC 162
Form W-9 .... 13, 166
Forms
    Expense report 50
    Petty cash book 36
    Petty cash transfer............................. 34
    Petty cash voucher 35
Full-time equivalent............................. 191

Global ACH... 45
Gross price method................................ 88

Hotel billings, analysis of.................... 125

Incorrect filings 165
Invoice numbering convention 27
Invoice numbering guideline.............. 116

Invoice paid stamp 117
IRS penalties 169

Job descriptions.......................................7
Job sharing 110

Keystroke logging 142

Layout analysis 105
Letter of credit.......................................47
Level III data.......................................131
Lifting fee...46
Lost card procedure...............................70

Magnetic ink character recognition.......38
Mail float...41
Manual check payments......................134
Manual check reduction 29
Matching discrepancies.........................28
Mileage claim review............................56
Mileage reimbursement.........................52
Mileage, analysis of 125
Missing receipts form..........................128
Multiple points of use certificate...........80

Negative approvals................................28
Net price method...................................88
Non-reimbursement expenses 55
Numbering convention, invoice 27

On-line expense reporting procedure 54
Open credits 32
Organizational structure 2

Paperless measurements......................193
Payables aging report............................32
Payables fraud.....................................138
Payables reconciliation 98
Payment analysis firm.........................120
Payment factory 144
Payment timing 83
Payroll cycle..1
Per diem meal review............................56
Per diem meals......................................52
Per diem reimbursement 135
Permanent part-time work...................110
Petty cash 34
    Book 36
    Box controls 133
    Controls...131

Reconciliation 132
Theft 140
Transfer form 34
Voucher form 35
Positive pay 117
Positive pay system 22
Process reviews 103
Processing float 41
Procurement card
Cancellation 130
Contracts 130
Control systems 128
Reconciliation 127
Spending limits 136
Statement reconciliation 127
Transaction log 127
Purchase authorization, avoidance of . 120
Purchase order approval 114
Purchase order release 19
Purchasing cycle 1

Receipt numbering, analysis of 126
Recurring payment audits 123
Recurring payment automation 29
Reverse lockbox 146

Sales cycle 1
Sales tax exemption 79
Schedule of activities 101
Second signature requirement 31
Separation of duties 129, 134
Signature stamp 31
Skills review 106
Spend management 61
Standby letter of credit 48
Stop payments 25, 135
Supplier
Billed price variance 189
Credit 18
Inactive designation 123
Invoice approval 113
Invoice recordation timing 115
Records, duplicate 122
Reduction 32

Statements, payments from 134
Trend analysis 119
Supplier invoice processing procedure 10, 15
Supplier invoice, aggregated 27
Supplier late fees 194
Supplier naming conventions 151
Supplier overbillings 139
Supplier portals 147
Supplier relations 110
Supplier-staff collusion 140
Supply chain financing 84

Three-way matching 12, 114
TIN matching 154
Training programs 107
Training, measurement of 107
Transaction error rate 190
Travel advances 52
Travel booking policy 135
Trend analysis 56
Two-way matching 16

Unauthorized shipments 139
Uncashed checks 98
Unclaimed property
Audit 174
Liability 171
Reports 176
Unpaid payables investigation 122
Use taxes 76

Value date 39
Vendor master file 13, 149
Access to 125
Change log 120
Void checks procedure 24
Void designation 25
Voided checks log 122

Wire transfers 24, 45
Wire transfers, approval of 118
Workflow analysis 105

Made in the USA
Thornton, CO
05/10/24 00:13:50

12efbe8e-c3d5-483a-832a-e28cf62c95dcR01